Disabled Policy

Disabled Policy

America's Programs for the Handicapped

A Twentieth Century Fund Report

Edward D. Berkowitz

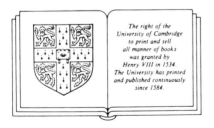

The right of the
University of Cambridge
to print and sell
all manner of books
was granted by
Henry VIII in 1534.
The University has printed
and published continuously
since 1584.

Cambridge University Press

Cambridge
London   New York   New Rochelle
Melbourne   Sydney

Published by the Press Syndicate of the University of Cambridge
The Pitt Building, Trumpington Street, Cambridge CB2 1RP
32 East 57th Street, New York, NY 10022, USA
10 Stamford Road, Oakleigh, Melbourne 3166, Australia

First published 1987

Printed in the United States of America

Library of Congress Cataloging-in-Publication Data
Berkowitz, Edward D.
Disabled policy.
Bibliography: p.
Includes index.
1. Handicapped – Government policy – United States.
2. Income maintenance programs – United States.
3. Vocational rehabilitation – United States.   I. Title.
HV1553.B47   1987   362.4'04561'0973   86-26388

British Library Cataloguing in Publication Data
Berkowitz, Edward D.
Disabled policy. – (A
Twentieth Century Fund Report)
1. Physically handicapped – Government
policy – United States
I. Title   II. Series
362.4'0456'0973   HV3023.A3

ISBN 0 521 34014 4

For Emily

Contents

Foreword

The nation's commitment to providing a minimum basic income for the growing number of aging people in our society has been subject to continuing scrutiny. Politicians and policymakers come under increasing pressure to ensure that Social Security is fiscally sound and that the benefits it provides are broadened. Concern also is expressed for disabled Americans; more than one hundred government programs offer help of one sort or another to the handicapped. The cost of these programs is high – and growing higher. In the early 1980s, the most recent years for which reliable figures are available, public and private expenditures for the disabled reached $122 billion a year.

Is this expensive and complex mix of disability programs truly meeting the needs of the disabled? Is it doing so efficiently and equitably? Are the funds provided by taxpayers being misspent or misdirected? How many who do not deserve disability benefits receive them? How many who badly need assistance fail to secure it? Is the right kind of assistance – financial support or rehabilitation – provided? Do the programs succeed in achieving their objectives? And are those objectives clear and appropriate?

The Twentieth Century Fund has a long history of sponsoring studies on retired workers. We have recently supported research on both the history and the future of the Social Security system. The growing burden of disability, and the fact that the largest disability program – Disability Insurance – is part of our Social Security system, have led us to focus on this aspect of the problem. We invited Edward D. Berkowitz to analyze and evaluate the disability programs currently in place, to measure their successes and failures, and to recommend feasible reforms that will best utilize the considerable financial investment in disability programs.

Berkowitz, a historian who served on the staff of the President's Commission for a National Agenda for the Eighties and an authority on disability, was a fortunate choice. He proved capable of making impartial assessments without neglecting the human side of the issue.

He has succeeded in presenting a sound history of the politics of disability policymaking, a reasoned evaluation of the programs that we have, and a careful look at what may be needed for the future.

It is Berkowitz's view that disability policy goals must shift from financial support for the retirement of the disabled to greater promotion of the participation of the handicapped in American life. While we do not expect everyone to agree with his prescriptions, we think that the wealth of information and analysis he provides will spark debate on an issue too often ignored and too important to leave to the specialists. We are grateful to him for his effort.

M. J. Rossant, Director
The Twentieth Century Fund
October 1986

Acknowledgments

I live in Baltimore and work in Washington. Although this arrangement poses occasional problems, it has proved ideal for writing a book on public policy toward disability. Since my book uses history as a means of understanding America's programs that serve the disabled, I have been able to do most of my research in the Baltimore–Washington area.

In Suitland, Maryland, I have consulted the records stored in the Washington National Records Center and benefited from the help of that institution's staff. In Baltimore, I have made use of the legislative collections in the Social Security Library and received considerable help from librarian Joyce Donahue. In addition, officials at the Social Security Administration have been kind in granting me interviews. In Washington, D.C., I have traveled to the offices of the Congressional staff-members who work on disability insurance and vocational rehabilitation.

Away from home, I have benefited greatly from the generous financial assistance of the Twentieth Century Fund. The Fund supported three particularly helpful research trips. One was to Texas, where I learned a great deal from Lex Frieden, who continued to show interest in this project after moving to Washington. Another was to Michigan, where I consulted sources in the Gerald Ford Library and learned once again how helpful archivists in presidential libraries can be. My friends Peter Ochshorn and Amy Kahn made this trip an enjoyable experience. The third trip was to Berkeley, where Judy Heumann, Ed Roberts, and many of their associates introduced me to the concept of independent living. Wendy Mercer efficiently handled the arrangements for these trips.

Working on a Twentieth Century Fund project is a collaborative effort. This book is not the one I would have written had I worked by myself. Instead, I collaborated with Pamela Gilfond, Beverly Goldberg, and Steve Andors. Pamela operated on a tight deadline and still managed to trim the length of the manuscript and make the presentation flow more smoothly. Beverly coordinated the progress of the manuscript through the Fund and into the hands of publishers. Steve read early drafts of the manuscript and made many helpful suggestions. These three individuals helped shape the book, changing it from a simple historical narrative to an exercise in policy analysis.

The process of collaboration consumed considerable time and occasioned many meetings in New York. Peter and Dale Demy provided me with an apartment on Park Avenue, pastry from the best bakeries in New York, and continuing good advice.

I would never have gotten support from the Fund without the help of W. Andrew Achenbaum and James A. Smith, to whom I owe my greatest debts. Andy went out of his way to bring my work to the Fund's attention, to provide me with advice on working with the Fund, to read and criticize my manuscript, and to make sure that the manuscript was reviewed by Cambridge University Press. At Cambridge, I might add, Frank Smith did a superb job of easing the manuscript into print. Without Andy's help I would not have had an opportunity to write or publish this book. Jim Smith was my program officer at the Fund until he left to write his own book on history and public policy. He read draft after draft of the original proposal, provided exceptionally good advice on the early chapters, and kept my morale at a reasonable level throughout the project. Jim, Andy, and I began our efforts as colleagues and have become close friends.

Other colleagues helped as well. At George Washington University this book became an important part of the Program in History and Public Policy, which I direct. I am grateful to Dean Henry Solomon and to the various chairmen of the Department of History, who gave me the time to write the book. Many students in the program also helped, in particular Anne-Marie Carroll, Steve Richardson, Susan LaMountain, Emory Luce, and Randy Grochowski. My colleagues William Becker and Leo Ribuffo, who supplied just the right mix of humor and support to get me through the project, made George Washington an enjoyable place to work.

As this book went through successive drafts, many scholars and participants in the field were kind enough to read it and offer comments. I appreciate particularly the advice of Blanche Coll, Harlan Hahn, Ida Merriam, Deborah Stone, William Roth, Richard Scotch, Tom Rose, Richard Burkhauser, Walter Trattner, and Carolyn Weaver. Frank Bowe, Arthur Hess, and Robert J. Myers deserve very special thanks. Frank Bowe read the entire manuscript with particular care and saved me from many errors. Arthur Hess reviewed closely the sections on the establishment of disability insurance and offered tape recorded comments that changed my view of the relationship between disability insurance and vocational rehabilitation. Robert J. Myers reviewed the sections on disability insurance with his usual care and attention to detail. All of these scholars and participants have my gratitude. Let me also exonerate them from responsibility for any errors that may appear in this book.

At home I owe a special debt to Jerry and Liza Frank, who entertained me and my ideas repeatedly throughout the project. They also took care of Sarah Elizabeth Berkowitz when the occasion demanded. I want in particular to mention the kindness of Frances Kleeman, who baby-sat, cooked lasagna, clipped relevant articles from newspapers, and did all that she could to allow me to reserve my strength for writing. Only those who know her can appreciate her extraordinary capacity for helping others and for assisting creative endeavors.

My parents, as always, were an important influence over this book. I have learned a great deal about many things from my father, and his ideas have helped me to formulate my own. His example of applying academic knowledge to practical endeavors has been very important to me. In a different way, I have constantly been encouraged, and encouraged to do better, by my mother.

As I have written a dissertation on disability policy, then edited a book on the subject, then used disability policy as an important example in my work with my friend Kim McQuaid, and finally written this book on disability policy, I have never stopped learning from Robert Wiebe. In a different way, I have also been inspired by Wilbur Cohen, who in my mind has always represented the highest ideals of public service. For this volume, he sat down with me and talked at length about his experiences with the disability insurance program. Years after our initial association, Robert Wiebe and Wilbur Cohen continue to motivate me.

Baltimore, Maryland   Edward D. Berkowitz
November 1986

Introduction

America has no disability policy. It maintains a set of disparate programs, many emanating from policies designed for other groups, that work at cross-purposes.

Born in many different eras, these disability programs reflect many styles of policymaking. Retirement policy intended primarily for the elderly, civil rights policy created for blacks and women, welfare policy aimed at the poor, and the legal system of torts and damages all govern disability programs. Duplication and confusion abound. The states and the federal government often perform the same function. Within Congress, responsibility lies scattered across innumerable committees and subcommittees that more often than not fail to consult with each other. Some programs rely on the courts and the private sector to transfer money to the disabled, while others operate through the tax system and the public sector. Some programs compensate people who have impairments; others attempt to eliminate disability. Civilians and veterans have their own sets of programs, federal workers have others, and railroad workers still others.

The nation pays a high cost for these programs, both in absolute and relative terms. In 1982, for example, disability expenditures in the public and private sectors amounted to $122 billion or 4.7 percent of personal income and 2 percent of all social welfare expenditures. Americans spent $67 billion on cash payments to the disabled and another $52 billion to cover medical expenses, leaving a comparatively meager $3 billion for other purposes. Almost none of that money prepared people for work or removed the architectural barriers that make so much of society inaccessible to the handicapped. The focus was on paying people not to work.[1]

Of the five disability programs that form the core of this study, two pay benefits to workers who have (temporarily or permanently) left their jobs, and three encourage workers to seek employment or to rejoin the labor force. Although the rehabilitation-oriented programs outnumber the other programs, the latter cost far more than the for-

1

mer. Workers' compensation, for example, which pays benefits to employees who have been injured on the job, costs employers $22.5 billion a year in insurance premiums. Only a small fraction of this money goes toward rehabilitating injured workers. Vocational rehabilitation, which attempts to restore the productivity of the handicapped by job placement and job training, costs the federal government about a billion dollars a year. It is by far the least expensive of the major disability programs.[2] Social Security Disability Insurance has emerged as the nation's most expensive disability program. This program paid $17.9 billion in retirement benefits in 1984 and another $11.7 billion in the form of health benefits to its 3.8 million beneficiaries.[3]

In 1973, as an amendment to the vocational rehabilitation program, Congress passed an ambitious civil rights program for the handicapped, making it illegal for programs or institutions receiving federal funds to discriminate against the handicapped. The civil rights program, along with independent living programs, marked an attempt to make society accessible to the handicapped.

Unless someone makes an effort to coordinate these programs and others like them, expensive, contradictory programs that perpetuate disability will continue to be the norm. As matters stand, there is little evidence that reforms are forthcoming. Americans continue to pile programs on top of one another without regard to the system they are creating. What passes for public policy toward disability stems from an almost casual sequence of historical events, beginning with the passage of industrial accident laws in the Progressive Era at the beginning of the century, continuing with the creation of Social Security in the New Deal, and concluding with the extension of civil rights coverage in the 1970s. The set of programs contains the very oldest as well as the very newest program; we live as much with the consequences of actions taken at the beginning of the century as with actions taken yesterday.

One of the main reasons for this lack of consistency is that, despite all the money devoted to them, disability programs have never attracted a political following. The contrast with programs to aid the elderly, who have many public champions, is striking. Highly visible congressional committees monitor public policy toward the elderly, but no congressional committees air the grievances and publicize the problems of the disabled. No leader of the handicapped community has risen to national prominence, nor have the handicapped received the sustained attention from the media that the elderly have.

A disabled person has a more difficult time securing entitlement to a pension and other benefits than an elderly person. Policymakers presume that the elderly have, because of their years in the labor force, earned the right to retire. The public has little fear of the elderly cheating the government by claiming benefits that are not rightfully theirs. It is easy to verify whether or not a person is elderly. And nearly everyone expects to grow old, so that the elderly, unlike the disabled, do not stand apart from the rest of the population. For all of these reasons, giving benefits to the elderly has gained universal acceptance in social welfare policy.

In contrast, the handicapped, who may never have worked, have not "earned" a right to benefits in the same way as the elderly. Those handicapped individuals who have worked and who wish to retire are, in a sense, asking for a special favor – to be let out of the labor force and to draw a pension from the state. Cheating is far more likely to occur among those seeking disability benefits than among those seeking old age benefits. And almost no one expects to become handicapped (the handicapped represent a far smaller segment of the population than do the elderly) before reaching retirement age.

Unlike old age, disability resists precise definition and measurement and therefore presents subtle problems. Identifying the disabled is an act of consummate skill. Disability represents a social judgment and, in some cases, a personal choice. It involves a combination of physical, economic, and psychological conditions that make the formation and administration of public policy difficult and complex. For example, people respond differently to the same physical condition. Most retire; Franklin Roosevelt did not allow a handicap to deter him from becoming president. Society could spend all of its money on disability programs and still not consistently influence a person's choice to retire.

The nation fights periodic wars on poverty and uses age as a convenient shorthand for need. Even as the nation's policymakers speak of ending poverty and creating opportunities for the disadvantaged to work, they choose to ignore the handicapped and the problems of disability (while at the same time spending a considerable amount of money on disability programs). Never regarded as a central concern of social welfare policy, disability policy has become fragmented among many programs. As a consequence, it lacks consistency. No one sees disability policy "whole": the welter of programs affords no vantage point from which to gain a panoramic view. These programs, by their very existence, limit public responses. Many of the choices in disability policy, in other words, have already been made, although ironically not much thought has been given to the effect of those choices on disability policy and on the handicapped.

When disability policy is viewed whole, a fundamental contradiction appears. Simply put, this nation spends most of the money allocated to disability on programs that provide the handicapped with tickets out of the labor force. At the same time, policymakers fund training programs and pass civil rights laws as an inducement for the handicapped to enter the labor force. Because disability has been subsumed under so many different headings, the contradiction goes largely unnoticed.

Recent events in the field of disability clearly reveal the contradictory nature of disability policy. Most people have seen the signs that bear the special symbol of a handicapped person in a wheelchair. Policymakers typically use the signs to reserve parking places for the handicapped or to announce that a facility, such as a public rest room, can accommodate someone in a wheel chair. Nearly always the signs are part of a policy strategy to make activities of daily life, such as shopping or working, accessible to the handicapped.

As these signs became common artifacts of daily life, the most-publicized event in disability policy involved a fight to keep people on the disability rolls and out of the labor force. In order to gain access to these rolls, people had to prove to the satisfaction of a state disability examiner, an administrative law judge, or a federal judge that they were unable to do any sort of work. When the Reagan administration suggested that some of these people could indeed work and removed them from the rolls, a furor erupted. Advocates for the disabled argued that the handicapped had a legal entitlement to a disability pension and should not be forced to seek work. They made no mention of efforts to facilitate the entrance of the handicapped into the work force. Thus the efforts to open up the labor force to the handicapped and the efforts to protect the rights of the handicapped to retire proceed in parallel, never touching one another.

One barrier to a more rational disability policy lies in the fact that, as used in public programs, disability has at least three different meanings. In the workers' compensation program and in the courts, disability means the damages that one person collects from another as a result of an insult or injury. In the Social Security Disability Insurance program, disability refers to a condition that links ill health and unemployment. And in the context of civil rights laws, disability connotes "handicap." Nor does the confusion end there. Policy analysts have spent a great deal of time puzzling over the distinctions among such terms as functional limitations, impairment, disability, and handicap. Despite the scholarly efforts, different people use the terms differently.[4]

The different definitions point to the many policy problems posed by disability. In the absence of a common definition people continue, for example, to associate disability with damages. In the judicial context, this use of the term perpetuates an anachronistic approach to the problem. The lengthy and expensive judicial process requires that a person demonstrate the extent of his disability rather than rehabilitate himself.* It concentrates money on recompense after the fact and detracts from the goal of preventing the hazard in the first place or promoting the independence of the handicapped. It also raises profound questions of fairness, since those with the most money – those who need damage awards the least – may have access to the most skilled lawyers and the most effective expert witnesses. In short, making disability a form of damages, and a legal concept for the courts to define, places a social problem in the framework of a personal dispute.

Efforts to end litigation have characterized disability policy ever since the creation of workers' compensation laws in 1911, yet litigation persists. As new work hazards arise, such as cancer caused by exposure to asbestos, workers turn to litigation for compensation. Workers in dockyards, for example, sue the manufacturers of asbestos for product liability because they believe that they will receive more from the courts than from disability programs. Further, the explosion of rights and entitlements in social welfare policy in the 1970s and 1980s has triggered disability litigation. As new rights are defined, people turn to the courts to secure them. Matters previously considered within the realm of professional discretion now become subject to litigation. As a result, many applicants for disability benefits hire lawyers to argue their

---

*To avoid awkward wording, the masculine pronoun "he" will often be used in the generic sense to mean "he or she."

cases before administrative law judges; the vocational rehabilitation program contains an explicit provision for dissatisfied clients to initiate legal action against the agency. In these ways, the use of litigation to secure disability benefits continues to grow. And as litigation persists, vested interests, such as lawyers who try disability cases, create barriers to the reform of disability policy.

Defining disability as the condition that links ill health and unemployment puts disability in the context of a valid ticket out of the labor force. If a person leaves the labor force as a result of a physical or mental condition, he is neither unemployed nor temporarily ill; he is disabled. Such a definition increases the subjectivity of the concept and makes disability that much more difficult to administer. The lines between temporary illness, permanent disability, and unemployment are difficult to draw. That, in turn, makes it hard to control the growth of entitlement programs that offer disability pensions.

The awarding of disability benefits, furthermore, is linked to other social forces. Recessions often lead to surges in the disability rolls because older "impaired" workers use disability programs to retire. During the 1970s, for example, when disability program officials appeared willing to loosen the definition of disability, employers used disability benefits as a way to ease out older workers and replace them with younger ones. In the 1980s, efforts to reduce social spending led to a decline in the disability rolls, even without formal changes in the program.

Cases arise constantly that test the boundaries between ill health, unemployment, and disability. Early in the Social Security Disability Insurance program, for example, a case arose that was typical of many to follow. The case concerned a woman, born in 1896, with a grade school education. She had worked for twenty-five years at odd jobs in a local Pennsylvania market, manning the cash register and helping to keep the books. In 1956, at the age of sixty, she retired.

She weighed 200 pounds. Both of her breasts had been removed in an effort to stop the spread of cancer. As a result of the surgery, she could not extend her arms or lift heavy objects. Despite the surgery, the malignancy had spread, so that more operations were necessary. In addition, she suffered from clots in her legs that, she said, prevented her from walking more than a block. Worried about her medical condition, distressed over leaving work, the woman suffered a nervous breakdown. When she entered a mental hospital, doctors discovered that she had been treated for mental illness in the late 1930s, at which time she had spent parts of two years in a state mental hospital, diagnosed as a paranoid. Her psychiatrist now reported that she had a fear of people, as well as an exaggerated fear of being bumped in the chest.

This woman was old, damaged, and distressed. She wanted a pension to tide her over until she could receive old age benefits from Social Security. The Social Security Administration (SSA) denied her disability benefits, telling her that if she had followed her doctor's advice and lost weight she might have "lessened her impairments" and found work. In other words, she failed to meet the SSA's strict definition of disability. She was ill and unemployed but not disabled.[5]

The woman's case and others like it created pressures to expand the disability rolls. For one thing, congressmen urged the Social Security Administration to interpret the law in a more lenient manner and passed laws liberalizing the definition of disability. For another, the courts began to undermine the strict definition of disability that had made it so hard for the woman from Pennsylvania to obtain benefits. Like other social welfare programs, the disability program grew throughout the 1960s and well into the 1970s.

Only in the 1970s did the size of the program become a political liability. In an age of concern about "uncontrollable" social welfare expenditures, expenditures for disability insurance consistently exceeded the expectations of policymakers. The growth of disability insurance put pressure on the entire social security system, which faced a series of financial crises in the mid-1970s and early 1980s. During the 1970s, for example, disability program expenditures grew from $3 billion to nearly $15 billion. In actual dollars, program expenditures doubled between 1967 and 1971, between 1971 and 1975, and between 1975 and 1980.[6]

The costs of entitlement programs such as disability insurance have dominated discussion of public policy toward disability and in the process obscured a more fundamental problem – the programs insist on withdrawal of a person from the labor force before they classify him as disabled. The benefits that most people want and that draw the most government funding lead to retirement rather than rehabilitation and independence.

At the same time, however, efforts to rehabilitate beneficiaries of disability insurance or workers' compensation have largely failed. Plans to merge income-maintenance and rehabilitation programs have en-

countered difficulties not unlike those of workfare programs designed
to put welfare recipients into the labor force. Rehabilitation plans have
foundered on the prejudices that older, impaired workers encounter in
the labor market and on the disincentives built into the income-
maintenance programs. Many workers who leave the disability rolls,
for example, lose their rights to health insurance and thus are deterred
from accepting a job. The fact that the disability system is so balkan-
ized further discourages efforts at rehabilitation. The vocational rehabilitation program is administered at the state level; the Social
Security Disability Insurance program at the federal level. The
congressional committees that authorize money for the vocational rehabilitation program have little communication with the committees
that oversee the social security program. As the example of the Pennsylvania woman makes clear, not every disability beneficiary or handicapped person can work, and drawing the line between those expected to work and those excused from working constitutes as difficult
a policy problem as any in the social welfare field. Nonetheless, the
structure of our public programs does little to encourage those who
can work to do so.

Because of the adverse reaction to the Reagan administration's attempts to remove people from the disability rolls – itself a reaction to
the growth of the disability rolls – the effort to rehabilitate disability
beneficiaries has reached a low ebb. As a result of a law passed in
1984, which protects the rights of disability beneficiaries, a person on
the disability rolls now has more chance of staying there until he dies
or reaches age sixty-five than ever before. The more Congress strengthens
the entitlement to disability benefits, the less chance disability policy
will emphasize rehabilitation rather than retirement. The more Congress widens the disability zone that lies between ill health and unemployment, the greater the chance the rolls will expand.

Equating disability with handicap leads to other problems. Someone
who looks or acts disabled is not necessarily unable to work. But many
people identify someone in a wheelchair, for example, as handicapped,
regardless of his abilities. Since the handicapped person cannot alter
this perception, one authority refers to disability as a "product of the
interaction between the individual and the environment."[7] From this
perspective, the problems associated with disability are not the result
of personal limitations so much as the consequences of a disabling
environment.

Disabling environments require correction at the community level, yet our disability policy focuses on handicapped individuals themselves. Instead of learning about environmental barriers to employment, rehabilitation counselors, trained in the methods of psychology, study the individual psyches of the handicapped. Counselors spend time matching the handicapped with jobs rather than expanding the range of jobs accessible to the handicapped. They do nothing to lower the barriers that exclude the handicapped from society; instead they adjust the handicapped to society and in this manner maintain, even legitimate, the barriers.

As many members of an increasingly militant handicapped community have come to realize, programs, such as vocational rehabilitation, develop for reasons that often have nothing to do with the people whom they serve. The programs have their own internal coherence, but they do not necessarily mesh with the lives of those they are intended to benefit. The handicapped have therefore tried to gain control over disability policy, to take power away from professional administrators, and to assume it themselves. This effort has led to the passage of civil rights laws and to the creation of independent living centers, which are largely run by the handicapped rather than professional rehabilitation counselors.

I find much to admire in this new generation of disability programs, for I believe that the existence of a physical handicap should not limit a person's participation in society. If prejudices stand in the way of employment, then handicapped people must be protected by the vigorous enforcement of civil rights laws. If physical barriers prevent people from working or from taking part in other activities, then public policy must seek ways to remove the barriers. For those whose conditions make work impossible, public policy should promote independence and self-care. Being handicapped should not be equated with being helpless. We need to move disability policy beyond retirement and toward the participation of the handicapped in American life.

As the persistence of litigation, the absence of coordination between income-maintenance and rehabilitation programs, and the inability of the vocational rehabilitation program to respond to modern conditions reveal, our present disability system lacks the structure to reach these goals. We do not have the institutional means to replace one program with another and to trade anachronistic practices for modern ones. The experts conduct their specialized work in isolation from each other, and disability programs have become so technical, complex, and detailed that, in the 1980s, it is virtually impossible for any one person to be current on all the programs, let alone the ways in which they interact.

The pieces of disability policy should form a coherent whole, but people cannot even agree on a common definition of disability, let alone create a disability policy that bridges the individual programs. Because these programs have been conceived and administered in isolation from one another, they are locked into an institutional structure that has proved resistant to change, even though the programs have failed to serve those they were intended to help. This collection of disparate programs should be replaced by a cohesive disability policy that reflects the high hopes the handicapped have for themselves.

Some day, perhaps, disability will receive the attention it deserves as an integrated policy problem, and policymakers will examine the system of programs rather than tinkering with one program in isolation from another. Some day policymakers may discover the importance of having a conscious disability policy rather than an uncoordinated set of programs that create unintended and undesired effects.

Before that can happen, however, we need to bring order to the labyrinth and expose the contradictions of our present approach. This book relies on a historical overview of five representative and important disability programs to achieve that objective. Rather than providing a strictly chronological account, the book concentrates on the development of policy problems, such as the conflict between advocates of handicapped rights and disability policymakers.

Part I considers income-maintenance programs, and Part II concentrates on programs that try to integrate the handicapped into society, primarily through the provision of special services or the enforcement of civil rights laws. In Part I, the state-run workers' compensation programs represent the first generation of income-maintenance programs. Social Security Disability Insurance marks the emergence of a second generation of these programs. Although this second generation of programs was created to remedy the problems of the first, analysis reveals that it failed to do so. In Part II, vocational rehabilitation, a state-run program started as an adjunct to workers' compensation, marks the first generation of programs designed to return disabled workers to the labor force. Civil rights and independent living programs reflect a second generation of efforts to integrate the handicapped into society; these second-generation programs emerged in reaction to the limitations of the first-generation vocational rehabilitation program. The analysis in Part II centers on the failure to blend these later programs with the income-maintenance programs.

In a final chapter, I turn from history to prognosis and attempt to make realistic recommendations for the improvement of disability policy. As a historian, I am aware of how yesterday's solutions have become today's problems and of how the same problems persist from generation to generation. Even so, I believe that the need for an efficient, equitable system that provides for the participation of the handicapped in society is more pressing than ever. We cannot continue to maintain a system that defeats itself and becomes progressively more costly to maintain.

I. Income-maintenance programs

How does American public policy respond to the circumstances of physical disability? That simple question lacks a simple answer. The federal and state governments run so many disability programs that it is difficult to know where to begin describing them. Elizabeth Boggs, perhaps the nation's greatest authority on programs that affect the mentally retarded, tells the story of being asked to produce a "Baedecker or Fodor" of public programs, "a guide to the labyrinth." Boggs, a woman of encyclopedic knowledge and enormous energy, struggled with the assignment, concluding that the labyrinth of disability programs was "psychedelic, constantly squirming and changing with the convolutions of Congress." She noted, however, that there was a "basic boney structure underlying those psychedelic streams."[1]

So the answer to the question about America's public policy toward disability may lie in the basic boney structure, which reveals a basic division among disability programs. Some provide cash to the disabled, others provide services.

The programs that pay cash stem from the movement toward social insurance against such risks as ill health and involuntary retirement that originated at the turn of the century. The most significant social insurance programs for disability policy are workers' compensation, started in the Progressive Era, and Social Security Disability Insurance, begun during the New Deal.

Part I of this book examines these two generations of income-maintenance programs for the disabled. They have indelibly stamped America's public response to the problem of disability.

1. Workers' compensation

Workers' compensation, begun in the states of Wisconsin and New Jersey in 1911, deserves to be called the nation's first modern disability program. Designed to aid workers who had been injured on the job, it removed control over the money, medical care, and other services given to injured workers from the hands of employers, the courts, and the community. It transferred that control to state governments.

Before the passage of workers' compensation laws, workers injured on the job struggled to collect what damages they could from their employers by suing them in court. Compensation amounted to a contest between employers and employees, mediated by judges and juries. Workers' compensation laws, which were on the books of every state by 1948, were passed in part as an attempt to avoid litigation over industrial accidents by equating a specific injury with a particular amount of compensation. Unfortunately, these laws failed to end the contest between employer and employee over industrial accidents. Disputes continued, in part because of the way in which the programs were financed. The laws required employers to buy insurance or to set aside reserves against the risk of injuring an employee, giving employers and their insurance companies an incentive to contest cases in which employees claimed to be disabled. If the employer won the case, he saved money on his insurance premiums or maintained the level of his cash reserves.

The fact that lawyers, insurance companies, trade unions, and state industrial commissions all acquired an interest in workers' compensation has made reform of the program exceedingly difficult. Benefits continue to rise with wage rates, but the program's basic structure, a product of the Progressive Era, remains unchanged. As a result, the program achieves old-fashioned social welfare objectives, such as compensating someone with an impairment – even though, in the face of medical improvements, this impairment may no longer be career threatening – at modern levels of expenditure. Nor does it appear likely that the state workers' compensation program will be federal-

15

ized or replaced with a more modern program in the near future. Worker's compensation, then, must be explained in terms of the historical circumstances surrounding its origins. Modern policy problems can be traced directly from the program's origins in the Progressive Era.

The origins of workers' compensation

In the nineteenth century, injured workers depended on the courts to recover damages from recalcitrant employers. In the first half of the century, judges provided employers with broad defenses, leaving many loopholes through which the employer could duck his responsibilities. The burden of proof rested on the employee, who had to demonstrate to a judge's satisfaction that the injury was not the result of the employee's wrongdoing (contributory negligence), that the employer's actions caused the injury rather than the carelessness of a coworker (the fellow-servant rule), and that the injury was not connected with an inherent hazard of the job of which the employee had advance knowledge (assumption of risk).[1]

The injured worker's situation, on the other hand, was never quite as bleak as the number of loopholes implied. When cases appeared on the dockets in significant numbers (only a few such cases had arisen in the early part of the nineteenth century; only one such case reached the Illinois Supreme Court between 1818 and 1854), workers began to gain the sympathy of judges and juries. As a consequence, the courts softened their application of the legal defenses available to employers. To illustrate, application of the fellow-servant rule won fewer and fewer cases for employers. In Illinois, for example, a foreman failed to qualify as a fellow servant; the courts attributed his negligence to the employer. Similarly, a worker temporarily outside of his usual place of employment could not be called a fellow servant; his negligence was also attributed to the employer. In other cases, the courts allowed the jury to decide whether a particular employee qualified as a fellow servant. The sympathy of the jury for the workers in such cases undercut the employer's fellow-servant defense.[2]

Adding to the workers' changing legal fortunes, some states legislated formal changes in employers' liability laws. Six states barred the use of the fellow-servant defense in work accident cases by the middle of the 1890s; sixteen states did so by 1908. Nearly twenty states passed laws stating that an employer's failure to follow safety regulations would cause him to lose the assumption-of-risk defense.[3]

By the end of the nineteenth century, the application of common law remedies to industrial accident cases came under heavy attack from many groups, including employers, the judiciary, and workers. Employers, facing increased probabilities of losing cases, perceived a need for insurance to cover their possible losses. As the demand for this insurance grew, it became progressively more costly. According to a crude estimate, it increased from $200,000 in 1887 to more than $35 million by 1912. At least part of the reason for this rise was the fact that workers were winning more cases and receiving generous settlements from juries. Of 307 personal injury cases that came to the Wisconsin supreme court in the years before 1907, for example, nearly two-thirds had been decided in the workers' favor by the lower courts. The combination of changing legal fortunes and rising insurance premiums sparked a change in employer attitudes.[4]

Members of the judiciary also grew dissatisfied with the common law approach. A Missouri judge, catching the spirit of the times, wrote that "the tendency of the more modern authorities appears to be in the direction of . . . a modification and limitation [of the fellow-servant rule] . . . as shall eventually devolve upon the employer . . . a due and just share of the responsibility for the lives and limbs of the persons in its employ." A Wisconsin supreme court judge stated in 1908 that the system was "all wrong in its basic features. It is illogical and wholly unadaptable to our complex industrial life. It should be displaced from its very foundation."[5]

Workers joined this chorus of dissatisfaction because the system afforded them no certain relief. Workers won many cases, but they also lost many, failed to bring suit in others, lost on appeal, had their cases thrown out of court, or settled out of court for less than their claim was worth.

A New York commission studying the problem of industrial accidents found that of 414,681 injury claims filed with nine of the largest insurance companies between 1906 and 1908, workers received compensation in only 52,427 cases. The Aetna Liability Insurance Company reported making payment in one case out of sixteen.[6] In 1907–8, Crystal Eastman concluded her classic investigation into the fate of injured and fatally injured workmen in the Pittsburgh area and found that 59 out of 235 families whose breadwinner had died in an industrial accident received no compensation from the employer; in a majority of cases the workers themselves bore a substantial part of the burden of disability.[7]

In this contradictory situation, late in the nineteenth century and early in the twentieth court dockets became jammed with accident cases brought by workers that the workers would, in all likelihood, lose. Despite the fact that workers lost far more cases than they won, the courts in the state of Washington spent half of their time on accident litigation in 1910 and 1911. In Wisconsin, accident cases easily constituted the largest single category of cases before the state supreme court.[8]

Crowded court dockets and the perceived inefficiency of the common law system bred discontent with the system on the part of reformers who professed an interest in "good government." National business and labor leaders, assisted by a group whom historians traditionally identify as progressive reformers, inched their way to a compromise. As a first step, many states appointed bipartisan commissions to investigate the problem and to recommend a solution.

Each commission included extensive evidence on delays in the court system as part of its report. The more severe the injury, those commissions found, the more likely an employee would be to contest the case at every stage of the judicial process and, therefore, the longer it took to settle the case. A worker never knew how long it would take to settle his case nor the size of his settlement. As the delays mounted, so did the pressure to settle out of court for less than a jury might award. Delays forced some workers and their families to rely on charity or public welfare while waiting for the conclusion of a case. In this manner, the system could be said to pauperize its beneficiaries. In Ohio, that state's commission discovered, it took two years to conclude the typical case involving a fatality. In Illinois, it was usually three years before an injured worker began to receive benefits. The Illinois commission report included case studies that powerfully condemned the court system. The report cited a 1903 case in which a worker in Moline got his arm caught in a conveyor belt. Although the worker ultimately received $11,000, the case consumed the time of four lawyers over a period of six years, producing considerable hardship for the employee.[9]

Not all those workers who persevered through the court system had something to show for their efforts. In 1909, for example, an immi-

grant worker living in Duluth severely injured his leg. A district court
awarded him $1,000 in damages in the summer of 1910. His employer
appealed, taking the case all the way to the Minnesota Supreme Court.
Not until the fall of 1911 did the court reach its verdict. Although the
court ruled in the worker's favor, he did not receive his money until
July 1912. Of the $1,000 plus $357 in interest that the worker received, he had to pay $635 to his attorney, $25 to an interpreter,
$73.20 in court fees, $313.14 to expert witnesses, and $147.40 to his
doctors. The settlement left him with less than $100 to show for his
efforts.[10]

The proponents of change – whose ranks included businessmen,
labor leaders, and those whom historians identify as progressives –
used these case studies to condemn the court system and to point out
the potential advantages of workers' compensation. Under the proposed new law, all industrial injuries would become the responsibility
of the employer, who would pay a fixed percentage of the worker's
earnings for the duration of the disability.

In most states, the commissions endorsed workers' compensation as
a prelude to the passage of state laws. By 1913, twenty-one states had
passed workers' compensation laws; by 1919, workers' compensation
laws existed in forty-three states.

The state of Washington's law contains a preamble that captures
the spirit in which the law was originally passed. The preamble states
that the common law approach to industrial injury is "inconsistent"
with modern conditions and is "economically unwise and unfair."
Workers' compensation removes industrial injury from "private controversy" and gives workers "sure and certain relief" by abolishing
the legal question of fault and making workers' compensation the exclusive remedy for industrial accidents.[11]

In the euphoria surrounding the passage of these laws, the proponents made extravagant claims about ending litigation over industrial
accidents and creating harmony between employers and workers. In
the state of Washington, one politician called the new law "a long step
toward getting the employer and employee together" and cited other
benefits, such as predictable insurance costs, "certain, prompt, and
adequate benefits," and, above all, the lessening of litigation. The Illinois commission stated that workers' compensation would tend, "of
course, greatly to reduce litigation. That, in turn, would tend to reduce
the cost of insurance. . . . With greater certainty as to indemnity, the

cost can be more accurately measured and the element of guess reduced."[12]

Caught up in the excitement of the moment, few realized how little
had changed. Although the passage of state workers' compensation
laws had established minimum standards that the states expected employers to follow, the existence of those standards failed to solve more
fundamental policy problems such as the persistence of litigation. At
most, the new laws made the outcome of cases more certain and limited the number of defenses on which an employer could rely. The
institutional arrangements remained largely the same. Insurance companies and private employers continued to pay compensation to injured employees and, in most states, the courts continued to rule on
disagreements between employer and employee. The new laws failed
to turn disability into an objective concept that could readily be applied to public policy. The state governments conditioned private actions but initiated no new public ones.

The persistence of litigation

Proponents of workers' compensation hoped to reconcile contradictory objectives and produce a new system that would be both more
informal and more professional than the old one. They believed that
the rules provided by workers' compensation laws would allow specialists to determine the facts of industrial accident cases and reach
decisions without involving lawyers or judges.

To keep the new law out of the hands of the old contestants, the
proponents urged that workers' compensation administration be removed from the courts. The situation in Minnesota was typical of that
in many other states. After the passage of the workers' compensation
law, the courts continued to hear disputed cases, much as they had
heard all cases under the old system, and to approve uncontested settlements. Insurance agents, who often failed to grant workers the benefits to which they were entitled, retained considerable power. Lacking
expertise in the new law, judges tended to accept settlements reached
between insurance companies and employees; they failed to scrutinize
the settlement to see if the worker received what the law said he had
coming to him. A special commission, established to explore this administrative problem, recommended that Minnesota follow the lead
of Pennsylvania and Wisconsin and establish an industrial commission

to administer workers' compensation laws.[13] Commissions of this type embodied the Progressive Era faith in professionalism. As one group of proponents put it, "The members [of a commission] become specialists. They get to understand problems that arise. . . . They work out a uniform administration of the law."[14]

Industrial commissions or industrial accident boards quickly took over the administration of workers' compensation laws. These commissions or boards worked out informal methods of hearing disputed compensation cases, often appointing hearing officers or arbitrators (referees) to settle cases. Mindful of their mission to reduce friction between workers and employers, the commissions strove to keep the hearings brief, informal, and unintimidating. The hope was to abolish "the slow, expensive and cumbersome procedure that had hampered execution of compensation laws by judges."[15]

In this spirit, A. J. Pillsbury of the Industrial Accident Commission of California expressed his desire to make procedures as "simple, as direct and inexpensive as possible." His commission's first report noted that three out of four cases did not require a lawyer. A referee (or arbitrator), who was permitted wide latitude in questioning witnesses, would elicit the facts in an informal hearing, and Pillsbury hoped that employers and employees could "adjust their own cases without delay or expenses."[16]

The lawyers who had played a significant role in industrial accident cases were not happy with this new informal approach. According to the California commission's first report, "There are members of the bar of this state who are unable to reconcile themselves to a procedure wholly different from that which characterizes trials in courts." The commission, wrote Pillsbury, was "subjected to constant pressure from bench and bar tending to make its hearings trials and its proceedings less summary than they should be."[17]

In time these pressures grew worse, and California and many other states succumbed to them. Persistent litigation, conducted under confusing circumstances and capricious rules, brought much criticism of the way in which workers' compensation laws were administered. The criticism that began as early as the 1930s continues to the present. In 1935, for example, federal bureaucrats characterized the administration of workers' compensation as "poor." That same year, a scholar of labor legislation wrote that, "Some of the most liberal workmen's compensation laws have been made largely ineffective by careless, inadequate, or incompetent administration." Lauded as revolutionary innovations in the Progressive Era, state workers' compensation laws languished in the New Deal and afterward. It was as if the progressives had grown weary, gone home, and left the industrial commissions to the lawyers and the politicians.[18]

In a classic study of workers' compensation administration in the mid-1930s conducted by legal scholar Walter Dodd, a sordid picture emerged. The industrial commissions of Illinois and New York were the worst offenders. In the Chicago office of the Illinois commission, four of the arbitrators had less than three months' experience, and they spent most of their time "keeping their political fences intact." (All owed their appointments to political connections.) Few of the arbitrators expressed any interest in the compensation law itself; some were illiterate.

Consequently, the justice that workers and employers received was less than perfect. "There is a great deal of obvious perjury in the testimony of many witnesses, but especially of the medical witnesses," wrote Dodd. The hearings lacked the compassionate informality for which the designers of the system had hoped. Instead they amounted to a "game of skill between opposing counsel" in which the arbitrator ruled, without particular competence, on the objections raised by the lawyers. Lawyers got to choose their arbitrator, a practice that created incentives for all sorts of corruption. Some attorneys solicited cases by sending out "runners" to buttonhole prospective clients in hospital waiting rooms or coroners' offices; they also sought clients through deals with insurance claims adjustors or by encouraging doctors to give patients their business cards. Even employees of the commission – supposedly impartial public servants – occasionally sent a worker to a lawyer for a split of the fee.[19]

Many of the same abuses occurred in the New York City office of the New York industrial commission. Workers' compensation was frenzied, with as many as fifty-five or sixty cases scheduled on a single day, and it was not free of corruption. The practice of sending "runners" to solicit business for attorneys endured in New York just as it did in Chicago. The foreign born constituted between 50 and 75 percent of the New York City caseload, and the runners concentrated most of their attention on this group. Immigrants crowded the hearing rooms, many unable to understand completely the questions being put to them by lawyers. Employees fended for themselves unless their unions intervened; the insurance companies nearly always retained counsel for a hearing. Further, as the workers' lawyers hustled for business, the insurance companies and their lawyers cultivated the referees. The commission made an effort to rotate the referees' calendars, so that a particular referee did not continue to hear the cases from a particular insurance company year after year. Still, the insurance companies maintained cordial relations with the referees and made it a regular practice to send the referees what Dodd refers to as "Christmas re-membrances." Some referees refused the gifts; most did not.[20]

In such circumstances, workers' compensation never engendered the hoped-for harmony between workers and employers. Over the years the number of contested cases rose rather than fell. At hearings, the representatives of employers and employees argued, among many other things, over whether injuries were work related and therefore covered under the workers' compensation act. For example, a case arose re-cently in the state of Ohio in which a woman slipped and injured her left foot about twenty feet from the entrance to her office. Her com-pensation claim was denied on the grounds that her injury did not occur in the course of, or arising out of, employment. She appealed her case and lost.[21]

Over the years, many other cases tested the boundary between work and leisure and led to disagreements that ended in litigation. Take, for example, a case in which a construction worker who also bowled and lifted weights in his spare time injured his lower back. As early as 1935, Dodd observed that back injuries were "the most difficult to adjudicate. They involve many hearings, disputed medical testimony, and become a burden upon the administration and a trial to everyone at interest." Today, in the state of Kansas, 42 percent of all workers' compensation expenditures are for back injuries.[22]

Bitter disputes also arose over the extent of a worker's disability – just how disabling was a particular injury? To paraphrase questions posed by Dodd: To what extent is the sight of the eye impaired? Has the use of the hand been lost? Shall compensation be paid for the loss of the finger or loss of half the finger? These decisions in turn involved the inherent subjectivity of disability – the fact that people reacted differently to the same physical problem. Because reaction to a physi-cal problem was so subjective, it became difficult to make rules that applied with equal validity to everyone. Debate over such questions took up an increasing amount of the industrial commissions' time and led to greater delays in the compensation process.

The situation in Maryland illustrated the general trend. During the first year of the workers' compensation law in the Progressive Era, 7.2 percent of workers' compensation claims were contested. In 1933, at the beginning of the New Deal, 20.2 percent of the claims were contested. The number of hearings increased from 273 to 1,776 per year.[23]

An increasingly contentious system bred formality by encouraging the participation of lawyers. The presence of lawyers, despite the efforts of early administrators to exclude them, defeated efforts to hold hearings with relaxed rules of evidence and cross-questioning. Nor did the harm end there. Because of the demands on the lawyers' time, their participation increased the delays in the compensation process and raised old questions about the financial status of the worker and his potential dependence on public programs. The participation of attorneys also invited concern about the competence of one lawyer compared with that of another and about the persistence of the mismatch between the comparatively rich insurance companies and the relatively poor workers.

Litigation: the situation today

In most states, it remains advisable for those seeking workers' compensation to employ the services of a lawyer. A Massachusetts industrial commissioner put the matter quite directly when he said, "The way our law is set up, it is worth it for the claimant to get an attorney."[24] A Michigan attorney who makes his living on workers' compensation cases said recently that the Michigan law was too complex for a worker to enter the system without an attorney. In Michigan, where it takes a year to schedule a workers' compensation trial, an appeal might take as long as four years. A Michigan worker, locked into this system, is often afraid to resume normal activities for fear of lessening his settlement. As time passes, the workers become more receptive to an out-of-court settlement. This alternative is often congenial to a lawyer as well as a worker since, regardless of whether the case is heard or is settled, the attorney claims his fee, just as he did under common law.[25]

Not all states passively accept the inevitability of litigation and de-

lay in workers' compensation. Some states wish to reverse the pattern
and seek alternatives. In Minnesota, for example, should an employer's insurance company deny responsibility for an employee's injury,
the employee has the right to file a petition with the Department of
Labor and Industry. A settlement judge reviews the petition; if he thinks
the claim can be settled without a formal hearing, he orders the parties
to attend a settlement conference, which provides an informal means
of adjusting the dispute. The state reports that one hundred of these
conferences are held each month and that settlements occur between
80 and 90 percent of the time.

Should an insurance company decide to discontinue a worker's benefits, the state of Minnesota holds what it calls an administrative conference. According to a state official, "Representation by an attorney
at this level should not be necessary; friends, spouses, union officials,
or others may attend as 'moral support.'" Should this conference fail
to resolve the matter, the parties can request a hearing before the Office of Administrative Hearings, at which lawyers often are present.[26]

The neighboring state of Wisconsin has made similar efforts to remove workers' compensation matters from the realm of litigation, with
mixed results. The state advises workers that lawyers are not necessary
in these cases, "unless a serious disagreement arises." But state officials also caution workers that should honest disagreement arise "over
the amount of disability or whether an injury is work related . . . you
and the insurance company may decide to settle your claim . . . and
after you agree to compromise, it is legally very difficult to change."
The prudent worker, after receiving this advice, would hire a lawyer
to bargain with the insurance company. In Wisconsin, as in many other
states, the no-fault workers' compensation system fails to operate as
originally designed.[27]

To illustrate in more human terms, let us observe a hearing conducted by Larry Tarr, deputy commissioner of Virginia's workers'
compensation program in Alexandria. He hears cases in the dignified,
formal atmosphere of a regular county courtroom. Although he dis-
dains the wearing of robes, he sits as a judge. Witnesses testify before
him as they would in a formal trial.

The case involves a carpet mechanic who claims to have suffered a
work-related injury. He states that while bending down to install a
carpet, he felt a pop in his back that caused him to fall to his knees.
The next day he was unable to work. He suffered a loss of feeling in

his legs and sometimes his legs went numb and he collapsed. He had difficulty getting from place to place. When his wife drove him to the doctor, he needed to lie down in the back of the car.

The bearded and muscular employee in his polyester suit and open shirt stands in contrast to the pinstriped lawyer who politely poses questions for him in Tarr's hearing room.

This lawyer contends that no accident arose out of the course of employment and that the employee has refused medical attention. A senior claims adjuster from the insurance company testifies that the worker's benefits have been denied because the carrier doubts that the injuries are as severe as the worker claims.[28]

Despite the fact that workers' compensation is designed to operate as a no-fault law in every state in the country, the carpet mechanic still has to prove that his injury is work-related before he can collect damages from his employers. Even then, he faces a disagreement over the extent of his disability. A system with such formal legal proceedings cannot be called a no-fault system.

As the case of the carpet mechanic reveals, even with workers' compensation laws in place, industrial accident claims continue to be contested by employers, who want to keep their losses or insurance premiums low, and argued by lawyers. Whatever merits those lawyers may bring to a case, they take away 20 to 25 percent of the award and their presence increases the time it takes to conclude a case. A federal task force estimates that the average contested case lasts more than a year.[29]

How benefits are awarded

Workers' compensation abounds with disagreements over what compensation payments represent. Some states regard them as damages, as payments to compensate the worker for the discomfort of enduring an injury. Other states see them as a form of income maintenance, as payments to compensate the worker for a definite economic loss that the injury has created. Each conception allows for arguments since discomfort and economic loss are difficult concepts to measure.

"The most damaging single trend in the modern compensation story has been the imperceptible shift, in many states, away from protection against actual income loss and toward cash payment for physical impairment," says Arthur Larson, the nation's leading authority on workers' compensation. The state of Washington, for example, bases its awards on "degree of bodily impairment and not on whether you can work." In the state of Kansas, if a person has an injury specifically mentioned in the workers' compensation law, "the total number of weeks [of compensation] is due the worker no matter how much time he may lose from work."[30]

That was not always the case. Under the earliest laws, such as the Illinois law, administrators determined compensation equal to one-half the difference between the average wages earned before the injury and the earning capacity of the employee after the injury. During the period immediately following an injury, a worker received "temporary total" benefits (subject to a maximum amount) based on his regular wages. When his condition stabilized, he received either "permanent total" disability benefits or, more likely, "permanent partial" disability benefits based on an estimate of his new earning capacity. To arrive at those estimates required considerable skill.

In order to simplify the process of determining compensation, many states moved from a wage-loss approach toward compensation for "permanent partial" or "permanent total" disabilities to a schedule of benefits. If, for example, a worker lost his fourth finger, he received a specified number of weeks of compensation, no matter what happened to his earning capacity. In 1913, Wisconsin adopted a schedule that included forty-two categories of injuries. The Wisconsin Industrial Commission noted that although estimating a person's loss of wages might be the theoretically correct principle for workers' compensation, it was difficult to put into practice and created many administrative quandaries; the schedule simplified things.[31]

Most states followed suit in adopting schedules, and the goal of compensating workers for lost wages went the way of reducing litigation. In both cases, the promise of the law failed to be realized; in both cases the law aggravated old problems and created new ones.

The schedules lacked uniformity. Some were elaborate, some were rudimentary. Some permitted generous benefits, others set stringent limits. California authorities decided to adopt and modify a schedule for compensation prepared in 1904 by the Medical Council of the Russian Ministry of the Interior. Concluding that a ditch digger used all of his physical functions equally, the California officials determined that a thirty-nine-year-old ditch digger would be the standard against which others would be measured. Then, after establishing a job requirement classification system, the board produced an elaborate scheme that converted a person's age, wage, and physical impairments into a compensation payment. The simpler schedules of most other states did not take age or occupation into account.[32]

The schedules may have begun as an effort to simplify the administration of workers' compensation by creating a straightforward relationship between an injury and payment and by making benefits less discretionary and more "scientific." (Here again a contradiction arose between the simple and professional approaches to public administration.) Disparities in the laws from state to state, combined with the politics inherent in any system of social benefits, soon mocked the effort at scientific administration. Viewed from a national perspective, the various schedules created a crazy-quilt pattern, with benefit levels wildly out of synchronization. One state, for instance, rated the loss of an arm at 78 percent of the whole body; another equated the loss of an arm at 29 percent of the whole body.[33]

Just as litigation persists in workers' compensation, so do the schedules. They give workers' compensation a curiously anachronistic quality. The Texas workers' compensation law, for example, awards benefits for "an injury to the skull resulting in incurable insanity or imbecility." The notion of incurable insanity jars modern sensibilities as does the idea that imbecility, or mental retardation as we would now say, relegates a person to a nonproductive life. If the Texas law can be excused on the grounds that its schedule is so old, more recent workers' compensation laws cannot escape censure so easily. The workers' compensation law in Hawaii, our newest state, also mentions imbecility.[34]

Even more problems arise in the case of injuries that fail to appear on the schedule and therefore require a different procedure for estimating the extent of a worker's disability. The state of Kansas, for example, lists its rules of workers' compensation on a wallet-sized card that contains a price list for injuries to various parts of the body. The law requires the employer to pay the cost of all medical care related to the injury. Unlike other benefits, medical benefits do not have a monetary limit. For the loss of an arm, a worker receives 210 weeks of compensation in addition to reimbursement for medical care; the loss of a great toe nets 15 weeks. Each member – arms, legs, ears – has its price, expressed in the number of weeks that a worker can receive compensation and a maximum total amount. This part of the

law is relatively straightforward, although it produces its share of disagreements. Workers seldom injure themselves as cleanly as the schedule implies. Parties at interest often disagree over whether a worker
has actually lost the use of his arm or over how much loss of use he
has sustained. The real trouble, however, arises when it comes to injuries to organs and systems that affect the performance of the entire
body, such as the back, heart, or kidneys.

In Kansas, injuries to these parts of the body fall under the heading
of "permanent partial general disability." The language of the law
expresses the complexity of the concept. "Permanent partial general
disability" is measured as "the extent, expressed as a percentage, to
which the ability of the workman to engage in work of the same type
and character that he was performing at the time of his injury has been
reduced." Basically, the Kansas law attempts to estimate, in a very
indirect way, an employee's loss of earning capacity. Instead of using
an employee's actual wages to make this estimate, the law begins with
the worker's impairment and translates that into a loss of earning capacity. Not only is this task extremely difficult, but it produces many
grounds for disagreement between employer and employee.[35]

In keeping with the heterogeneous nature of workers' compensation, the state of Minnesota has a slightly different way of compensating permanent partial and other disabilities. The state maintains an
impairment schedule that equates particular impairments with a percentage of total disability, thereby eliminating the need to estimate a
worker's loss of earning capacity. The state attempts to encourage
workers to return to work by offering "impairment awards" and
"economic recovery benefits." Even if a worker returns to work, he
still gets his impairment award, the level of which is determined by the
severity of his injury. A worker who stays out of work receives economic recovery benefits. A worker who goes back to work gets his
impairment award in a lump sum (which increases its value) as well as
his wages. A worker who is out of work receives only his weekly compensation payments. In the Kansas system, a worker may well reduce
his benefits by returning to work. The hope in Minnesota is to make
it advantageous for the employee to get back to work.[36]

Impairments that affect a distinct part of the body – such as the loss
of the use of an arm – lend themselves better to the Minnesota approach than do impairments that affect the performance of the entire
body – such as heart disease. Unfortunately, impairments that affect

the whole body have become increasingly prominent in workers' compensation cases, and fewer cases involve losses of a "member." In Hawaii, for example, workers in 1982 had more heart attacks than they did injuries that required amputations. Sprains and strains were far more prevalent than the loss of use of a finger, toe, or other "member." The most common type of accident involved overexertion rather than a fall or an incident in which a worker caught part of his body in a machine. Even in the face of these trends, many states continue to base workers' compensation benefits on schedules computed from outdated formulas that express impairment as a percentage of total disability. Fewer states – Florida is a notable example – attempt to compensate a worker for actual wage loss.[37]

Occupational diseases and disability

Like impairments that affect the performance of the entire body, occupational diseases present profound problems for workers' compensation because the system was not designed for them. Occupational illnesses only gradually came to be associated with work-related disability as public health researchers discovered links between working conditions and industrial diseases. Even when such links could be proved, employers argued that by compensating workers who contracted such diseases they would be converting the disability program into a general health insurance system, since every illness or death could conceivably be attributed to some occupational cause. As late as the 1930s, only eleven states offered disability compensation for industrial diseases, and six of those states confined compensation to a specific list of diseases.[38]

If a statute failed to mention industrial diseases, the state courts often decided that workers could not receive compensation. A Maryland court ruled in a 1925 case, for example, that an "occupational disease differs from an accidental injury, which is an unforeseen event occurring without design, in that disability comes on gradually and cannot be fixed at any particular time and by any certain event." Lacking this proof, the court ruled that industrial disease was not covered by state workers' compensation law.[39]

Because the disabling effects of a health hazard may not show up for years, the relationship between a person's employment history and his state of health is difficult to determine. To protect employers from an onslaught of claims from older workers, eleven states have statutes of limitations in their workers' compensation laws: After a number of years have passed, a worker may not instigate a claim for workers' compensation benefits that is based on occupational illness caused by prior working conditions. Other states have attempted to minimize the number of occupational illness claims by stipulating that an employee must have been exposed to the hazard for a minimum amount of time or by restricting claims to diseases that the state considers characteristic of the worker's occupation.[40]

Although workers' compensation laws operate on the principle that an employer is responsible for work-related injuries, occupational diseases present special problems. For example, a worker may have been exposed to a risk while in the employ of many employers. In most states, the responsibility for compensation falls on the last employer to expose the employee to the hazard. This principle of law helps resolve disputes but does not appear to be based on compelling logic. The workers' compensation laws also impose a heavy burden of proof on the employee, who must demonstrate that it was the job, not his life-style, that caused the illness. Further, benefits received for occupational illnesses are sometimes based on the benefit levels that prevailed at the time of the employee's last exposure, not on current benefit levels.

Because of these complexities, occupational diseases embroil workers' compensation programs in disputes. In the only existing study of closed cases in several states, investigators found that 63 percent of occupational disease claims were disputed by the employer; more than half ended with compromise settlements.[41]

A recent federal task force report features a case study that illustrates the difficulties that occupational illnesses pose for workers' compensation. The case involved a woman with an incurable cancer called mesothelima, which is nearly always the result of exposure to asbestos. Her exposure occurred over a period of fifteen years. Although she had never worked directly with asbestos, she did deliver occasional telephone messages to a room in which asbestos was cut. She also had a forty-year history of smoking. The case went through three hearings over the course of a year before it was decided. Ultimately, she received financial compensation, which was based on her salary at the time of exposure.[42]

Many asbestos-related cases have reached the courts in recent years.

Frustration with the compensation system has led 200,000 workers to file tort actions against the manufacturers of asbestos insulation, following a 1973 court decision that allowed such a claim on the grounds of product liability. Congressman George Miller of California, representing a district in which many dockyard employees work with asbestos insulation, argues that such legal recourse is to be expected since "workers' compensation laws governing occupational disease and disability do not in many cases provide prompt, adequate, and equitable compensation." In addition, attorneys, who stand to obtain a higher fee from a successful court case than from a compensation case, may advise workers to sue. Further, courts hold more closely to the common law principles of damages than do workers' compensation programs, which may demand that the worker demonstrate an actual economic loss. Moreover, tort liability awards, unlike workers' compensation payments, are not in any way linked to benefits from other government programs. (Someone who is retired and is receiving social security, for example, may not be able to collect workers' compensation but may be able to win a court case.)[43]

The court system has provided relief for many workers such as Anthony Piscano. A fifty-two-year-old resident of Baltimore, Piscano had worked for more than thirty years as a shipyard pipefitter, twenty-six of them in Bethlehem Steel's repair yard. Piscano claimed that, as a result of his exposure to asbestos on the job, he suffered permanent damage to his lungs and required a continuous flow of three liters of oxygen a minute. Since Piscano did not know which manufacturer made the asbestos to which he was exposed, he sued a dozen manufacturers and reached a settlement with all but one of them.[44]

Although Piscano won his case, many workers end the process with nothing to show for their efforts. Even when workers are successful, many of them give up nearly half their award to their lawyers. The circumstances resemble those that produced workers' compensation laws early in the century – there is an epidemic of litigation, rising costs, and a perception that the system does not treat people fairly.

Congressman Miller claims that, with more than 21 million people exposed to asbestos, the system for compensating asbestos cases is unworkable. He believes that the solution lies not in reforming state workers' compensation programs, but in creating a new federal program, such as the one that covers lung ailments from which coal miners suffer. In 1984 he sponsored a bill that would bring asbestos claims under federal control.[45]

Because workers' compensation programs have failed to respond adequately to occupational diseases and disability, tort actions, costs, and delays have all increased. At the same time, enough attention has been focused on the problem to generate a proposal for new federal legislation that, in turn, has sparked efforts to reform workers' compensation. The result of this cycle remains unknown. For now, in the case of asbestos and of other industrial hazards, the alternatives of increased litigation, reforming workers' compensation programs, or a new federal program coexist uneasily with one another.

The survival of workers' compensation

The failure of workers' compensation to realize its initial objectives and to respond to modern problems raises a fundamental question: How is it that workers' compensation, a state disability program born in the Progressive Era, has survived so long without being replaced by a new program, perhaps a federal program? The answer lies in the force of bureaucratic continuity, as can be seen in past efforts to reform the program.

Although authorities recognized the inadequacies of workers' compensation as early as the 1930s and contemplated replacing it with a federal disability program, efforts at reform did not begin in earnest until the Eisenhower administration, which took office in 1953. Early in that administration, the Department of Labor – which, although it exercised no direct control over the state programs, served as a federal watchdog and as a clearinghouse of information – made workers' compensation a priority. Arthur Larson, the department's under secretary and already an authority on workers' compensation, decided to use his influence as a force for change. Reflecting Larson's influence, the department's 1954 annual report noted that "most injured workers . . . suffer acute financial hardship along with their injuries" and stated that in the coming year it would give workers' compensation "special emphasis." By the end of 1954, Larson spoke with enthusiasm about the model workers' compensation act that he and his assistants were preparing. Not since the dawn of the compensation era in 1911 had something of this sort been attempted.[46]

By 1956, Larson's model compensation act – an effort to put the best of all the different state statutes into one exemplary law – lay totally discredited, the victim of political sniping by state officials, businessmen, and their allies in the administration. The parties at interest interpreted it as an attempt at a federal takeover of the state compensation programs, and they resented it. The New England Daily Newspaper Association called it "a new approach to the welfare state via the employer's pocketbook." The administration quickly squelched further discussion.[47]

The politics of workers' compensation proceeded as usual. During the 1950s, labor forces in Mississippi tried to pass a bill that would have raised the $25 maximum weekly payment for temporary total disability and included coverage of occupational diseases. Regarded as too liberal by the Mississippi Manufacturers Association, the law failed of passage.[48]

Arthur Larson fared no better when he proposed a new version of his model compensation act in the 1960s. Despite the endorsement of the Council of State Governments and other prestigious bodies, the states rejected this version just as they had the previous one.

The situation approached stalemate: Workers' compensation laws were inadequate, but reform appeared out of reach. Efforts to expand federal disability laws at the expense of the state workers' compensation laws met with sanctimonious resistance. Legislatures in Idaho, Illinois, Iowa, and North Carolina, for example, passed resolutions that declared they were "opposed to any legislation by the United States Congress which would infringe on the right of this [state] to enact and administer its own Workmen's Compensation laws and to further federal encroachment into the field."[49] The states resisted a federal takeover because workers' compensation was different from other public welfare laws. State legislatures often perceived welfare as a costly burden on the state treasury. They therefore entertained with sympathy proposals to federalize welfare and, later, medicaid. Financed by the employers, workers' compensation required relatively little public expenditure, and it provided employment for local doctors and lawyers. Indeed, it was not unlikely that some workers' compensation lawyers served in the state legislatures. Furthermore, few of the proposals to federalize workers' compensation promised to relieve employers of compensation costs. On the contrary, these proposals threatened to increase employer and insurer costs by raising the level of benefits they were required to pay.

Despite the barriers to the federalization of workers' compensation, efforts to replace workers' compensation with new federal laws gained ground by the end of the 1960s. Passage of the Occupational Safety and Health Act (OSHA) in 1970 raised the possibility of a federal takeover of the compensation system. Stopping short of this alternative, the OSHA legislation authorized the creation of a national commission to study the state workers' compensation laws.[50]

When the commission met in 1971 and 1972, talk of the end of the workers' compensation program ran rampant. The president of the National Indemnity Company opened the 1970 meeting of the International Association of Industrial Accident Boards and Commissions by stating that what was adequate in 1920, 1940, or 1960 was no longer adequate. If the laws were not upgraded, he warned, the system would be taken over by the federal government. At the next year's meeting, James E. Bailey, legislative counsel of the American Society of Insurance Management, reported, "I'm afraid that if the states don't do more and make improvements in needed areas quickly you may see federal regulations or intervention within three years. That would be disastrous." John V. Keaney of the Maine Industrial Accident Commission told the American Bar Association, "Just because that state system has been in existence for more than half a century, just because it is our nation's oldest social insurance program – just because it is a state system – are not justifiable reasons for its continued existence."[51]

The extension of federal social welfare programs at the expense of state programs appeared almost inevitable. As one compensation official told the American Bar Association, "We will undoubtedly have a national health act." With the passage of such an act, the federal government might well decide to make health care for industrial injuries part of national health insurance. Monetary benefits could be handled through the social security program or through an expanded welfare program, such as President Nixon's Family Assistance Plan, which was then under serious discussion.

Both union and management leaders spoke of the possibility of the federal government taking over workers' compensation. The union leaders sometimes appeared less than reluctant to part with the program. Fred Huntsinger, president of the Portland local of the International Longshoremen's and Warehousemen's Union, for example, complained that "the benefits for injured workmen are far too low and everyone knows it. Unless some drastic changes are made soon, the entire program will be scrapped." Management saw similar threats to the program and took them more seriously. Carl J. Vogt of the General Tire and Rubber Company, for instance, predicted, "with tears in my eyes, that the states will lose their . . . exclusive jurisdiction over this benefit area."

John Burton, a liberal Republican trained as both a lawyer and an economist, chaired the National Commission on State Workmen's Compensation Laws. A perfect choice for the job, Burton was a man of sharp intelligence with a deft sense of humor who was able to maintain cordial relations with insurance companies, labor unions, and state administrators alike.

He presided over a form of government body not known for producing results. Blue-ribbon panels of this sort often served as lightning rods drawing attention away from the president or Congress and were a politically convenient means of ignoring problems. This commission did have an advantage over others in that all of its members knew a great deal about workers' compensation; ceremonial appointments to appease one constituency or another were kept to a minimum.[52]

Survival of the program dominated the commission's early discussions. Burton was well aware, as he put it, that "somebody outside the system looking in at it [might say] why don't we just collapse this whole system and fold part of it into the negative income tax and part into national health insurance?" He was equally aware of the need to take that question head on. James O'Brien of the American Federation of Labor (AFL) and Congress of Industrial Organizations (CIO) agreed: "We can continue to talk and give the states more time, but I don't think it will have much of an impact unless this Commission makes positive recommendations to the Congress to do something about workmen's compensation." Samuel Horovitz, a Boston lawyer specializing in workers' compensation, considered a federal takeover inevitable: "They are going to do away with workmen's compensation, and the federal government will run it all. I would at least like the public to know that we had brains enough to foresee it and disagree with what is going to come." Other members of the group, such as William Moshofsky of the Georgia Pacific Company, dismissed the idea of a federal takeover. He understood the power of the constituencies that supported workers' compensation. "When you get down to the constituency, labor and management, they are going to be wasting their time," he said.

Burton urged the commission to include a formal defense of the workers' compensation program in its report, and he prevailed. "I think that to the 18 of us that may be something that is obvious. . . . But I think one of the major tasks of this report is to convince a lot of other people who do not agree that there is a continuing rationale for workers' compensation and that it should continue."[53]

The commission members agreed, as had the members of the various interest groups in the past, on the survival of workers' compensation, on the need for its improvement, and on little else. More than fifty years after the creation of the program, it proved difficult to get these representatives of various interest groups to concur even on the program's basic objectives. One commissioner suggested that the benefit levels were intended to be uniform, "everybody's arm was the same." Burton disputed this version of history, arguing that the original laws tied benefits to wage levels, and that not everyone should get the same amount for the same injury. The dispute illustrated how muddled the program had become and how difficult it was to reform.[54]

Even the experts on the commission nearly strangled on the complexity of workers' compensation. The bewildering variety of approaches to compensating disability made coherent explanation almost impossible. For example, state laws embodied at least three different notions on permanent partial disability. Some states subscribed to the indemnity theory, providing compensation on the basis of physical loss alone. Others followed the principle of wage replacement, trying to ensure that a worker's post-injury wage approximated his pre-injury wage. Still others adhered to the theory of wage-earning capacity, attempting to pay the worker the difference between what he earned prior to his injury and what he could earn afterward. A commission staff member concluded that there was "almost no rhyme or reason that you can see in the various states."[55]

Even when the group agreed on some area of compensation in general, specific recommendations came hard. For example, the group achieved consensus on the coverage of farm workers, only to encounter questions on whether a farmer's son who had hurt himself on the family tractor, but who was not entitled to compensation because he earned nothing, should receive coverage. Similarly, the group favored including domestic workers under compensation laws, but foresaw difficulties covering a person who worked for several employers. Nor was it clear at what point to draw the line: What about babysitters or a person who shoveled the driveway?

The group realized that there were some matters on which it would never come to agreement. Insurance coverage was such an issue. Some states allowed private companies to supply employers with workers' compensation or allowed employers to insure themselves by setting aside reserves against the risk of a worker's injury; other states permitted competition between private and state-owned insurance; still others granted a monopoly to a state-run insurance fund. Arthur Williams, an expert on insurance coverage who served as a consultant, convinced the commission that "it is far better to worry about the maximum level of weekly benefits than it is to worry about insurance arrangements." The commission decided not to choose one arrangement over another. As Burton put it, the issue generated "more heat than light. . . . It is not a two-party camp here. We have got the employers; we have got the private insurance industry; and we have got the state funds."

How to compensate for permanent partial disability – the most "fundamental" question confronting workers' compensation – was another intractable issue. When the case was raised of a man who had lost an arm but continued to work, Burton asked if the man deserved money simply because he lost his arm. The commission members agreed that, even if the man resumed work at his same job at the same wage, he deserved some compensation. As one commission member put it, "Are you going to tell me that I am going to lose my arm and I cannot tie my tie and you are not going to give any benefit for that? I might want to hug my wife." But the group decided not to take a stand on how to determine the permanent partial disability benefits.[56]

How to compensate heart disease represented another troubling issue. Burton wanted the group to agree that heart disease should be compensable. "If you have a heart disease, you get your workmen's compensation benefits. You do not have to prove it is work-related." The employer representatives balked. Moshofsky of Georgia Pacific related the case of a man who came to work, sat down at a tractor, pulled a gear, and suffered a heart attack. A jury awarded him compensation. Such cases, Moshofsky claimed, "just turned people off the system." Mr. Flournoy, a state administrator from California, suggested that the problem might be too complex for the commission to handle. "Cases come to us where an individual might have been a carpenter, and they say that [his job led to a heart attack]. We'll have a doctor that will say, 'Yes, this developed,' and another doctor on the other side says, 'It's impossible.'" Heart disease presented the commission with a problem that was beyond its competence, and the group quietly laid it aside.[57]

To its credit, the commission decided to ignore such issues as well as most others on which it anticipated that consensus was out of reach. It held no illusions about correcting all of the program's faults.[58]

On April 17, 1972, the commission ended its deliberations and began to vote. Its final report, issued in the summer of 1972, concentrated on benefit levels, leaving the philosophical and more intractable issues for others. The report featured a vigorous defense of the workers' compensation program. Even in the face of the program's ineffectiveness, the commission concluded that, since none of the proposed new federal programs paid cash benefits for short-term disabilities or for longer-term partial disability, "there is a substantial and vital role for workmen's compensation in contemporary America."[59]

The commission's essential recommendations constituted a nut-and-bolts guide to the improvement of the workers' compensation program, stressing the need for adequate benefits and urging the states to increase their benefit levels. The commission became quite specific on the subject of adequate cash benefits, stating that permanent total disability benefits should be at least two-thirds of a worker's gross weekly wage and 80 percent of a worker's spendable weekly earnings. It also set specific standards for the maximum levels of benefits. In the case of permanent total disability, the commission recommended that by July 1, 1973, the maximum be at least two-thirds of the state's average weekly wage; by July 1, 1975, it should become at least 100 percent of the state's average weekly wage; and by the middle of 1981, 200 percent of a state's average weekly wage. Temporary total disability benefits received the same specific treatment.[60]

The commission offered the states a deal. It gave them until July 1, 1975, to comply with the commission's essential recommendations. If the states failed to reform the program, the commission recommended that Congress impose federal standards on them. It offered the carrot of the program's survival and the stick of federal regulation should the program fail to comply with the commission's recommendations.[61]

The commission's approach produced substantive results. Although the states never met all of the commission's recommendations, they made major efforts to raise their benefit levels. For the first time since the 1920s, workers' compensation appeared to be enjoying a revival. The fact that it continued to do so even after the threat of federal takeover receded solidified the program's achievements and its security.

With the commission's report as a spur, the program performed better. Burton, appearing at Senate hearings on the federalization of workers' compensation in March 1976, spoke with pride of how thirty-three of the states met the commission's demanding standards for temporary total disability as of July 1, 1975, "the best record for benefit maximums in the post–World War II period." By April 1984, more than half of the fifty-one state jurisdictions maintained maximum weekly benefits exceeding 100 percent of the state's average weekly wage for temporary total disability, permanent total disability, and death.[62]

Benefit levels have risen, but the program's basic structure remains the same, undisturbed by eighty years of history. Although the commission's actions may have ensured the survival of the program, those actions did little to change it. In fact, the commission owed its success to its decision not to change the program, but simply to make it pay more adequate benefits.

The persistence of litigation remains an unresolved problem. Workers' compensation programs in many states continue to award benefits on the basis of physical impairment, rather than on the basis of a loss of wages or a lessening of the ability to work. Ignoring medical improvements and incentives for rehabilitation, the workers' compensation program clings to the outdated notion that benefits should reflect damages. Paying benefits to injured workers who can work is costly, and making payments available for impairments discourages rehabilitation and recovery.

As a consequence, the nation faces new problems in the area of disability with old programs. This is not to say that change is impossible. The New Deal saw efforts to create new social welfare programs that would eliminate many of the problems inherent in workers' compensation. As Chapter 3 reveals, however, the second generation of programs has not eliminated the problems of the first, nor has it been able to avoid creating entirely new problems.

2. The origins of Social Security Disability Insurance

Workers' compensation, limited to physical impairments that arose out of accidents in the work place, left a large gap in public protection against disability. To some extent, Social Security Disability Insurance, passed in July 1956, helped to fill this gap. More ambitious in scope than the state workers' compensation programs, disability insurance offered uniform national coverage for total disabilities, regardless of their origins. Although more universal in its coverage, disability insurance defined disability more narrowly. It paid benefits only to those who could demonstrate they were unable to hold any job, anywhere in the country, because of a permanent physical or mental condition.

The administrative problems of separating those truly unable to work from those merely out of work colored the debate over disability insurance and delayed its passage. Under discussion since the late 1930s, the program did not receive congressional sanction until the mid-1950s. When finally passed, it reflected the caution of depression era planning (in its strict definition of disability) and the political conservatism of the Republican resurgence in the 1950s (in its administrative structure). Proposed originally as a strictly federal program, disability insurance, as passed, allowed the states to make the initial determinations of eligibility. As a result, individual states awarded disability benefits for which the federal government paid all the costs. Proposed as a program to cover people of all ages, it emerged from the political process as a program only for those fifty years of age or older. Consequently, disability insurance became closely associated with the retirement of older workers.

For all of that, disability insurance soon became the nation's largest disability program, both in the number of people it covered and in the amount of money it cost. Some of the reasons for its growth and some of the differences between disability insurance and workers' compensation are illustrated by the case of a thirty-eight-year-old man who traveled to a Social Security hearing room at the edge of Chicago's loop on March 21, 1984, hoping to receive disability insurance.

The man, who weighed 275 pounds and who lived at home with his parents, had not been injured or made ill as a result of his work. He had once driven a beer truck, the only job for which he was equipped, as he told the administrative law judge. He had to quit because of his recurring mental illness, clinically defined as "bipolar manic depression." The man described himself as "hyper" and complained of an inability to sleep. Although stabilized by a drug called lithium carbonate, which enabled him to spend some time outside of mental institutions, he could not hold a job. He said that inside work was too "confining" and that he needed work with few responsibilities. In fact, he never looked for work, he told officials, and instead spent most of his time watching television or reading the newspaper. He had tried to attend college but quit after a few months. His marriage had ended in divorce.[1]

The man's case presented a modern disability dilemma. Although medicine allowed him to function outside of a medical environment, it could not make him well enough to be able to hold a job. Stable for long periods of time, he remained dependent on the social welfare system for survival.

Workers' compensation would not have met his needs because he could not demonstrate a connection between his job and his mental illness. However, the Social Security Disability Insurance program did award the man benefits because he was — regardless of the cause — unable to hold a job. Because he once paid into the social security trust fund, he had earned the right to retire in the event of disability. He would, therefore, receive benefits from the federal government and not a private insurance company.

This case not only reveals some of the differences between the two generations of income-maintenance disability programs, but it also shows some of the similarities. For one, litigation has not disappeared; although most people received benefits without recourse to a lawyer or litigation, the man was required to attend a hearing in which a lawyer argued his case. Further, differences from state to state have not been eliminated; the federal government would pay the man benefits, but the decision came only after two thorough reviews of his case by the state of Illinois.

The very beginnings and disability redefined

The social security program began in August 1935 when Congress passed an omnibus piece of legislation that put most of the nation's federal social welfare laws under one statute. Congress included three new federal programs in the Social Security Act: the modern welfare system, the unemployment compensation program, and the old age retirement or insurance program. This last program became so central to the operations of the Social Security Board and its successor – the Social Security Administration (1946) – that it came to be called social security.

Congress included these three programs in the same legislation but no two were administered in the same way. The federal government gave grants to the states for welfare programs; it allowed the states to administer their own unemployment compensation programs; and it put old age insurance under complete federal control. Aware of the innovation that old age insurance represented, Congress started the program slowly, beginning the collection of contributions in 1937 but not allowing the first pensions to be paid until 1942. Further, Congress limited the program to commercial and industrial workers.

As this caution demonstrated, old age insurance was an experiment, and no one knew if the federal government could make it succeed. Nothing on this scale had been attempted in Washington before. Existing retirement programs covered civil servants, veterans of the nation's wars, and railroad workers. True, foreign countries, such as Germany and England, ran retirement programs, but the circumstances were far different from those in the United States.[2]

Not only was old age insurance far from firmly launched when employees of the newly created Social Security Board first tried to define disability, the United States was also in the most severe depression of its history. The high unemployment rate made tickets out of the labor force, even third-class tickets to a mean existence, extremely desirable. The demand for the tickets that disability pensions represented could create political pressure strong enough to undermine a disability insurance program before it became solidly established.

When officials of the Research and Statistics Division attempted to define disability in 1935 and 1936, therefore, they recognized the importance of establishing firm but workable controls. I. S. Falk, the public health expert who did most of the Social Security Board's theoretical work on disability and health insurance, called disability an "elastic concept," sensitive to the level of unemployment in the economy. The higher the unemployment rate, the more people who would regard themselves as disabled. If the government tried to control disability by being strict about its definition, administrators might interpret the strict definition in a liberal manner. "Too strict a system invites pressure to swing in the opposite direction," said Falk.[3]

As the concerns of Falk implied, the officials of the Social Security Board and its successor recognized the lack of precision in the concept of disability. Arthur Altmeyer, the former Wisconsin workers' compensation administrator who headed the social security program from 1936 to 1953, conceded that determining disability was not an exact science but a matter of "conjecture," because the state of disability rested not on a set of facts but on the conclusions that were drawn from the facts. Social workers, administering the welfare programs, agreed, stating that efforts to distinguish between employable and nonemployable applicants and between temporary unemployables and permanent unemployables had proved "impossible." Altmeyer's actuaries also told him bluntly that "precision" was "impossible."[4]

So the officials realized that they could be neither as precise nor as humane as they would have liked. Still, the concept of disability required definition. Researchers assigned to Falk turned to other public programs for guidance and discovered a choice. The federal civil service program permitted a worker to retire if he was unable to do his customary job. It did not require the worker to find another job. Railroad retirement legislation, passed in 1935, and a life insurance policy offered to veterans of World War I required that workers be unable to do any job, to be "disabled for hire."[5]

Falk and Altmeyer decided to put this stricter alternative into the Social Security Board proposal for disability insurance. Disability, Altmeyer stated, should enable workers to withdraw from the market only when it was "impossible for them to support themselves through their own efforts."[6] Of the available definitions, Falk and Altmeyer chose one from the War Risk Insurance Act that defined disability as "any impairment of mind or body which continuously renders it impossible for the disabled person to follow any substantial gainful occupation, and which is founded on conditions which render it reasonably certain that the total disability will continue throughout the life of the disabled person."[7]

This definition made no mention of partial disability nor of compensating someone for an impairment alone. The Social Security officials believed that physical impairment posed a problem only to the extent that it caused economic hardship. A loss of "strength, disfigurement, or diseased condition" would not be enough to initiate benefits; to qualify, the impairment would have to sever the person from the labor market and cause a "loss of earning power for work in general."[8]

Adopting a definition of disability answered only one of many questions. How could administrators decide whether an impairment caused a loss of earning power for work in general at a time when it was so difficult even for the able-bodied to get work? This question forced officials to consider the difference between unemployment caused by imperfect labor markets and unemployability caused by a physical condition. One possibility was simply to assume that the labor markets were perfect and to let other policies and programs correct the imperfections. As the International Labour Office, which monitors disability laws around the world, expressed the perfect labor concept: "The fact that a disabled worker is in practice unable to find employment is immaterial." Physically handicapped persons had to prove that their physical condition made it impossible for them to work, regardless of the general level of employment.[9]

Realizing that the American labor market was far from homogeneous and that it did not meet all of the conditions for perfect competition, Falk and the others at Social Security rejected the "perfect labor market" assumption "in which all marketable capacities to perform work are utilized."[10] They recognized, for example, that obsolescence of technical skills and the problem of racial prejudice could defeat a person's attempts to secure employment. They decided that if a person's physical condition allowed him only to perform jobs that were obsolete, then he could collect disability. Also, a black man capable of performing work inaccessible to blacks because of racial prejudice in his particular area would not have his claim turned down.

As these discussions, which took place between 1936 and 1948, implied, the Social Security Administration would adopt a definition of disability that took personal, economic, and social circumstances as well as physical impairment into account. Two people in the same physical condition would not be treated in the same way. Take, for example, a violinist who had hurt his hand and lost his livelihood. If he were an educated man who could still do other things, he would be considered ineligible for disability insurance. A common laborer with the same injury might receive disability benefits, particularly if he were "illiterate, advanced in age, and had always worked at heavy labor," because he could no longer perform any work for which he was in demand. According to the Social Security Administration, "the degree of physical or mental impairment which a worker must suffer in order to meet the definition of extended disability would vary with the individual's ability, training, age, and to a limited extent regional economic conditions."[11]

To illustrate, the Social Security Administration used the classic comparison between white- and blue-collar workers. A manual laborer with a severe heart condition might qualify for disability benefits, but a "desk worker with an identical heart condition might be able to continue at his work or some other occupation." Variables considered relevant included sex, race, urban or rural residence, occupation, and experience. The inclusion of these variables implied that disability insurance would act as a safety net into which marginal labor force participants could fall.[12] Considerations of this sort made disability insurance a far more complex undertaking than old age insurance.

Because the Social Security Administration wished to use the old age insurance program as a political base for the proposed disability programs, it ignored the differences and continued to emphasize the parallels. Between 1935 and 1956, the agency repeatedly argued that old age and disability resembled one another. According to one official, "invalidity occurs mainly among older workers. It may be regarded as premature old age." In the late 1930s, a memorandum of the agency stated that the disabled person "leaves the labor market in the same sense as does the aged person." Permanent disability could, therefore, be considered a period of "declining physical vitality and loss of earning power terminating in death," just as old age could. "The purpose of both systems," wrote the chairman of the Social Security Board in a frame of mind typical of the depression, "is to enable workers with reduced earning capacities to retire from gainful work and to fill the vacancies created by their retirement with workers of unimpaired efficiency."[13]

This equating of old age and disability held major consequences for America's public policy toward disability. In the first place, the planners equated disability with retirement. In so doing they tended to regard disability as a permanent condition, like old age. This line of reasoning emphasized income maintenance (paying benefits to those who do not work) rather than rehabilitation (trying to restore people's productive capacity so that they can work). At the time this emphasis represented the realistic choice; medical rehabilitation, for example, had not yet been invented, let alone perfected. Only during World War II would rehabilitation emerge as a field of medicine and bring new respectability to the idea of rehabilitating the handicapped within policy-making circles.

In the second place, Social Security officials based the size of the disability benefits on the same formula as those that determined old age benefits. In a state workers' compensation program, benefits varied according to the severity of an injury, a worker's average wage, and the size of his family. In the proposed disability insurance program, benefits varied only by a worker's average wage and the size of his family, not by the severity of his injury. Consider two workers with identical wage records and the same size families, each of whom suffered an accident on the same day. These two workers would receive exactly the same disability benefit, even if one worker had lower back pain and the other became a paraplegic. As long as the physical conditions resulted in permanent disability, the disability insurance program would not differentiate among those with no arms and legs, those with lower back pain, and those with manic depression.

The planners did make some exceptions. The blind, for example, would receive special treatment in the proposed disability insurance program, just as they already did in the welfare program. A blind person was considered automatically entitled to disability insurance benefits. According to a 1946 Social Security memorandum, a person would be considered disabled if he "(1) is blind or (2) is afflicted with any impairment which continually renders it impossible to engage in any substantially gainful work." Could a blind person go on the disability rolls any time he wished? The Social Security officials decided the answer was yes. "Admittedly," conceded the officials, "this is one of the disadvantages in specifying by law that any given handicap shall result in automatic entitlement."[14]

Favorable treatment of the blind contrasted with harsh treatment of the mentally ill. Although Falk and his coworkers recognized that mental illness was a leading cause of disability, the earliest drafts of the disability insurance program specified that a person suffering from mental illness would not qualify for benefits. Social Security officials justified excluding the mentally ill on the grounds that many were being taken care of in public hospitals and institutions and that certain types of mental illness were too difficult to diagnose and, by implication, to police. Falk cited evidence from Sweden where there was a problem in the handling of disability benefits for people suffering from "neurosis."[15] Too many people in this category entered the Swedish disability rolls. Although the Social Security Administration later relented and allowed the mentally ill to be covered under the disability insurance program, these discussions revealed that certain groups among the handicapped were considered more worthy of aid than others. In the case of the blind, the Social Security Administration believed that automatic entitlement "would not result in malingering"; in the case of the mentally ill, the threat of malingering precluded them from even receiving benefits.[16]

For those planning the Social Security Disability Insurance program, workers' compensation was not only a comfortable precedent but also the base from which Altmeyer and many other Social Security administrators of his generation got their start. As an expert on state workers' compensation laws, Altmeyer had no desire to create a federal program that would, in effect, supercede them.[17] As Altmeyer and his colleagues put their state government experiences behind them and took a cold, hard look at workers' compensation, they eventually began to see its flaws.

By the late 1930s and early 1940s, disparaging workers' compensation became a popular sport at the Social Security Administration. According to the federal officials, the states, left to their own devices, had created uncoordinated programs with many gaps in coverage. Workers' compensation excluded too many disabilities. There was too much litigation. The state of Mississippi had not even passed a worker's compensation law. Worst of all, the program suffered from "poor administration in many states."[18]

The Social Security Board employees began to believe that they could improve upon workers' compensation. The growth of this self-confidence can be traced in successive drafts of the proposed disability legislation. For example, the earliest drafts contained provisions resembling the lists of permanent total disabilities in state workers' compensation laws. When combined with unemployment, the loss of the use of both feet or both hands created an automatic entitlement to disability benefits. The first drafts also stated that benefits were to be awarded only for illnesses and injuries "not arising out of and in the course of employment," on the theory that those disabilities were better handled by the workers' compensation program. Both of these provisions were deleted from later drafts and are nowhere to be found in the actual legislation. The relationship between workers' compensation and disability insurance remains a troubled one that has generated its share of political controversy. By the early 1940s, however, federal officials were convinced that their program was superior to the state workers' compensation program.[19]

Ultimately, Social Security Administration officials came to regard workers' compensation programs as a political force to be accommodated rather than as a model worthy of emulation. The federal authorities realized that the disability program they were proposing was fundamentally different from workers' compensation. Workers' compensation paid damages to injured workers according to a rigid set of rules that varied with the impairment. The proposed Social Security Administration program called for an individually tailored consideration of a person's social and economic circumstances as well as the person's physical condition.

As a consequence, Social Security officials abandoned the use of a schedule of disabilities. "It seems hardly feasible to devise a schedule which will give due weight to all these diverse elements," such as training, previous experience, and education, Altmeyer stated. "Any schedules or tables . . . would be used as guides" rather than "final criteria" and had "no formal standing, are subject to constant change, are not binding, are not publicly printed, and are not available to claimants." In this way, the Social Security Administration emphasized an informal approach to the determination of disability that was not possible under workers' compensation.[20]

Plans for administration

"As in every other country which contemplates the expansion of its social insurance system," Altmeyer stated, "the first question is where the new program might be most advantageously placed within the existing social insurance structure." His statement reflected the obsession of the Social Security Board with dividing responsibility between the federal government and the states. By the end of the 1930s, the board had decided that the federal government should administer social welfare programs. The board expressed a desire to create a unified system of social insurance, complete with health and disability coverage.[21] Falk, among others, defended that decision, arguing that "there are so many advantages of thinking of a single system of disability compensation, all administered by the federal government." Any proposed disability programs, therefore, should be administered by the federal government.[22]

In the months before Pearl Harbor, the Social Security Board designed enormously ambitious plans for a federal system of social insurance. The plans called for the creation of permanent disability insurance; the end of the state, and the beginning of a federal, program of unemployment insurance; and the start of new federal programs of temporary disability and hospital insurance. The board also had hopes of ultimately reducing the retirement age of women to sixty and of extending social security coverage to nearly everyone in the labor force.[23]

It remained to be decided just who would declare a person disabled. From the beginning, the planners agreed that a person's doctor should not have this power. In England, giving power over disability determination to personal physicians had led to a run on the rolls. So the planners made a distinction between the federal health insurance programs, in which a person could choose his own doctor, and certification for disability insurance, in which he could not. Even the cautious and conservative American Medical Association (AMA) agreed with this principle. In 1938, one of the AMA's ad hoc committees declared that it was in the "interest of good medical care that the attending physician be relieved of the duty of certification of illness and of recovery."[24]

If not a person's personal physician, then who would act as the gatekeeper for the disability insurance program? The Social Security Administration regarded disability determination as a matter of teamwork. One of its proposals, for example, suggested that the decision be made by a triumvirate consisting of a reviewing doctor who would comment on the medical evidence, an examiner with skills in the vocational field, and another examiner with legal skills. This team approach to administration went hand in hand with the individual, multidimensional approach to the definition of disability.[25]

Finally, there was the question of how centralized the operation would be. When the Social Security Board began to pay old age benefits in 1940 (two years earlier than planned), it relied on local field offices to gather information and on centralized payment centers. The field office played a significant role, yet the agency was reluctant to extend this role to the determination of disability. Altmeyer explained, "if the determination of disability is left to several different disability boards, the likelihood is that their decision will lack uniformity." As a result the Social Security administrators believed "it advisable to centralize operations, at least initially." Either way, however, the Social Security authorities believed that "the determination of the existence of disability should rest with the Administrator." In other words, final authority should rest with the federal government.[26]

Barriers to passage

The laboriously drafted plans for the disability insurance program influenced the carefully crafted law in some ways but not in others. Congress accepted the Social Security Administration's strict definition of permanent disability without agreeing to centralized administration under total federal control. In part, the changes reflected differences in political outlook between Congress and the bureaucracy. Congress had to accommodate a much wider range of political interests, which, in the case of disability insurance, included insurance companies, doctors, and state governments.

Private insurance companies had tried to offer permanent disability insurance and failed. In 1936, when Falk and his fellow planners at the Social Security Board made the first tentative studies of permanent and total disability insurance, the outlook for private insurance companies in this area appeared grim. As the bureaucrats cast their statistical net, the accountants at the Travelers Insurance Company recorded some distressing numbers. Travelers lost $1.5 million on disability insurance in 1936; the year before they had lost more than $6 million. An actuary at the Social Security Board called these losses "impressive" and admitted the "seriousness" of the situation.

Three years later, as the Social Security Board contemplated a major expansion of social security, the situation for the insurance industry remained unimproved. The fifty-seven life insurance companies doing business in New York received more than $52 million in payments for permanent total disability contracts in 1939, a not unimpressive sum in late depression America. The money these companies paid out to people claiming to be permanently and totally disabled, however, was even more impressive: $69 million. Total losses came to more than $29 million on permanent total disability insurance in 1939. The loss for the entire insurance industry could only be estimated. One authority figured that between 1926 and 1946, the ten largest insurance companies lost more than half a billion dollars.[27]

The Social Security Board set out to discover the reasons for the insurance companies' losses. By 1940, the federal planners thought they understood what had happened. Beginning in 1906, the life insurance companies had offered special provisions to cover the risk of permanent total disability. If policyholders became permanently and totally disabled, they did not have to continue their premiums but could collect on their policies later as though they had made all of the payments. In 1915, the companies began to offer cash payments for permanent total disability in the form of annual payments of 10 percent of the face value of the policy, without any deduction from the amount payable at death. Later, in a competitive scramble, the insurance companies increased these payments to 12 percent. In 1921, the companies liberalized the definition of permanent total disability. If a person's disability persisted for three months, he qualified as permanently disabled. By the end of that decade, the insurance companies had signed contracts that promised the payment of $3.2 billion should all of the beneficiaries become disabled. These promises involved about as much money as the federal government spent in a year.

The roof fell in on the companies during the depression. They tightened the definition of disability, lengthened the waiting period before a disabled person could begin to receive benefits, refused to sell policies to women, and restricted benefits to those who became disabled under the age of fifty-five. In other words, they offered limited protection and attempted to take only the very best risks. Even so, they lost money. Most discontinued the sale of permanent disability insurance.[28]

Falk and his colleagues expressed criticism of the private insurance carriers' approach to disability. Falk argued that the companies did not take the risk of disability seriously enough. Since it remained a sideline, the companies failed to develop appropriate actuarial data or to set adequate rates. They misunderstood the risks that people faced, such as the emerging problems of automobile accidents and of degenerative diseases related to the aging of the population. Even more significant, they lost control over the certification process. People denied disability benefits took the insurance companies to court. Sympathetic juries, reacting to a struggle between the largest companies in America and sick individuals, struck blows for the common man. Publicized court cases increased public awareness of disability clauses in insurance policies and spurred people to press claims with greater frequency.[29]

Two problems in particular doomed the life insurance companies' involvement with disability insurance. In the jargon of insurance, these problems were called "adverse selection" and "moral hazard." Adverse selection refers to a problem common to all types of health insurance. Since health insurance is costly, people tend not to purchase it unless they have reason to believe they might need it. The more bad risks the company takes, the more money it pays out, and the more costly the insurance becomes. The more costly the insurance, the more selective people are in purchasing the insurance and the worse the problem becomes.

Moral hazard, in plain English, refers to the fact that people cheat. They claim to be disabled when they are not. To protect against cheating, the insurance companies try to make sure that a policyholder will not receive more income from being on the disability rolls than he would if he continued to work ("overinsurance").

Under any circumstances, disability posed a severe moral hazard problem since, as Falk put it, "the very nature of disablement makes it hard to judge its genuineness." During the depression, with wages falling and many people losing their jobs, the moral hazard problem grew that much worse. A large number of policyholders became overinsured as the real value of their disability benefits rose and the amount of money available through working fell. Conditions were ripe for the problem of moral hazard. When the insurance companies lost their tight control over the process of declaring someone disabled, they were inundated with claims and put out of business.[30]

The actuaries at the Social Security Board read a great deal into the experience of the private insurance companies. W. R. Williamson, the board's first actuary, noted that when the Metropolitan Life Insurance Company offered group insurance packages that included old age and disability pensions during the 1920s, the two pensions began to resemble one another. Disability came to be regarded as a permanent condition like old age. In Williamson's vivid phrase, disability was like "living death." He believed, therefore, that a person who became disabled at a young age would remain on the rolls from the time of his disability through the date of his death.[31] If the Social Security Board tried to "hedge" or limit the costs of the disability insurance program with "restrictions," then Falk's elastic concept would snap and the "adjudication [would] be liberal."[32] Like the Metropolitan Life Insurance Company, the Social Security Board would discover disability insurance to be an expensive and uncontrollable program.

Robert Myers, who served as the chief actuary of the Social Security Administration from 1947 until 1970 and remains one of the nation's greatest authorities on social security, shared Williamson's concerns. Myers prided himself on being exceptionally precise and careful and on supplying realistic, accurate data to the Social Security administrators. Other leaders in the field readily conceded that Myers was the foremost technician who best understood how to apply the formula in the social security law to compute benefits and to conduct other complex calculations that were part of social security.[33]

Complexity did not daunt Myers, but disability did. Asked to supply data on the incidence of disability, Myers insisted that it was impossible to make estimates for a disability insurance program until the program was in operation. He argued that in contrast to the figures on old age and survivors insurance, which possessed "a much higher degree of accuracy" and deserved the designation of estimates, "those for disability would more properly be termed illustrations."[34]

Falk, who also prided himself on his knowledge and his accuracy, did not read the private insurance companies' experience with disability insurance in the same way. To him, and to many others who believed in social insurance, disability insurance represented a need best met by the public sector; the failure of the private sector only confirmed this conviction. Since social security was compulsory, the adverse selection problem would be eliminated. Everyone would be covered, not just those who presented the greatest risks. Spreading the risk, guarding the determination of eligibility through "efficient administration" to eliminate "unjustified claims," and protecting against overinsurance would enable the public sector to overcome the problems of the private sector.[35]

Executives of the private insurance industry disagreed with Falk strongly enough to oppose disability insurance. They believed that if they could not administer disability insurance, then no one could. The Social Security Board's insistence that federal bureaucrats could be the agents of efficient administration struck the insurance executives as naive.

M. Jarvis Farley of the Massachusetts Indemnity and Life Insurance Company argued that any insurance line with a severe moral hazard could not be written in the absence of the profit motive. He claimed that the success of disability insurance hinged on "strong discipline." "The profit motive provides that discipline in a private insurance organization," he declared, "but I know of no substitute in government administration. I believe that a government would fail to obey the moral hazard."[36]

In a sense, both sides misjudged the other. The private insurance executives discounted the dedication and sincerity that administrators like Altmeyer brought to their jobs. The Social Security officials tended to assume that the private insurance executives put profit above the public interest. Dialogue between the two sides became strained.

In the early 1940s the actuaries at the Social Security Administration held meetings aimed at conciliation between the the insurance executives and the Social Security administrators, but the two groups talked past one another. The insurance executives spoke with a cynicism inspired by bitter experience. One executive from Travelers, for example, approved of the idea of rehabilitating the disabled and sending them back to work but "didn't expect much of it." Other executives said the depression had created the "common attitude that money received from the state could be accepted without apology."

The Social Security officials argued that the separation between unemployment and disability would be easier under social insurance because the state unemployment compensation programs would take some of the pressure off the disability program. The insurance executives replied that the federal officials did not even begin to understand the pressures they would face if Congress passed disability insurance. With the courts watching over the Social Security Board's shoulder, they argued, liberalization would be inevitable. The private executives saw themselves as the voices of experience; the Social Security officials regarded them as negative voices from the past. The two groups learned little from each other.[37]

Soon they abandoned the informal private discussions and met instead in congressional hearing rooms, where each tried to counter the

testimony of the other. In February 1945, the social security committees of the American Life Convention, Life Insurance Association of
America, and the National Association of Life Underwriters recommended that if the Social Security Administration insisted on setting
up a program of disability insurance, it should be limited to those over
the age of fifty-five. By 1950, these same groups took an even harder
line and opposed the establishment of federal disability insurance entirely.[38]

The 1938 advisory council

The political battle over disability had begun as early as 1938, when
an advisory council appointed by the Senate Finance Committee to
study the financing of social security provided an opportunity for a
confrontation between the supporters and opponents of disability insurance.

Edwin Witte and M. Albert Linton were the chief protagonists on
the council. Witte, the Wisconsin professor and executive director of
the committee that designed the original social security legislation, defended the old age insurance program. Linton, an executive with the
Provident Mutual Insurance Company, attacked it. They argued over
the advisability of putting the system on a pay-as-you-go basis, as Linton wanted, and over using the money already collected for the expansion of the program, as Witte wanted.

Witte took a pessimistic view of the council's work, believing that
most of the members shared Linton's viewpoint. He stated that the
council "undoubtedly has a clear majority of the critics of the Social
Security Act" and vowed not to let "our Republican and insurance
friends use this report as a vehicle to hit the administration" with an
attack on the financing provisions of social security. Witte regarded
Linton, who enjoyed a reputation for integrity, as someone who
"stubbornly holds to his ideas, without compromise."[39]

Disability insurance remained peripheral to the advisory council's
agenda, which focused on what became the 1939 amendments to the
Social Security Act: money for a worker's survivors and increased benefits for married workers and workers with dependent children. Disability came into the discussions late, indicating that the Social Security Board wanted the advisory council to validate the idea of disability
insurance rather than to recommend the immediate adoption of a spe-

cific plan. Nonetheless, the moment was an important one. It marked the first public exposure of the Social Security Board's permanent disability plan. Altmeyer and Falk hoped for a favorable reaction, a letter of recommendation that they could later take to Congress.[40]

Almost everyone was a little afraid of the disability insurance plan when it was introduced on October 21, 1938, and when it was voted upon on December 10, 1938. Douglas Brown, the Princeton labor economist who chaired the council, thought that recommending disability would make the advisory council's proposals too expensive. He wanted to protect the credibility of the advisory council's report. Although sympathetic to the Social Security Board's plans, he opposed disability insurance. Even Altmeyer was somewhat wary of the administrative burden of disability insurance, although he concluded that, "If you have a restricted definition of permanent total disability, our judgment is that it can be met."[41]

Albert Mowbray, an actuary from the University of California at Berkeley, feared the pressures that would be brought to bear on a social security disability insurance program. He gave his fellow council members a graphic picture of the moral hazard problem in late depression America. "You will have workers like those in the dust-bowl area, people who have migrated to California and elsewhere," he said, "who perhaps have not worked in a year or two, who will imagine that they are disabled. . . . Unless you have a very highly qualified medical staff and you put every case through the mill, my judgment is that the cost is going to be far above anything that can be forecast." Linton, for his part, worried that the private sector's experience with disability insurance merely foreshadowed a worse situation for public disability insurance.[42]

The actuaries at the Social Security Board were afraid for their professional reputations. Before the advisory council members were given a copy of the disability insurance plan, Williamson and Falk met to agree on a cost figure for disability insurance. Wilbur Cohen, then an assistant to Altmeyer and later the program's chief congressional liaison, described the discussion as "tense, hectic, and emotional." Williamson took the position that the Social Security Board should not give a definite estimate of the cost of disability insurance. He said that he could not possibly give one estimate and "maintain his professional integrity." This breach in the ranks caused serious concern. Cohen feared that Williamson would "practically refuse to give one cost es-

timate." Even worse, Linton already knew that Williamson's cost figures had a "range from one to ten."[43]

When the disability program was proposed to the council, Williamson maintained his professional integrity by siding with Linton and
emphasizing the potential costs of disability insurance. "It seems almost inevitable," Williamson stated to the advisory council, "that when
men are laid off and cannot work, with nothing in sight, no earning
power whatever, they will be judged disabled."[44]

The liberals on the council tried to stand their ground. William Haber, a professor at the University of Michigan, argued that mere administrative difficulty should not be allowed to delay the passage of
disability insurance. Lee Pressman of the Congress of Industrial Organizations emphasized that, "when a problem arises such as disability protection and it is admitted that it is a socially desirable thing to
cover that problem, there is no better time to start covering the problem than the present."[45]

By November, Witte was convinced that the cause of permanent
disability insurance was lost. He reported to fellow liberal Gerald
Morgan that there had been very little discussion of disability insurance at the council's recent executive committee meeting. The other
executive committee members appeared convinced that the council had
already turned down disability compensation.[46]

By December, the Social Security Board had nearly lost control of
the situation. Morgan proposed that the council recommend extending welfare coverage to include disability rather than creating a new
form of social insurance. Welfare, he argued, had the advantage of
getting money into people's hands quickly. Paul Douglas, a University
of Chicago economist who later became a U.S. senator, picked up
Morgan's idea. He noted that the blind already were covered by the
welfare program. It made sense to add other physically impaired groups.
"Obviously, a person who has lost both legs is more or less out," he
argued. "If you have lost both arms, you are more or less out. As you
come down, if he has one leg or one arm, that is a border-line case."[47]

"I counted noses and concluded we were licked," Witte later wrote
to Altmeyer. During the course of the meeting, Haber told Witte that
disability insurance stood no chance of passage. So Witte persuaded a
relatively anonymous council member to present a compromise that
Witte had devised. Brown wanted the council to recommend that the
administrative provisions of disability insurance "warranted delay"

and that in the meantime disability should be covered by an expanded
welfare program. Without mentioning welfare, Witte, acting through
the compromise motion, put the council on record as believing disability insurance was "socially desirable" and as disagreeing only on
when the program should begin. "At the council meeting I said that I
was convinced that a majority of the Council favored disability compensation but when I said it I feared the worst," Witte wrote Altmeyer.
Somehow the motion carried, and the council endorsed disability insurance in a lukewarm way.[48]

In the years that followed, the Social Security Board cited the advisory council's report as a recommendation for disability insurance,
knowingly concealing the council's ambivalence over the issue. As the
Social Security Board's self-confidence about its administrative ability
grew, it sought endorsements for its disability insurance program, not
critiques or advice. The advisory council's report became part of the
sales pitch.

With a heady sense of optimism, Cohen said, in the spring of 1941,
that he was "enthusiastic" about the Social Security Board's plans,
particularly those for disability insurance, which he considered "administratively feasible" and "socially desirable." In the Social Security
Board's 1941 report to the president, it "strongly recommend[ed] the
inclusion of permanent total disability insurance in the federal system." Soon the board's plans became legislative proposals.[49]

By then the politics of disability insurance featured not only the split
between the federal government and the insurance companies but also
emerging differences between the federal and the state governments.
Reinhard A. Hohaus, an actuary of the Metropolitan Life Company
and a friend of social security, urged the Social Security Board to be
cautious in its dealings with both of these groups. He advised the federal bureaucrats to work on extending social security coverage first
and then to press for disability insurance. If disability insurance were
considered essential, he suggested that coverage begin at age sixty and
that the board begin by preserving the retirement rights of disabled
workers.[50]

Falk and the other social security planners would take none of this
friendly advice. Falk sought continuity of coverage; he envisioned a
federal social insurance program that would carry a worker through
unemployment, sickness, disability, and old age. In the past there had
been "the need to mark off rather sharply state and federal adminis-

trative functions." Now, he said, "there are so many advantages of thinking of a single system of disability compensation, all administered by the federal government." He saw no reason to compromise. Falk dismissed Hohaus's suggestion to restrict disability to those over age sixty: "It is many shades better than no disability plan, but that does not . . . warrant our giving it currency."[51]

The war brings delay

For reasons not yet fully unraveled, the war made it more difficult for the Social Security Board to realize its ambitions. Witte noticed a change even before the United States entered the war. When the fighting began in Europe in 1939, he wrote that "everything else seems to be of little moment." Witte predicted that the United States would join the war and that the social security program would drop out of public sight. Witte believed, however, that should the war last long, "our Social Security system will become a national one." He saw the war as drawing the nation together, putting more emphasis on the federal government and less on the states. Three months after Pearl Harbor, Williamson made the opposite prediction. He believed that the end of the depression would make it more difficult to expand social insurance because it could no longer be sold so readily on the basis of need. "Arguments which would have sounded reasonable a few years ago no longer click," said Williamson, who proved to be the more correct.[52]

In the short run, though, the war expanded the responsibilities of the Social Security Board, just as Witte predicted. On February 6, 1942, President Roosevelt gave the Social Security Board $5 million to compensate civilians for casualties sustained in enemy attacks. Through executive action, Roosevelt started a minidisability program. When enemy attacks failed to materialize, however, federal officials dispatched the minidisability program to the archives, where it continues to gather dust.[53]

Special projects aside, the war forced the Social Security Board to put its disability plans on hold. Although the head of the Old Age Insurance Bureau announced his total loyalty to the board's plans to expand social security, the war had created what he called "administrative implications," among them an employee turnover rate of 75 percent. This turnover made implementation of a disability program expected to handle a million claims in its first year impossible. Even Falk worried whether there would be sufficient medical personnel.[54]

Economic considerations also argued for delay. In the depression, liberals encouraged the federal government to spend money and stim- ulate private investment. Now the nation needed to raise money for the war. The Treasury wanted to take money out of private circulation as a barrier against inflation and as a means of paying for the war. Disability insurance would violate the war effort.[55]

Altmeyer, anticipating a postwar recession, wanted disability insur- ance and the other components of an expanded social insurance pro- gram passed during the war years so that they would be in place after the war.[56] The din of the war prevented Altmeyer from being heard, however, and the lack of a postwar depression rendered his message irrelevant. The war and the ensuing prosperity made the labor force a more secure and attractive place to be. Tickets out of the labor force lost some of their appeal.

So the Social Security Board faced an unfortunate paradox in its plans for disability insurance. Hard times made for good politics, good times made for bad politics. Depression brought political success and affluence produced political failure. The Social Security Board, which had tailored many of its policies to an atmosphere of depression, now needed to change its strategy.

Temporary disability: a case study

The fate of temporary disability insurance, a measure linked closely with permanent disability insurance, illustrates how the war enabled private insurance companies and the states to defeat plans for a federal system of social insurance.

Planners had always separated disability insurance into two parts: permanent disability and temporary disability. Temporary disability meant "sickness." Since a person recovered from being sick, his afflic- tion was considered to be temporary. The social security planners drew the line at half a year. If an impairment forced someone out of the labor force for up to half a year, he was a candidate for temporary disability benefits. Longer illnesses fell into the domain of permanent disability.[57]

The Social Security Administration planners proposed the creation of a federal temporary disability program as part of a unified social insurance system in 1942, but the states acted before Congress could. Although only one state, Rhode Island, passed temporary disability insurance in June 1942, it preempted the field. Federal officials remained under orders not to start new benefit programs that would fuel inflation during the war. Rhode Island officials, under no such restrictions, had no difficulty initiating a program on behalf of its heavily unionized, newly prosperous work force.

S. E. Carroll, vice-president of an Omaha insurance company, expressed the insurance industry's reaction to the Rhode Island law when he characterized it as a "whirlwind of disaster" that "penalized the industrious." The fact that the law created what the trade called an "exclusive state fund" disturbed the insurance industry most. Under this arrangement, the state collected employer and employee contributions and paid benefits without allowing the private insurance companies to participate.[58]

In contrast to the insurance industry officials, John B. Andrews, veteran of efforts to pass state labor laws from the Progressive Era to the New Deal, greeted the passage of the Rhode Island law with enthusiasm. He praised it as "evidence of a recent tendency of States to assert more vigorously their desire to assume local responsibilities without federal complications." Andrews believed that the center of gravity in labor legislation was shifting away from Washington and toward the state capitals. "The administration at Washington had its opportunity and muffed it," he concluded.[59]

During the war years, conditions appeared to favor the passage of temporary disability laws in a number of states. J. Douglas Brown explained the forces leading to the passage of such laws in a letter he wrote to a New Jersey state official. First Brown noted the existence of large reserves in the New Jersey unemployment insurance fund. He said that the state and federal planners, used to the depression, were too conservative in their employment estimates for the wartime economy. Then Brown called the official's attention to a feature of the New Jersey unemployment compensation law that required employees to contribute into the unemployment compensation fund. "In order to satisfy labor in paying the employee contributions," he wrote, "New Jersey can well afford to be liberal in being a pioneer in temporary disability insurance." Brown was also aware of the fact that the local medical societies welcomed the idea, since temporary disability insurance would enable workers to pay their medical bills. For all of these reasons, Brown advocated a temporary disability insurance law for New Jersey.[60]

In 1946, Congress passed an amendment to the Social Security Act that allowed employee contributions to state unemployment insurance funds to be used for temporary disability insurance. With the passage of this amendment, other states that required employee contributions became more interested in temporary disability laws. For example, the law hastened the passage of a California law that initiated a state temporary disability insurance program in the spring of 1946. The California law, unlike the Rhode Island law, allowed employers to purchase private insurance to meet their temporary disability obligations in addition to establishing a California state temporary disability fund.

Altmeyer now had two reasons to be displeased with the course of events. First, the more states that passed temporary disability laws, the less chance the federal government would pass such a law. Second, allowing private insurance companies to provide temporary disability coverage increased the private sector's influence over social security policy, and, in Altmeyer's view, this would result in uneven coverage that left serious gaps in coverage. In 1948, he pleaded that employees in states with temporary disability insurance laws not be permitted to "contract out" to private insurers. In other words, employers should be required to participate in exclusive state insurance funds. The success of social insurance, he claimed, depended on "the widest pooling of the risk." If the states allowed private companies to participate, he argued, temporary disability would become a chaotic, uncontrollable program in the manner of workers' compensation.[61]

When New Jersey passed its temporary disability insurance law on June 1, 1948, it permitted contracting out; so did New York in its temporary disability insurance law passed in the spring of 1949. New York's Governor Thomas Dewey portrayed the law as a bulwark of private enterprise. "It is not a tax-supported program," Dewey said; "it is privately-provided social insurance. It not only permits continuation of existing voluntary plans, but encourages the formation of new voluntary plans." The law allowed for "the very minimum of government interjection in the field of social insurance."[62]

By 1955, plans for a federal program of temporary disability insurance had faded completely. About one-fifth of the nation's workers were covered by various state laws, and more than half of those were protected by private insurance plans. The war had cut the ground out from under the Social Security Board. The newfound prosperity allowed state governments and private insurance companies to expand their operations while the Social Security Board took a vow not to increase its spending. As a consequence, protection against the risk of temporary disability came to be provided by the private sector more often than by the public sector; that remains true today.[63]

The 1948 advisory council

In 1943, the Social Security Board drafted a bill for Senators Robert Wagner (D.-New York) and James Murray (D.-Montana) and Representative John Dingell (D.-Michigan). The bill asked Congress to create a unified system of social insurance, with permanent disability, temporary disability, and national health insurance all under federal control. Congress declined. In May 1945, a similar bill appeared, and again nothing happened.[64]

With the political situation so discouraging, the Social Security Board needed to stir up support for permanent disability insurance. The 1946 elections, which returned the first Republican Congress since the era of Herbert Hoover, offered little encouragement. Cohen, speaking before the American Bar Association in the fall of 1947, reported little enthusiasm for the Social Security Board's plans. With their hopes unraveling, the board cooperated with the Senate Committee on Finance in the appointment of another advisory council. "We expect to be able to make some progress through this Council," Cohen wrote Witte.[65]

Witte told Cohen not to be so sure. Witte, who was not appointed to the council, noted immediately that Linton was. "With Mr. Linton on the [council]," he said, "it is a safe guess that nothing will be recommended which even remotely would make social insurance a competitor with private life insurance." Witte thought that Linton might agree to an extension of social security coverage and an increase in benefits, since Linton was smart enough to make recommendations "which he hopes will keep Congress from making changes in the [old age and survivors insurance] system which might mean some competition for the insurance companies."[66] As for the others on the council, though Witte called them "good friends," he doubted they would be able to stand up to Linton.

If nothing else, the 1947–8 advisory council brought some new faces to the social security scene. Robert Ball, who later served as commissioner of Social Security (1961–73), was the council's staff director, although the insurance industry worried that he "might not carry out the program the Senate Finance Committee had in mind." Nelson Cruikshank, who directed social insurance activities of the American Federation of Labor, emerged as a national figure in social security through his appointment to the council. For the next twenty years, he acted as a lobbyist on the program's behalf and faithfully served on advisory councils. More than anyone else, he helped organized labor to overcome its traditional suspicion of the federal government's social welfare activities.[67]

The council held its first meeting at the beginning of December 1947. Following the lead of the earlier council, it appointed an organizing committee to facilitate its work. Sumner Slichter of Harvard, Brown, Linton, Marion Folsom (an Eastman Kodak executive and later the secretary of the Department of Health, Education, and Welfare), and Cruikshank served on the committee. Edward R. Stettinius, a United States Steel Company executive and former secretary of state, chaired the committee. Businessmen formed the largest single group, just as they did on the council itself.[68]

Disability insurance appeared prominently on the council's agenda. Cohen believed "disability insurance is going to be the most controversial item." Further, Social Security officials were no longer seeking a simple endorsement of permanent disability insurance, as they had in the earlier council. They not only expected endorsement of the idea now, but also wanted the council to approve a disability insurance plan that included workers of all ages, not just workers fifty-five or older.[69] Since more than half of all permanent disability cases occurred among workers under fifty-five, "when the worker has heavy family responsibilities and has not had the opportunity to build up adequate protection through savings or insurance," Altmeyer urged the council to recommend a disability insurance program for workers of all ages.[70]

Linton was strongly opposed. The closest he had come to accepting disability insurance was when he testified before the House Committee on Ways and Means in 1946. At that time he said that if disability insurance benefits were adopted, they should be restricted to those fifty-five or older. He now joined the insurance industry members of the council in retreating from this position and coming out against permanent total disability altogether. Instead of a federal social insurance law, Linton suggested a welfare law. Cohen understood Linton's change of position. "After all," he noted, "if disability protection is good at age fifty-five, why is it not good at fifty, forty, thirty and eventually twenty?"[71]

The fight for the soul of the advisory council shaped up as a battle between Linton and Altmeyer. The neutral members of the council were bombarded with propaganda from both sides. Ernest C. Young, for example, a dean at Purdue University, received a visit in his home-town from a local Social Security agent who urged Young to consider the problems the absence of disability insurance caused in social se-curity. Young had never thought about disability insurance before at-tending the December meeting of the advisory council. Intrigued and eager to take his service to the nation seriously, he solicited advice from members of his faculty, from doctors, and from workers' com-pensation administrators. "Go slow it is dynamite," the experts told him. The agent told Young that under existing law a person could become disabled, drop out of the labor force, and as a consequence lose his old age benefits. The agent referred to the discussion as "pro-ductive"; Young supported disability insurance.[72]

On March 29, 1948, the council's organizing committee decided to eliminate dependents' benefits from any disability insurance recom-mendation that might emerge, a restriction that Cohen called "unde-sirable" because it conflicted with the goal of family protection. The council members also compromised on what they called the "work requirement." They decided to include a provision that limited dis-ability benefits to those who had worked for at least a year and a half in the three years before they became disabled. With these concessions, the liberals hoped to get a unanimous recommendation from the coun-cil, including the vote of Albert Linton.[73]

The organizing committee asked Myers to estimate the cost of their proposed disability plan. He estimated the cost would be in the range of 0.1 to 0.3 percent of payroll, which meant that the costs of disabil-ity insurance could be met by raising the social security tax a little. For those who preferred their estimates in cold, hard cash, Myers re-ported that a disability program would cost $15 million in 1950 and reach no more than half a billion dollars by 1970. He also warned that cost estimates were deceptive. "The controversy," he said, "did not hinge on the low cost" of the limited disability program, "but rather [on] the belief that all restrictions will have to be removed and costs will hence become very large." If the disability insurance program were to be expanded, the initial numbers meant nothing. By promulgating them, the council would put a false scientific gloss on a fundamentally subjective concept.[74]

With the numbers in and reassuring, the council debated disability insurance on April 9–10, 1948, and approved the limited disability insurance proposal. Neither side was entirely satisfied. Cohen regretted the loss of dependents' benefits. To Cruikshank's disgust, Linton, who objected even to the limited proposal, insisted that a memorandum he had written be included in the report as a dissent. For the first time, then, an advisory council report featured a dissenting opinion by "two members." Although not identified at the time, they were Linton and Folsom.[75]

It was one of Linton's most effective essays in persuasion. He pointed out the likelihood that the system would break down during periods of high unemployment. He argued that workers would come to regard benefits as rights and that attitude in turn would create incentives to pay borderline claims. Women, he stated, would present particular problems, with complaints of physical ailments that could not be disproved and their less-than-steady attachment to the labor force. In addition, he contended that the present proposals were merely the entering wedge for more liberal proposals. The solution to the problem, he said, was the creation of state welfare programs for the disabled, funded with federal grants. He concluded by stating that, because of the subjective nature of disability, the handling of "total disability cases belong peculiarly in the realm of the individual States and not in the realm of the Federal government."[76]

Linton found an ally in Mary Donlon, an administrator from New York's workers' compensation program, who also served on the council. She shared Linton's concerns about the expansion of the federal government and the effect it would have on state governments. She insisted, therefore, that the federal government's responsibility be limited only to the totally disabled. The rest, she said, should be left to the states.[77]

When the advisory council's report appeared, it did little to dissipate the political tensions over disability. The insurance industry and the state governments still objected to it or failed to support it warmly. The American Medical Association feared that disability insurance might be the entering wedge for national health insurance. The advisory council tried to reassure these groups by emphasizing increased control over claims that "could be objectively determined by medical examinations and tests. In this way, the problems involved in the adjudication of claims based on purely subjective symptoms [a euphemism in the disability literature for pain] can be avoided." The insurance industry remained unpersuaded by this rhetoric; so did the doctors who were, in any event, less concerned about controlling disability expenditures than they were about government intervention in the field of health care.[78]

Linton's dissent made it clear that the opponents of disability insurance had a counterproposal. They wanted the federal government to assist the states in aiding the disabled who were poor enough to qualify for welfare. With this counterproposal, they not only managed to overcome the criticism that they did not care about the handicapped, but also were able to form a tentative alliance with workers' compensation administrators and other advocates of state control over disability programs.

Even though the second advisory council endorsed permanent disability insurance in more positive terms than the first, this time the report contained a dissent, which suggested welfare as an alternative to social insurance. The first time around, Witte and his allies had contained Linton and talk of a welfare program. This time, with Witte watching from Wisconsin, Linton put his views down on paper for all to see.

The freeze

Altmeyer and his colleagues now had a tougher fight on their hands; not only did they still have to push hard for their disability insurance program, but they also had to contend with Linton's welfare proposal. Not everyone, however, was persuaded by Linton. Jane Hoey, the director of the Bureau of Public Assistance, for example, scoffed at the idea of creating a welfare program for the disabled. The states and localities, she said, lacked the administrative capability to handle the problem. Hardened by years of observing the state welfare agencies, she dismissed Linton's proposals as unrealistic, motivated more by politics than by genuine concern for the disabled.[79]

With the departure of the Republican congressional majority in 1948 and with the recommendation of the advisory council, Altmeyer hoped once again to interest Congress in permanent disability insurance. Almost as soon as Congress convened, "Muley" Doughton, a veteran Democrat from North Carolina reclaiming his place as chairman of the Committee on Ways and Means, announced the beginning of a legislative drive to expand social security. He asked Altmeyer to testify on permanent disability insurance. By this time Altmeyer could have testified in favor of permanent total disability insurance in his sleep. He paraded the arguments of need, administrative feasibility, and low cost before the committee. Taking a slap at the insurance industry, he said that although disability could not be predicted on an individual basis, "in the aggregate it is a predictable, insurable risk." The Ways and Means Committee included a limited disability insurance plan, along the conservative lines suggested by the advisory committee, in a bill that was passed by the full House in the fall of 1949.[80]

The lobbying against disability insurance now began in earnest. The AMA, increasingly worried about the passage of national health insurance, took the lead in opposing disability insurance, arguing that it would perpetuate the condition of sickness and would work against rehabilitation. Further, the AMA said, the law would allow the federal government to supervise the doctors who examined the disability applicants. Who knew where that practice might lead? The solution to the problem of disability, the AMA claimed, was to eliminate it, not to encourage it.[81] The war had produced a new branch of medicine that restored a disabled person to his highest functional capacity. Rehabilitation medicine to help people help themselves represented, according to the AMA, a much more positive approach than disability pensions.

In the fall of 1950, Altmeyer appeared on a radio broadcast and debated disability insurance with Judd Benson, president of the National Association of Life Underwriters. The entire debate centered on rehabilitation. Benson argued that disability insurance "retards" rehabilitation. Altmeyer countered that the country needed both rehabilitation and disability insurance.[82]

Though Altmeyer doubted Benson's sincerity, and that of others in the insurance industry, he recognized that the rehabilitation argument worked well for the opponents of disability insurance. He toyed with the idea of reworking the disability proposals to eliminate conflict between rehabilitation and income maintenance. At first, the disabled would receive "rehabilitation and interim payments"; they would get permanent disability benefits only if efforts at rehabilitation failed.[83]

These proposals came too late to save the disability insurance legislation from being killed by the Senate Committee on Finance. Instead, the committee recommended, and Congress ultimately passed in 1950, a welfare program for the disabled called Aid to the Permanently and Totally Disabled. As in the other welfare programs, the federal government made grants to the states, and the states gave money to people who could prove they were permanently and totally disabled and poor.

The 1950 legislation, which also expanded social security coverage to the self-employed and increased benefit levels for everyone, marked the most significant changes in social security since 1939. Still, Congress proved willing to pass only a welfare program and not a disability and health insurance law. In the minds of the Social Security administrators, these proposals came next. Unlike earlier efforts to create a complete federal social insurance program with one legislative stroke, a series of laws might now prove to be the best approach, perhaps beginning with a permanent disability law that did not pay benefits to dependents and that did not appear to conflict with efforts to rehabilitate the handicapped.

Compromise on disability insurance had never appealed to the Social Security Administration. Social Security officials believed that most of the alternatives, such as expanding public assistance, did damage to the disabled, since Congress might perceive these measures to be permanent solutions to the problem. Still, compromise appeared the only way to proceed.

One compromise, called the "freeze," which had been considered "inferior" in the 1930s, began to look more attractive. The freeze preserved a disabled worker's rights to social security at age sixty-five. Under its terms, persons who became disabled had their benefit records "frozen." If they qualified for benefits when their records were frozen, they received them when they reached retirement age, even though they had been out of the labor force and paying nothing into the social security trust fund.

Altmeyer was convinced that the freeze represented the best alternative in the chilly political climate. Although it might meet opposition from the AMA and the insurance companies (since it required the federal government to certify someone as disabled), it seemed so fair and reasonable that it would be difficult to oppose. Furthermore, it closely resembled the practice of offering a "waiver of premium" to disabled policyholders of private life insurance contracts. The private sector precedent might undercut some of the insurance companies' op-position. The freeze also had another advantage. Rather than trying to start a new disability insurance program, it would build on the old age and survivors insurance program, a program of which even Linton approved.[84]

Altmeyer suggested the idea to Doughton, who, by now close to retiring, presented the idea to his House colleagues. The House passed the freeze in 1952. The Senate Committee on Finance, once again blocking the Social Security Administration's plans, opposed it. This set the stage for Doughton to bring the freeze proposal to a conference committee.

The conferees found themselves deadlocked over the disability issue. The House wanted the freeze, the Senate opposed it. Cohen, by now a senior member of the Social Security Administration staff, shuttled between the two sides. The House wanted to move toward a full dis-ability insurance program; the Senate wanted to halt the progress of disability insurance, short of the freeze. At this moment, Congress had arrived at the boundary of the disability insurance program. If Con-gress agreed to a freeze, the federal government would have gained the right to declare workers disabled and this action would mark the be-ginning of a disability insurance program, however limited. There ap-peared to be no way to resolve the impasse. Even Cohen, who pos-sessed nearly unlimited energy, extraordinary political sensitivity, and extreme technical competence could do little.

Then an idea arose that Arthur Hess, a career Social Security em-ployee, called a "flash of genius." Someone suggested letting the states make disability determinations. The states ran the vocational rehabil-itation, workers' compensation, and public assistance programs. By linking disability determinations to these established programs, the House conferees hoped to overcome the opposition of their Senate counterparts to the freeze. The states would have the option of using their welfare departments, their workers' compensation bureaus, or their vocational rehabilitation agencies as the institutional home of their disability determination units. Even the AMA and the insurance industry approved of the state-run disability programs. Cohen has-tened to work out the details.[85]

Allowing the states to declare someone disabled appeared to ex-haust every avenue of compromise, and still the two sides remained adamant. Cohen came up with one more idea to which he managed to obtain the assent of the Senate conferees. As Cohen later recalled, he acted instinctively, without even contacting Altmeyer for approval. His proposal was one of the most unusual in the history of social welfare legislation. The Senate agreed to a freeze in return for an agreement by the House not to implement it. Under the compromise agreement, the freeze would end on June 30, 1953, but no applications would be accepted before July 1, 1953. So the freeze ended before it began. The House won in principle, the Senate in practice. In the clubby atmosphere of Congress, the freeze became a tribute to Doughton, who joined a parade of retiring congressman whom the Social Security Administration used over the years to introduce legislation that the AMA opposed.[86] Although the Senate had resisted another attempt to start a disability insurance program, it had succeeded only by the barest of margins.[87]

The concessions of 1952 appeared at the time to be harmless political maneuvers, yet they created a dangerous precedent. Neither the freeze itself nor the political games over the starting date of the freeze mattered much in the long run. It was allowing the states to make disability determinations that left its permanent mark on American disability policy. It put the administrative burden of disability insurance on forty-eight individual states, the District of Columbia, and several odd territories, a scheme that could only lead to inconsistency from state to state. Unlike nearly every other limiting feature of the 1952 legislation, the Social Security Administration never undid this mistake. From 1952 forward, state participation in disability provided a comfortable cover of precedent under which Congress could legislate.

When the Republicans returned to power in 1953, eager to do something constructive on social security, but feeling cautious, they seized on the old idea of a disability freeze. By this time Altmeyer, Falk, and the other Democratic stalwarts had left the Social Security Administration. Of the Social Security insiders, only Cohen and Ball remained. In the summer of 1954, the Eisenhower administration passed the disability freeze, with the states holding the power to determine eligibility, just as it was written in the 1952 law.[88]

The Eisenhower years exposed tensions between the White House and the Social Security Administration. The Eisenhower administration issued public statements that indicated support for the freeze as a means of solving problems related to disability. What the freeze failed to do, an expanded rehabilitation program would accomplish. The Social Security Administration, even minus Altmeyer and Falk, never abandoned its drive to pass disability insurance. For the Social Security Administration, the freeze represented a step along the incremental path to disability insurance.

These differences produced annoyances on both sides, as when Assistant Secretary of Health, Education, and Welfare Roswell Perkins, who did most of the work on the freeze for the Eisenhower administration, discovered that the correspondence section of the Social Security Administration continued sending letters that lamented the failure to enact disability insurance. Capturing the Eisenhower administration's point of view, Perkins wrote that the standard letter "makes no mention of the administration's philosophy that the first line of attack on disability should be rehabilitation, in order that people be restored to useful and productive lives . . . rather than merely being recipients of cash benefits."[89] These differences of emphasis between Perkins and his nominal subordinates at the Social Security Administration made it clear that the struggle over disability insurance was far from over.

The final battle

In order to secure a disability insurance program, the employees of the Social Security Administration assumed the role of double agents. Although part of a Republican administration that was opposed to a disability insurance program, they worked almost openly with the Democrats to pass disability legislation.

The Democrats in Congress now regarded disability insurance as their policy, and they wanted the credit for bringing this benefit to the public. Since Eisenhower brought a Republican congressional majority with him, the Democrats had to wait until 1955 before they could mount a serious move. That year, Jere Cooper (D.-Kentucky) replaced Republican Dan Reed (who had replaced Doughton) as the chairman of the Ways and Means Committee, and by summer he stood ready to assemble his committee in executive session to tackle disability insurance. He called the lack of disability insurance the "greatest shortcoming" in social security. As expected, the committee endorsed disability insurance, just as it had in 1949. This time, however, the committee made a significant concession to the forces of incrementalism by proposing disability insurance only for those over the age of fifty.[90]

In the past, the Social Security Administration had vigorously opposed this kind of age limitation on disability insurance. Now, in the interest of making some headway, it endorsed it eagerly. The insurance industry had scored an unprecedented and unsolicited victory. In the mid-1950s, the Social Security Administration was reduced to advocating the position the insurance industry had taken in the mid-1940s.

Those members of the Ways and Means Committee who supported disability insurance knew that those who opposed it in the Senate Finance Committee would emphasize rehabilitation and argue that disability benefits substituted expensive cash payments for efforts to rehabilitate the handicapped. The committee recognized the need to address the problem directly. "We believe," the committee reported, "that everything possible should be done to support and strengthen vocational rehabilitation. . . . Important as rehabilitation is, it cannot be a substitute for disability benefits."[91]

As expected, the committee measure passed the House and, as expected, the House measure failed to clear the Senate Committee on Finance. Although the Senate and the Finance Committee had Democratic majorities, Dixiecrats (southern Democrats), who often sided with the Republicans, enjoyed considerable influence. Senator Harry Byrd, the chairman of the Finance Committee, caucused with the Republicans. Said Nelson Cruikshank, "This not only serves to carry on the negative legislative activity of the Administration but gives it a Democratic coloration."[92]

Unable to wait any longer, the Social Security Administration decided to attempt to pass disability insurance on the floor of the Senate. By this time Cohen, who had left the government to work at the University of Michigan, was serving as a lobbyist on behalf of the legislation, free from any conflicts of interest. As he modestly put it in a letter to Witte, he tried "to keep in close touch with the legislative situation." He also kept his ties open to Robert Ball and Alvin David in the Bureau of Old Age and Survivors Insurance and to Marion Folsom, now secretary of Health, Education, and Welfare. At first he had hoped to convert Folsom and work through the administration. Failing at that, he threw himself into the preparation for the floor fight.[93]

The proponents of disability insurance enjoyed several advantages that they had not had before. By 1956, the states had already made 106,130 determinations under the disability freeze program without the sky falling in. The large number reflected the fact that the freeze was retrospective; it applied to people disabled since the early 1940s. This bit of information greatly strengthened the argument that disability insurance was administratively feasible. Further, the fact that social security trust funds were in robust shape and the economy appeared to be doing well boosted the argument that the cost of disability insurance plus all the other items in the legislation (such as reduced retirement age for women) amounted to less than 1 percent of covered payroll. In addition, the fact that social security featured what the actuaries called the "level earnings assumption" made the program seem even more affordable. The actuaries assumed that earnings would not rise; if earnings rose, more money would flow into the trust fund. In the mid-1950s, earnings appeared certain to rise.[94]

Other advantages were more political in nature. As a result of the merger between the AFL and CIO, Cruikshank now lobbied for the entire labor movement. He already knew George Meany, the AFL leader chosen to run the merged organization, and he succeeded in convincing Meany of the importance of disability insurance. As Cruikshank recalled, "We consciously made the decision that this would be the first thing on which the united labor movement would work."[95] The new labor movement wanted to win its first battle.

The next person Cruikshank had to convince was Senator Walter George of Georgia. Respected, conservative, and retiring, George was a perfect candidate to lead the floor fight. Cruikshank called George "the only one who could do it." Still, George had opposed disability insurance in 1950, and, according to Cruikshank, the relatively liberal CIO was "unable to get near him." The AFL, on the other hand, had supported George, even when President Roosevelt had wanted to purge him from Congress in the 1930s. As a result, Cruikshank and fellow labor lobbyist Andrew Biemiller managed to get an appointment to see George, even though they were told he "wasn't seeing anyone." When they met, they brought up his retirement and urged him to support disability as a "parting gift for the American people."[96]

Meany followed this presentation with a letter. He thanked George for his distinguished service and then ventured "to predict that in the years to come as you review the work of a long and distinguished career in the Senate you will enjoy no greater satisfaction than that justly derived from your having contributed your notable leadership to this much-needed rounding out of our social security program." George swallowed it.[97]

The Senate floor debate took place on July 17, 1956. Cohen came to Washington to compose arguments and marshal votes; Cruikshank roamed the corridors off the Senate floor hoping to pick up votes. Richard Nixon made an infrequent appearance as presiding officer of the Senate, dispatched by the administration to vote against disability insurance in case of a tie vote. Lyndon Johnson kept discipline among the Democrats, telling them that "this is one of our most important positions."

George offered his amendment, and Senator Byrd presented his rebuttal. Byrd argued that people would regard disability benefits as retirement pensions, payable at age fifty. Although the program might start off in good financial shape, the restraints would probably come off and this would lead to serious fiscal troubles: "This temporary balance on hand will be seized as justification for liberalizing the program by eliminating any age requirement, providing additional dependents' benefits, and perhaps providing for partial disability." He pointed out that someone might be disabled for one job but not for another; he cited examples of handicapped people who had managed to rehabilitate themselves. Quoting the president of the American Medical Association, he contended that, "the positive, constructive approach to disability is rehabilitation, not cash benefits."[98]

It appeared as though the vote would be very close, and Cruikshank, Cohen, and the others would need a handful of Republican votes to carry the measure. Johnson delayed the vote until the Democrats could muster the necessary majority. At one point, Johnson gave Cruikshank one hour and told him to find six more votes. Cruikshank induced representatives from influential unions to approach senators from their home states. He arranged, for example, for a representative of the railroad unions to approach Senator Milton Young (R.-North Dakota); he prevailed on other union leaders to talk with Senators George Malone (R.-Nevada) and Wiley (R.-Wisconsin). In a similar manner, lobbyists from the AMA, an important local influence for each of these senators, brought doctors and hospital administrators into contact with the senators.[99]

Johnson, with his exquisite political timing, moved toward a roll call. The amendment, with its provision for disability insurance, obtained the vote of forty-one Democrats and six Republicans, carrying 47–45. One change of vote would have created a tie that Nixon would have broken.[100]

The gallery erupted. Observers from the Social Security Administration could no longer restrain themselves. Cruikshank reported to Altmeyer, who was at home in Wisconsin, that "Ball and some of the others were literally dancing in the aisles and it didn't seem to bother them that Rod Perkins [from the Eisenhower administration] was looking down at them down the full length of his nose."[101] With the vote concluded, Cruikshank bumped into his counterpart from the AMA. They greeted one another. Cruikshank said, "How are you?" "How do you think I am," the AMA man replied. "This is the end of the medical profession."[102]

Altmeyer gave Cruikshank the credit for the victory. Witte thought Cohen deserved the credit. Leaving the government had strengthened Cohen's position, according to Witte. Whichever was right, they had both identified a remarkable feature of the 1956 legislative fight. Never before had a major social security amendment passed Congress with the opposition of the administration in power. The double-agent strategy had worked.[103]

On August 1, 1956, President Eisenhower signed a disability insurance program into law, and the long political struggle ended. Beginning in October 1956, the Social Security Administration would accept applications for disability benefits, and payments would begin in July 1957. Eisenhower, himself the victim of a heart attack, promised to administer the new law "efficiently and effectively" in cooperation with the states. He also pledged "increasing emphasis on efforts to help rehabilitate the disabled so that they may return to useful employment."[104]

In essence, the new law built directly upon the provisions for a disability freeze. The same state agencies would make the disability determinations, although Congress expected the secretary of Health, Education, and Welfare "to assure uniform administration of the disability benefits and to protect the [newly created] Federal Disability Insurance Trust Fund from unwarranted costs." The definition of disability remained essentially the same as it had appeared in social security proposals for almost twenty years. To obtain benefits, a person needed to demonstrate that he was unable to engage in gainful activity by virtue of a medically demonstrable impairment that was expected to last for at least a year. The only difference in definition was that the new law made no mention of the blind. For the time being, the blind, who had previously received special treatment, would be treated the same as everyone else.[105]

In the initial euphoria over the passage of the law, the Social Security Administration failed to recognize the price it had paid. The opponents had secured, at least temporarily, stringent conditions governing the disbursement of benefits, the most critical of which was the age limitation. Only people aged fifty or older qualified for the disability insurance program, although everyone realized how arbitrary this choice of age was. Disabled people under age fifty could have their wage records frozen and receive benefits at age fifty. The opponents also succeeded in securing a critical role for the states in the disability insurance process, as it would be the states, not the federal government, that would determine eligibility for benefits.

Although the social security planners had devised a definition of disability and a plan for permanent disability insurance with federal administration in mind, Congress had brought the states into the picture, complicating an already difficult problem in public administration and making it that much more difficult for the program to succeed.

In this manner, the Social Security Disability Insurance program joined workers' compensation in offering public protection against disability. In part because of the circumstances attending its origins, and in part because of the inherent nature of disability, disability insurance developed some of the same problems that haunted workers' compensation.

3. The administration of Social Security Disability Insurance

As a result of Congress's actions in 1956, the nation gained a major new disability program. In theory, this law marked an improvement over workers' compensation and the first generation of income-maintenance programs. Unlike workers' compensation, for example, disability insurance applied one definition of disability to the entire nation and eliminated differences in treatment of the disabled from state to state. Furthermore, as part of social security, disability insurance was financed by a tax on employers and employees and not by private insurance premiums. If a worker went on the disability rolls, it cost his employer nothing. Indeed, the way that fringe benefits were designed, an employee might even save his employer money by going on disability insurance. For this reason, employers would have no incentive to contest cases. Since cases could not be contested, the process of obtaining benefits would be quicker and more equitable than under workers' compensation.

As this account of the administration of disability insurance reveals, however, the advantages of disability insurance over workers' compensation have failed to materialize. Congressional desires to the contrary, disability insurance has developed problems similar to those in workers' compensation. Just as in workers' compensation, decisions on a person's eligibility differ from state to state, and many decisions engender legal disputes.

How did the new 1956 law develop these old problems? The answer lies in the complex administrative system that the law created and in the expansion of government social welfare programs since 1956. The states, administrative law judges, and the courts all play a role in the administration of disability insurance. By the 1970s, these various administrative actors had substantially altered the original conception of the law.

79

An overview

As reflected in the debate that preceded its passage, disability insurance relies on a tough definition of disability to determine eligibility. As amended in 1967, the law requires that a person have an impairment of "such severity that he is not only unable to do his previous work but cannot, considering his age, education, and work experience engage in any kind of substantial gainful work which exists in the national economy, regardless of whether such work exists in the immediate area in which he lives or whether a specific job vacancy exists for him or whether he would be hired if he applied for work." This definition has occasioned many disagreements. People wonder whether Congress intended the definition to be as tough and restrictive as a simple reading of it implies.

For, despite the severity of the definition, many people qualify for disability benefits. By the end of 1984, the Social Security Disability Insurance program was paying benefits to 2.58 million workers, their 0.92 million children, and their 304,000 spouses. A total of 3.82 million people received disability benefits that averaged $471 a month for an individual, $131 for his spouse, and $139 for his children.

The process of awarding these benefits worked as follows: An individual filed an application in a Social Security Administration district office, which reviewed his employment record to see if he was covered by disability insurance and then sent the application to a state disability determination office for an initial decision on eligibility. If the person was denied disability benefits, he could ask the state to reconsider. If still denied, he could bring his case before a federal administrative law judge. If still declared ineligible for benefits, he could then take his case to the Appeals Council of the Social Security Administration and finally to a federal district court, with full right of appeal through the courts. If benefits were granted, they were paid by the Social Security Administration in monthly installments.

The result was a complicated system utilizing a multistage process to implement the tough definition of disability and containing built-in checks and balances. Because administrators at the various stages brought different perspectives and incentives to the process, the administrative structure underlying disability insurance was unstable. Administrators often worked at cross-purposes and disagreed on the decisions they should make about particular claims.[1]

The states' role

The partnership between the Social Security Administration and the states began under strain and remained troubled. The first problem concerned the failure of the states to rehabilitate those who applied for disability benefits. The second involved the failure of the states to process disability cases as quickly as the Social Security Administration would have liked. Backlogs mounted. By October 1956, the states had yet to settle 120,000 cases from the disability freeze program of 1954. By November 1957, they were overwhelmed by 400,000 applications for disability benefits. The Social Security Administration reported that the states had encountered problems "in acquiring sufficient staff and know-how to keep pace."[2]

Given all of the problems connected with the federal–state relationship, why has it lasted? After all, it began as a compromise, and it ran into problems almost immediately. Why has it survived?

Initially, the parties at interest respected the compromise that Congress had reached and made a sincere effort to make it work. The Social Security Administration and influential congressmen such as Wilbur Mills understood how much importance physicians and businessmen attached to state administration. Neither Mills nor Social Security leaders such as Arthur Hess, who administered the program, or Robert Ball, who ran the agency, wanted to create unnecessary ill will with these groups.

Today, more practical concerns limit the possibilities for reform. Simply put, it is difficult for a congressman to propose that a state government agency be federalized; such an action would increase the size of the federal bureaucracy and leave the state employees in an uncertain situation. If the federal government agreed to hire the state employees, the costs of the program would increase since federal pay scales are, on the average, higher than state pay scales. All in all, it hardly seems worth the political trouble. The state–federal arrangement persists and seems likely to survive in the future.[3]

Since the arrangement is a historical artifact, it produces anomalies when viewed in its modern context. The state disability examiners base their eligibility determinations on a paper record that does not contain so much as a picture of the applicant and on pages and pages of rules stored in flexible notebooks and known as the "Program Operating Manual System." The state disability determination office often resembles a warehouse, with more paper than people. The examiners must reduce all the paper in the file and all the rules to a simple decision: yes or no.

The state disability examiners award sizable benefits that will be paid entirely from federal funds and in many cases be spent entirely in the examiner's state. The more money they award, therefore, the more money that is likely to flow to the state. The federal government tries to control the flow of funds by making binding rules that, it is hoped, will restrict the number of benefits granted. Although the federal government makes the rules, it has little control over the people who apply them because they work for the state. One state director of a disability determination service said that "he would probably be discharged if he follow[ed] a strict interpretation of SSA [Social Security Administration] guidelines." Another employee of a state disability determination service adds, "We are state employees; therefore, we don't have to pay attention to what the SSA regional office . . . or any other federal agency says." As these state workers realize, if the state does not grant disability benefits paid for by the federal government, the applicant may well apply for general assistance grants that are paid for entirely by the state government.[4]

The only hold that the Social Security Administration has over the states is the right to approve their annual budget for disability determination. That leaves the states considerable freedom to manage the disability program in their own way. As a result, the fifty-four state (and territorial) agencies reside in different government departments, lack uniform training programs, and follow different procedures.[5]

The diversity means that eligibility decisions vary from state to state. In the case of workers' compensation, the diversity stems from differences in the laws themselves; in the case of Social Security Disability Insurance, the differences involve variations in the ways in which the same law is administered. In the workers' compensation program, the differences concern the amount of money a worker receives, in Social Security Disability Insurance, the differences affect whether a worker receives any money at all.

The interstate diversity in disability insurance is illustrated in a study conducted in 1976 in which the General Accounting Office gave 221 disability claims to ten states and asked them to adjudicate them. The states agreed on only 48 of the claims. The rate of approval ranged from 47 to 31 percent and of denial from 41 to 19 percent.[6]

A great deal of evidence can be cited to show that eligibility determinations vary among the states from year to year. In 1974, for example, the state of Alaska denied eligibility to 63 percent of the cases it received, while the state of Iowa denied only 36.6 percent. In 1975, New Mexico turned down 61.9 percent of the applications for disability insurance, whereas the state of Iowa rejected only 34.4 percent. In 1980, the state of California dismissed 68.1 percent of its disability cases, and South Carolina rejected 52.7 percent.

In time, the states adopted a tougher attitude toward disability and denied a larger percentage of applications. Connecticut, for example, denied 41 percent of disability cases in 1974; but six years later rejected 63.6 percent of the cases, even though no changes in the law had occurred during those years. During that same period, the national average of denied cases rose from 50.5 to 67.4 percent. Of those granted disability benefits, a much greater percentage in 1980 than in 1974 qualified on the basis of medical considerations alone rather than on a combination of medical and vocational circumstances. Some states purchased medical evidence to supplement an applicant's file in 50 percent of the cases; others considered it essential in less than one case out of ten. As these examples reveal, states have not reached a consensus on what constitutes adequate documentation, nor do they arrive at the same conclusions.[7]

These statistics, through the fault of no one state, tend to discredit the performance of all of the states. They strengthen the impression of one federal analyst that the "state agencies may be operating more like fifty-four autonomous independent units than as sub-units of organizations that have contractual responsibilities with the Federal government."[8]

Changes in administration

Although the states do not treat disability claims uniformly and seem unable to carry out their basic mission of rehabilitation, they have received more responsibility, rather than less, as the disability insurance program has evolved. Further, the federal government has spent less time supervising the states and checking their decisions. The 1970s, in particular, marked a time of loosening federal supervision.

The looseness stemmed in part from the rise in applications for disability benefits. By 1974, the system had 1.2 million applications to manage, and the sheer volume of the applications defeated efforts at administrative control. Social Security administrators emphasized the need for quick decisions, and there remained little time and few resources to check state decisions and to review the growing disability rolls to make sure that those receiving benefits continued to deserve them.

One indication of the decline in administrative control was the falling recovery rate. Whereas in 1967 there were 30 recoveries per thousand beneficiaries, by 1976 there were only 15 recoveries per thousand beneficiaries. Despite an increase of 900,000 disabled workers on the rolls, the number of recoveries increased by only 2,000.[9]

Another indication of the loosening of administrative control in the 1970s was the number of state decisions the federal authorities decided to review. Before 1972, federal examiners checked about 70 percent of the cases in which the states recommended granting disability benefits. The federal review occurred before the applicant was told of the favorable decision. If the federal authorities questioned awarding benefits, the states reexamined and in most instances rejected the cases. The system changed in 1972, however, when the Social Security Administration, pressed for manpower and money, began reviewing only a random sample of the states' decisions. Instead of reviewing 70 percent of the favorable decisions, the federal government now saw only 5 percent of the cases, and it saw those cases only after a person had been informed of the favorable decision. The federal government also checked the status of a smaller percentage of those already on the disability rolls. In the early 1970s, the percentage of cases checked fell from 10 to 4 percent.

Even as these changes were occurring, Congress entrusted the states with two important new assignments. The first involved the black lung compensation program, the second a new welfare program called Supplemental Security Income (SSI).

The black lung program filled a gap in the nation's disability system. In 1969, Congress discovered the limitations of state workers' compensation programs in covering occupational diseases such as black lung, which afflicted the nation's coal miners. As a consequence, Congress created a special federal program to provide assistance to miners suffering from black lung disease. Congress put black lung claims filed before 1973 under the administrative control of the Department of

Health, Education, and Welfare (HEW), which entrusted the state–federal disability determination service with examining these claims for compensation and determining eligibility.[10]

SSI marked a point of departure from traditional welfare practice. The nation's welfare system began in 1935 with the creation of individual state programs to aid the needy elderly, dependent children, and the blind. Without exception, a person needed to pass a "means test" – prove he was poor – before he could receive welfare benefits. Social insurance benefits, by way of contrast, came to people as a matter of right, no matter how poor or rich they were. Although the states received money and advice from the federal government, they ran the welfare programs by themselves and paid the benefits, which varied widely, depending on a state's economic conditions and its attitudes toward welfare. In 1950, Congress created a new welfare category: aid to the permanently and totally disabled. This situation persisted until 1972, when SSI was created.

Beginning in 1974, SSI replaced the old state-run programs for the blind, the permanently and totally disabled, and the elderly with a new federal program that guaranteed all three of these groups a minimum income. Although the states could choose to supplement the minimum payment, the federal government assumed the basic responsibility for funding and administering SSI. Congress entrusted the Social Security Administration with running this new program, and the Social Security Administration placed responsibility for determining eligibility for the blind and disabled under the control of the state–federal disability determination system. In most states that meant that the process of declaring someone disabled and eligible for welfare was transferred from the state welfare department to the state disability determination unit, usually housed in the state's rehabilitation agency.

Congress gave these administrative logistics little thought, preferring to focus on how the new welfare program would affect the elderly. In this it showed a lack of foresight, since the disabled rather than the elderly soon made up the bulk of the SSI caseload. In 1984, for example, the number of people on SSI was a little more than 4 million; 2.4 million of those people were disabled and another 80,524 were blind. In 1979, the Senate Finance Committee estimated that 80 percent of the applications for SSI came from people who wished to qualify on the basis of disability. The disabled also received much of the money paid by the program. In 1984, the disabled took $7,143,212 of the $10,371,790 paid in benefits. SSI therefore became primarily another program for the disabled.

Congress failed to consider the effect that SSI would have on other disability programs. For example, even though the disability insurance program was showing signs of strain, Congress applied that program's definition of disability and system of determining eligibility to SSI. Using the same process and definition for disability insurance (a form of social insurance that people received as a right) and for Supplemental Security Income (a form of welfare that only poor and disabled people received) would produce serious consequences a decade later.

Even in 1974, the introduction of SSI put a massive amount of pressure on the states. The Social Security Administration, which in the past had weeded out many applicants for disability insurance on the grounds that they did not have proper wage records or might not have worked a sufficient number of quarters before becoming disabled, now referred many more applicants to the states. Many who might not be eligible for disability insurance but might be poor enough and disabled enough to qualify for welfare were encouraged by Social Security officials to file applications for SSI. Furthermore, Social Security officials discovered applicants for SSI whose wage records made them eligible to apply for disability insurance. Social Security officials in district offices sent both types of applications to the state disability determination units.

As a consequence, the number of applications the states had to process rose dramatically. In 1974, for example, 1,369,500 people applied for SSI on the basis of disability or blindness, 1.2 million people filed applications for disability insurance, and 500,000 applications were received for the black lung program. With so many applications arriving, the states spent less time scrutinizing each case and found it more difficult to maintain the tough standards for disability written into the law. As the Senate Finance Committee commented, the states responded by "speeding up the processing of cases," an action that the committee believed led to "a decline in the quality of decisions which were made."[11]

It took several years for this situation to attract public concern. Distracted by other questions, the members of Congress failed to distinguish between Social Security's old age insurance and disability insurance. Unlike the administration of old age insurance, disability determination was a complex matter, whether performed by the states or the federal government, and the federal government had already ceded much responsibility for this function to the states, even in programs (such as disability insurance) that most people though of as purely federal programs.

Worried about the cost of disability programs, the Carter and Reagan administrations did make some tentative and ultimately unsuccessful efforts to reduce the states' autonomy. The Carter administration wanted the states to sign a new contractual agreement that gave the federal government more supervisory power. Among other things, it provided the secretary of HEW with the right of access to state agency premises and the authority to set educational and other standards for disability examiners. Some states simply refused to sign and were allowed to continue their work under the terms of the existing contract. The state of Wisconsin threatened to terminate its contractual agreement with the federal government altogether. Hale Champion, Carter's under secretary of HEW and a former California state bureaucrat, wanted to call Wisconsin's bluff and have the federal government run the state agency. Stanford Ross, Carter's commissioner of Social Security and a distinguished tax lawyer, favored federalizing the entire system. Neither Ross nor Champion prevailed, and Wisconsin agreed to resume its duties under the existing contractual arrangements. During the Reagan years, relations between the states and the federal government grew even worse, despite the passage in 1980 of a law that gave the federal government more regulatory control over the states.[12]

The administrative law judges

The states occupy only the first layer of the disability determination system. At the next layer are the administrative law judges (ALJs) who, like the state disability examiners, face contrary pressures. Nominally the employees of the Social Security Administration, they are expected to decide whether the Social Security Administration has reached a fair verdict. Without exception, the ALJs are lawyers with seven or more years of legal experience. They bring elements of legal training and judicial reasoning to this system of mass justice.

The ALJ has much more freedom in deciding a case than the state disability examiner. He does not have to follow the strict procedures contained in the Program Operating Manual System. Instead, he interprets the law directly from the statutes and the regulations. Whereas the disability examiner almost invariably works in full view of others, as part of a team, the ALJ decides cases in his own office, by himself. Unlike the employees of the state disability determination unit, the ALJs have the privilege of rank, and lawyers treat them with the stylized courtesy they reserve for judges.

Far more than the disability examiner, the ALJ has an opportunity to consider the plight of the individual who has filed the disability application. The disability examiner never sees the whole man; he reads from a paper record about medical symptoms, about jobs held and lost. The record removes the examiner from the overwhelming sense of need that motivates the person to cash in his working life and seek benefits. The ALJ sees the whole person. He sees his pain, his inability to move with fluidity or to think with clarity, his fear and despair. When the ALJ goes home at night, he knows that it is up to him to decide. More than the disability examiner, therefore, the ALJ feels the pressure to err on the side of compassion.

A confidential memorandum from one ALJ to his supervisor recording the ALJ's impressions of a case shows how subjective considerations may influence an ALJ's decision. The case was extraordinarily tangled, involving veterans benefits, workers' compensation benefits, conflicting dates of employment, and many other complexities common to disability cases. Before the hearing, the ALJ happened to look out the window and see the applicant arriving. His attorney drove the car, and his wife helped him out. He climbed the steps to the hearing in obvious pain. He wobbled as he entered the room and approached the hearing table. "He appeared to be frail and sickly," the judge observed, and "he had considerable difficulty in understanding some of the questions directed to him and some moderate difficulty in answering." After observing the applicant face to face, the ALJ brushed legalisms aside and declared him disabled. Without the opportunity for face-to-face observation, with only the paper record on which to rely, the state disability examiner had reached the opposite conclusion.[13]

The ALJ's supervisor sent him a reprimand, telling him that he was not to use such subjective evidence. What would have happened, the supervisor asked, if the person had bounded up the steps to the hearing room with great vigor? In either case, the supervisor told him, the judge should reach a decision on the facts before him, not on what he had seen while glancing out the window. Despite the reprimand, the decision stood.

Personal observation, in this case, made the ALJ sympathetic to an applicant in obvious distress. The fact that the ALJ had a chance to observe the demeanor of the witness made a difference. Few of the applicants who presented themselves to the ALJs after being rejected by the state agencies were cheating. They regarded themselves as disabled. The ALJs had to review many tough cases, ones that could go either way. In addition, they judged claims after the state had reviewed them, so that, with the passage of time, the claimant's condition might have worsened.

The people who came before the ALJs included Ed Pullam. He was married and had six children. He had worked in the coal mines. The mine he had worked in closed on December 15, 1959. When it re-opened, his employer refused to rehire him. The employer said Pul-lam's physical impairments caused him to work too slowly; also, be-cause of Pullam's age, the employer feared his insurance premium would increase if he rehired this man. Pullam drew unemployment compen-sation, then filed for disability. He was fifty-three years old, too old to take his sixth-grade education and seek other work. Pullam was a flesh-and-blood example of what the social security planners had called the perfect labor market hypothesis. Even though he could not get a job, he had the ability to work. The Social Security Administration had resolved not to award benefits on the basis of unemployment alone. The states had been suitably tough with Pullam, turned down his ap-plication, and refused to reconsider it. To the ALJ, however, before whom Pullam appealed the decision, the case represented a close call. Pullam was unemployed and impaired. Ultimately, the ALJ had to look Pullam in the face and say, no, he was not disabled.[14]

Emphasizing the need to address the particular circumstances of cases such as Pullam's, an ALJ has commented that he is "not an accoun-tant," who must keep the needs of an entire system in mind. As Victor Rosenblum of Northwestern University notes, the ALJs do not stand "at the apex of a hierarchy of decision makers" but function as "ex-pert independent factfinders and legal analysts."[15]

As these descriptions imply, the ALJs introduce a litigious note into the Social Security Disability Insurance program. When the applicant takes his case from the mass claims-handling apparatus of the state disability determination units to the ALJ's personal hearing room, the case changes from a routine administrative matter of verifying facts to a legal contest between the applicant and the government. In the process, as well, disability insurance joins workers' compensation as a program that has failed to end the litigious nature of disability policy. Litigation, in various institutional forms, lies close to the surface of that policy.

The passage of disability insurance led to an epidemic of litigation in the social security program. Before 1956, the social security system permitted a disgruntled applicant to appeal a case and appear before what were then called referees. Some took up the offer but most realized the futility of such a move. Facts were facts. Whether or not a person was sixty-five allowed little leeway for argument. In the disability insurance program, by way of contrast, facts were not quite facts. They were pieces of information that led to a conclusion over which reasonable men might differ.

When the disparity among the states in interpreting facts became an accepted part of the system, the grounds for disagreement grew. Between 1955 and 1958, the years in which the disability insurance program got under way, requests for hearings in the social security system increased by more than 500 percent. The number of ALJs the Social Security Administration needed to hire rose from 30 in 1956 to 110 in 1960. By 1959, requests for hearings reached 1,300 per month. That marked only the beginning of the rise in litigation. By 1965, the Social Security Administration received 23,323 requests for hearings. By 1970, requests numbered 42,573; by 1980, 252,023.[16]

As these numbers suggest, the role of the ALJs became increasingly important over the years. In 1964, for example, state disability determination units accounted for 97.5 percent of the admittances to the disability insurance program. The ALJs admitted most of the other 2.5 percent. In 1982, the states denied 72 percent of the disability insurance and SSI applications they received. Forty-six percent of the applicants appealed, and the ALJs reversed more than half of the states' decisions. More than one out of every five people admitted to the disability rolls employed the litigation process to get there.[17]

Hearings entailed the participation of lawyers, who escalated the level of formality and contentiousness. Although both the disability insurance and workers' compensation programs hoped to institute a highly informal, unintimidating, and inexpensive hearing system that would not require the presence of lawyers, the element of informality lessened and the role of lawyers increased as the programs matured.

Consider what happened in the depressed coal mining areas of West Virginia and Kentucky, which led the way in the use of lawyers for social security disability cases. These areas produced many impaired and unemployed claimants who regarded themselves as disabled. The cases that resulted occasioned many disagreements between the applicants and the states and, as a consequence, the applicants turned to lawyers for help. In 1960, one ALJ complained about the lawyers in a letter to his supervisor: "Inasmuch as the southern half of West Virginia and the eastern half of Kentucky are very depressed areas, with thousands of able-bodied coal miners out of work, I feel that the caseload will be heavy for several years to come. . . . On my last trip to Pikesville, Kentucky there were lawyers representing eight out of the fourteen cases which I heard." The ALJ noted that a district court had allowed many disability applicants to receive benefits. "This has not escaped the eyes of the legal fraternity, nor of prospective clients," he wrote.[18]

As late as 1970, lawyers were seldom present, except in sections of the country burdened by problems of high unemployment, an aging labor force, and a fading industrial base that contained a diminishing number of jobs that, even in the best of economic times, took their physical toll on workers. In the nation as a whole, claimants appeared with attorneys about 20 percent of the time. After 1970, for reasons that remain hard to identify, lawyers appeared more frequently.

Today a resident of Baltimore flips through the TV guide in the Sunday paper and reads, "Social Security Denied? Call Disability Specialists Jenkins and Block – Former Social Security Staff Attorney; Free Consultation; No Money Up Front; No Recovery/No Fee." This sort of advertising increases what the social security planners used to call "claims consciousness," and it increases legal representation at Social Security hearings.[19]

The numbers substantiate these impressions. One can infer that lawyers appear in at least half of the disability cases and probably more. The law permits attorneys to collect a percentage of the back payments due a claimant. In 1981, the Social Security Administration paid $62.5 million in fees for attorneys who successfully represented 60,000 claimants. An organization devoted to the needs of attorneys who practice in the field of disability insurance has 13,000 members. No wonder that the *Wall Street Journal* reported in January 1982 that the legal representation of disability claimants "now bears all the earmarks of a growth industry."[20]

In the tradition of administrative law proceedings, Social Security hearings are intended to be informal. The government is not represented by legal counsel. The ALJs do not wear robes, and they permit wide latitude in the questions put to the people who testify. As with other disability programs, however, the growth of the system has strained its informal qualities. It seems that the lawyers, by their very presence, increase the level of formality. Without a lawyer representing the person seeking benefits, an ALJ can chat with the applicant: ask him how he is feeling, sympathize with him, and assure him that he will receive a fair hearing. A lawyer puts the ALJ on his guard and forces him to think about proper procedure.

No two ALJs conduct hearings in exactly the same way. Some rely heavily on medical consultants; others lean more on the testimony of vocational experts. Some ask for medical examinations nearly all the time, and others never do.

A comparison of hearings conducted in Chicago and Baltimore helps to illustrate the point. Thomas Ploss, a Chicago judge, unlike James Cullen, his counterpart in Baltimore, regularly conducts a minimedical examination as part of the hearing, asking the applicant to perform simple physical actions, such as raising his arms over his head.

A woman enters his hearing room. She is black, obese, an unmarried mother of five children, four of whom are under the age of sixteen. "My backs and legs hurt me so bad. I hurts all over," she says. "It be like something pulling me down. I vomits." The judge asks her to describe the medications she is taking, and she pulls out a collection of medicines from her oversized handbag. She puts a bottle of medicine for "nerves" down on the table; next she pulls out another bottle and appears at a loss to explain its purpose. For her high blood pressure, she thinks. The judge, watching with a glacial expression on his face, breaks the silence and asks, "the [Social Security] administration says that you could operate a feather cutting machine. Could you do that?" "What's a feather cutting machine," she answers.[21]

Judge Cullen hears cases in Baltimore, Maryland, in a pleasant office that forms part of a shopping complex in one of the more affluent areas of the city. Unlike Judge Ploss, Cullen relies heavily on the advice of experts. When he is hearing a case involving a heart attack, for example, he often seeks the advice of a famous doctor at nearby Johns Hopkins University Hospital. The doctor almost never testifies at the hearings; his time is too valuable. Vocational experts, on the other hand, often testify at Cullen's hearings. They provide evidence on the jobs available for a person with particular skills, who can withstand certain amounts of stress and expend limited amounts of exertion. Cullen runs brief hearings and prides himself on not taking his work home. He presides over a very different type of operation than does Judge Ploss.[22]

This variety from judge to judge grates on the sensibilities of the Social Security Administration and produces problems. The judges do not follow the same standards as do the state disability examiners, and the judges do not employ the same standards among themselves. As a result, since applicants perceive a more lenient attitude on the judges' part than on the part of the state disability determination units, many cases are appealed. In addition, since treatment can vary from judge to judge, inequities result. More than one-quarter of the judges grant disability insurance to between 26 and 45 percent of the cases before them, but more than 17 percent of the judges award disability insurance to between 66 and 89 percent of the cases they hear.[23]

In response to these problems, the Social Security Administration has made periodic efforts to institute a single standard for the entire disability system, from initial application to final decision, and it has attempted to improve the flow of cases by monitoring the number of decisions and the outcome of the decisions that each judge hands down. In fact, however, just as the Social Security Administration does not have much control over the states, it lacks the ability to manage the judges.

The judges object to being monitored, and many politicians share their concerns. The "management programs or Administration policies which they [the Reagan administration] are pursuing are adversely affecting the ability of the judge to provide fair hearings," argues Charles N. Bono, the president of the Association of Administrative Law Judges. ALJ Francis O'Byrne disagrees with the emphasis that the Reagan and Carter administrations have put on the high reversal rates of state decisions. He notes that, under present law, "Such cases are heard de novo. The evidence before the judge is rarely the same evidence upon which the State Agency bases its decisions." In other words, the record remains open after the state decision, and the applicant has the right to add evidence to it. For that reason, it makes no sense, according to O'Byrne, to complain when judges disagree with the findings of the state disability determination units.[24]

Senator Howell Heflin of Alabama, who agrees with O'Byrne, has introduced legislation that would make the ALJs independent of the Social Security Administration. The legislation would pave the way for the creation of a disability court or some other entity to hear disputed cases.[25] At present, however, disputed disability cases pass from the state disability determination units to the ALJs to the Appeals Council of the Social Security Administration and finally to the domain of the regular federal courts.

The ALJ, who does not relish the prospect of being reversed by a higher court, strives to develop a record that will support his eventual decision. At most ALJ hearings, a clerk operates a portable tape recorder that preserves a record. Swamped with so many cases, the Social Security Administration does not even bother transcribing the records. If a case reaches federal courts, however, the tape is transcribed, and it becomes part of the court record. When the ALJ makes his decision, he keeps in mind the opinions that the federal court in his jurisdiction has handed down and anticipates its possible objections to his ruling.

On October 16, 1959, for example, the United States District Court of Appeals for the Seventh Circuit handed down its decision in the case of *Teeter* v. *Flemming*. The decision reversed that of the ALJ against the applicant (Teeter), stating that the ALJ had not refuted the testimony of a medical doctor who claimed that Teeter was disabled. Although in the Social Security Administration's view doctors are not considered the disability insurance program's gatekeepers, the court possessed binding power over the case. The Social Security Administration therefore moved to prevent damage in future cases. It told the ALJs to explain in their opinions why they did not find a particular doctor's testimony to be persuasive. In the Teeter case, the doctor had testified that Teeter was unable to "carry on his former occupation." The disability program, on the other hand, used a more stringent test for disability, and the ALJs needed to point such things out.[26]

One bureaucrat assessed the situation this way. "Once the hearing process is started, the Hearing Examiner . . . must be forever conscious that this case may result in litigation where a federal judge . . . is asked . . . to support a disallowance." This consciousness affected the way that the ALJS did their work.[27]

Furthermore, the ALJs were aware that the more the applicants regarded them as figures of authority, the less likely they were to appeal; the more that an ALJ looked and acted like a judge, the less chance that a rejected applicant would take his case to a federal judge. According to one official, an applicant walked out of a hearing held in a small business office and felt as though he had "simply had a discussion with another clerk." This applicant was more likely to request a review. If the same hearing was conducted in a more judicial setting – a county court room, perhaps – the applicant would react quite differently. "He feels that he has had his day in the court, and the chances of his requesting a review of an unfavorable decision are materially lessened."[28]

The federal courts

Although the ALJs strive to give claimants their day in court, some disability decisions become federal cases. Like the ALJs, federal judges decide on the cases before them without regard to the amount of money in the disability insurance trust fund and with little regard for national consistency. Both the federal judges and the ALJs have been described as "chancellors at equity." The only difference is that the Social Security Administration retains some control (although it is not very much) over the ALJs; it can do nothing about the dictates of the federal court.

The law binds all parties in this complex system together. Through each level of appeal the definition of disability remains the same. By the terms of this definition, last significantly modified in 1967, a person who wishes to receive disability benefits has to be unable, because of a medically determinable impairment, to do any sort of work that exists in the national economy for which his age, education, and previous work experience qualify him. Although the definition of disability is the same for the state disability examiners, the ALJs, and the federal judges, each actor in the disability determination system interprets it differently and applies it in different ways to particular cases.

Congress, wishing to act as a force for consistency, has tried to be explicit about the meaning of "work that exists in the national economy." The work should "exist in significant numbers either in the region where such individual lives or in several regions." A congressional committee noted that whether or not an applicant might be hired for the jobs that exist in the national economy could not be used "as the basis for finding an applicant to be disabled in this definition."[29]

Congress also has felt pressure to be more explicit about its intentions because of the huge numbers of disability cases that wind up in the courts – and because of one court case in particular. This case, *Kerner* v. *Flemming*, is similar to many other disability cases and serves as a good illustration of the way in which the courts have influenced the disability program.

Mr. Kerner worked on the edges of the labor market as a carpenter, salesman, and furniture repairman. Suffering from diabetes, heart disease, and a great deal of anxiety, he applied for disability benefits. The state disability examiners told him that he could do light, sedentary work, and the ALJ agreed. Kerner discovered, however, that the job opportunities for a sixty-year-old man with his medical problems were limited.

Judge Friendly took a sympathetic view of Kerner's problems. He asked the Department of Health, Education, and Welfare to show explicitly what work Kerner was capable of doing. In the process, Friendly created what came to be known as the Kerner doctrine. Friendly wrote that "mere theoretical ability to engage in substantial gainful activity is not enough if no reasonable opportunity for this is available." Friendly suggested a more pragmatic test of disability. "What can the applicant do," Friendly asked, "and what employment opportunities are there for a man who can do only what the applicant can do?"[30]

By 1963, the Kerner doctrine started to "filter backward" into the entire disability system. The ALJs began to use vocational experts as witnesses more often, so that they could put the applicants' vocational capabilities on the record. The Kerner doctrine lacked clarity, however, and despite the best efforts of the ALJs, the law became "confused," in the word of the House Ways and Means Committee staff. Did the jobs have to be in the applicant's neighborhood, his region, or anywhere in the country? How many of them did there have to be? These questions could not be answered precisely.[31]

Reacting to the many court decisions that used the Kerner doctrine, Congress made the law more explicit in 1967. Essentially, it stated that the ability to work rather than the condition of being employed should determine a person's eligibility for disability benefits. A person who could work was not entitled to disability benefits, even if no one would hire him or if there were no vacancies in the fields in which he was qualified. Despite this clarification, however, judges continued to interpret the law in ways that were different from the Social Security Administration, the state disability determination units, or the ALJs.

More fundamental forces appear to be at work than a simple case of a judge trying to loosen the definition of disability and Congress and the Social Security Administration countering by tightening the definition. No matter what the statutory definition is, the system encourages people to take their disability cases to court, and the courts and Congress look at disability in fundamentally different ways.

Since the federal judges sometimes award benefits to people who have been turned down at each of the lower levels, it pays an applicant to pursue his case. The costs of appeal are low, since lawyers operate on a contingency basis and the applicant is out of work. The logical course of action is to press a case as far as it can go or as far as a lawyer wishes to take it. As the House Ways and Means staff wrote in 1974, the statistics "highlight the wisdom of continued appeal." This wisdom, it might be added, reduces incentives for rehabilitation. After all, why engage in rehabilitation when a case is being appealed if successful rehabilitation means an unsuccessful appeal? This approach also increases the level of litigation.[32]

The passage of disability insurance began a movement of social security cases toward the courts. For example, in the second quarter of 1962, of 114 district court cases involving the social security system 98 involved disability. Between 1963 and 1967, applicants filed 4,299 requests for court hearings; 85 percent of this litigation involved disability. By the late 1970s, people spoke of disability as a "burden" on the court. In 1973, 2,226 disability cases were filed; in the first six months of 1983, the number had risen to 11,000.[33]

As the number of court cases rises, the time it takes to conclude a case also rises. According to former congressional staffer and veteran disability program–watcher Fred Arner, it takes, on the average, a month and a half to obtain an initial decision, two months for a reconsideration, half a year for an ALJ decision, and another year for a district court decision.[34]

The federal judges operate from a "substantial evidence" rule. According to the terms of the rule, the court must accept the findings of the secretary (which means the ALJ who reaches decisions in the name of the secretary of Health and Human Services) as to fact, if those findings are supported by what the law calls "substantial evidence." In such a subjective area as disability, however, the substantial evidence rule becomes difficult to apply since disagreements can arise over the meaning of a particular fact. Thousands of individual cases heard over the years by thousands of judges in hundreds of locations have therefore left their mark on the disability insurance program.[35]

An examination of the cases in the Social Security files illustrates the different ways in which the courts have interpreted the disability statute. Consider the case of *Kachmar* v. *Celebrezze* heard by the district court in the early 1960s. Andrew Kachmar had a third-grade education and had worked in the coal mines for thirty-three years. In the summer of 1959, at the age of fifty-one, Kachmar applied for disability benefits. He complained of shortness of breath and was diagnosed as having emphysema and anthrasilicosis.

Kachmar's doctor testified that the coal miner was totally disabled. The state sent Kachmar's file to a consulting physician who stated that Kachmar might do work "of a general nature." In the face of conflicting medical testimony, the court pointed out that vocational considerations assumed added importance in this case because Kachmar's community was "recognized by both the national and state governments as a depressed area." Kachmar had a clear impairment, and he was out of work. The court thought those facts were enough to entitle him to disability and it awarded Kachmar benefits.[36] Although the earlier findings of the secretary had been supported by substantial evidence (the opinion of the consulting physician), the federal court did not find it sufficient to deny Kachmar disability benefits.

The case of *Hall* v. *Celebrezze,* a case from the United States Court of Appeals for the Sixth Circuit decided in 1963, also underscores the importance given the opinion of the treating physician by the courts, even though Congress did not intend them to have this authority.

Ora P. Hall had worked as a wood and plaster patternmaker in Kentucky before he became disabled, or claimed to have become disabled, in December 1956 at the age of fifty-three. The doctors told him that he had "minimal arthritis of the spine and a moderately severe kidney ailment." Approaching old age and lacking a high school education, Hall considered these medical problems sufficient to entitle him to disability benefits and he pressed his case through the system. When the ALJ denied his claim, Hall filed an action in the district court of Kentucky. When the district court upheld the ALJ's decision, he appealed, and the court of appeals sent the case back to the lower court for more documentation. When the lower court reaffirmed its previous denial of benefits, Hall appealed once again. This time the court of appeals awarded him benefits.

Hall won because of the testimony of the many physicians who had examined him. One testified, "I have advised that he undertake no physical work"; another stated, "I am positive that Mr. Hall is 100 percent disabled for work of any kind, and I heartily recommend that he be given social security." That recommendation was enough for the court. In its ruling, the court stated that Hall "had no way of establishing his case if his credible medical evidence was disregarded. While the Secretary may have expertise in some matters, we do not believe he supplants the medical expert."[37]

As the judicial seal was being put on the Hall case, the United States Court of Appeals for the Third Circuit began hearing the case of *Farley* v. *Celebrezze*. Like many disability applicants, Cecil V. Farley had done heavy labor and broken down. At the age of fifty-three, he suffered what the record describes as a "crushing injury" to his right arm, which damaged his muscles and nerves so that he was unable to grip. In the language of workers' compensation, he had lost the industrial use of his right arm. In addition, Farley was already impaired. As a child, he had lost the last joints of the thumb and two fingers of his left hand. Nor did the harm end there. Farley also developed what the psychiatrists called "traumatic neurosis" as a result of having suffered so much physical trauma. Despite all his injuries, however, Farley's own physician said that he might be able to do work that did not require the use of his right arm.

Farley, like many disability applicants, suffered from what the literature calls a "cluster" of impairments. The court of appeals recognized this fact and ruled that it was necessary to consider the effect of all of Farley's impairments. With only the paper file, the state disability examiners found this type of evaluation difficult to make. Doctors, after all, concentrated on one body system or disease and had difficulty determining the effect of several minor impairments on the whole man. Heavily dependent on the doctor's report for a sense of the applicant's medical condition, the state disability determination system, on the one hand, added the impairments in a manner unsympathetic to the applicant. The court, on the other hand, looked at Farley and saw a sixty-year-old cripple with a seventh-grade education in a state of obvious decline. He was hurt, and he was demoralized; the court ruled that he was disabled.[38]

As these cases, all from the same year, reveal, the court exercised an important influence over the administration of the disability program.[39] Lance Liebman of the Harvard Law School has argued that the chief difference between the approach of the courts to disability and that of the Social Security Administration lies in what he calls the "job gap." In many cases, the court saw people who were able to perform certain jobs but who could not get hired to do those jobs. The court tended to award benefits to those who fell into the resulting job gap. The courts believed that it was reasonable to construe the statute liberally. In this manner the courts expanded the disability insurance program and presented problems for the Social Security Administration, which saw its role as maintaining consistency across cases and keeping program costs within the congressionally mandated limits. Unlike the courts, the Social Security Administration believed that people who fell into the job gap should not be awarded disability benefits: unemployment benefits, yes; disability benefits, no.[40]

Basically, the courts and the Social Security Administration disagreed over the intention of Congress. The disagreement was an old one, going back to court interpretations of life insurance policies. The courts refused to interpret such phrases as "totally helpless" literally. As one court noted cynically, "If a person should suffer the loss of his arms and legs, his eye and his hearing, he might have his trunk conveyed to a busy street corner and make a little money by selling such small objects as post cards, candy, or cigars." Courts reasoned that neither the holders of insurance contracts nor the beneficiaries of disability insurance should have to sell candy on the street corner and that Congress did not intend to have them do so. The courts tended to give policyholders, whether of public or of private insurance contracts, the benefit of the doubt. As one court noted, "the rule of law which comes before us as expressed by the [state] examiners repeatedly seems to be that if the person involved can do anything at all and is not a hopeless mental or physical wreck, then he is not entitled to the benefits of the Act. This we do not believe is the purpose of the Act nor the intention of the Congress which passed it."[41]

Eligibility guidelines

The Social Security Administration believed that efficient and consistent administration of the disability insurance program would prevent both bankruptcy and an uncontrollable flurry of litigation. The ALJs and the courts were more concerned about equity, about giving applicants a fair chance to receive benefits.

Although Congress, particularly the House Committee on Ways and Means, resented having its legislative authority usurped by the ALJs and the courts, it was far from unsympathetic to the notion of using due process of law to ensure the rights of disability applicants. Special hearings conducted in 1959 and 1960 marked the beginning of a long period of congressional concern over the rights of applicants to the disability insurance program. A House subcommittee, led by Representative Burr Harrison of Virginia, which probed the handling of disability cases, discovered that as many as one-third of disability insurance applicants had not been told they had a right to a lawyer. The Harrison committee also questioned the rationale for not making the disability standards available to the public.

The Social Security Administration had always regarded the list of impairments that entitled someone to disability as confidential. It did not want to create an automatic entitlement to benefits merely because an unemployed person had a particular medical problem. Robert Ball informed Harrison that the standards were "only guides," and that the administration granted benefits in 10 percent of the cases in which applicants did not suffer from listed impairments. In addition, the medical advisory board to the Social Security Administration insisted on confidence on the grounds that it was undesirable for "examining physicians throughout the country to have available to them exactly what it is that makes it possible for a person to qualify."[42]

Harrison argued that keeping the rules confidential put applicants at a great disadvantage: "We have this average man who is poor and ignorant of his rights and sick, and he has the primary responsibility of getting up a medical legal record which must be so complete that the evaluator can look at it and say that it is or is not within the law." The subcommittee's report concluded that "it is essential that the convenience of confidentiality not be extended to the basic rules of the game." It recommended that materials related to the disability insurance program be published and that the applicant have the advantage of the confidential state manual, the decisions of the Appeals Council, and other "precedent" material.[43]

Social Security personnel continued to resist. Arthur Hess, who was in charge of the disability insurance program, admitted the existence of guidelines that described 130 impairments and showed the symptoms and clinical and laboratory findings that usually existed when the condition was severe enough to cause permanent and total disability. He refused to name those impairments, and they remained confidential. In some cases, he explained, applicants who did not suffer from the listed conditions, but whose education, training, and work experience combined with their impairments qualified them as disabled, were granted benefits. Most cases, perhaps 70 percent, he reported, were decided on the medical guidelines alone.[44]

Congressional committees continued to call upon the Social Security Administration to publish its specific disability standards. In 1974, Fred Arner, who had served as staff director for Harrison's subcommittee, prepared a major report on the disability program for the House Ways and Means Committee. This report again called upon the Social Security Administration to publish clear and concise regulations that both examiners and applicants could use. The manner in which the states applied vocational factors was of particular interest to the staff of the Committee on Ways and Means. The Social Security Administration delayed. Not until 1979 did it publish a list of impairments along with the specific numerical values of clinical tests required for disability insurance and a specific set of rules that explained the application of vocational considerations to disability determination. This set of rules came to be called the grid.[45]

The grid was the last of a five-stage sequence. First, the state disability examiners asked if the applicant was engaging in "substantial gainful activity." In other words, they looked to see how much money he was earning. If he earned over a set limit, he could not get disability benefits. Then they asked whether the applicant had a severe impairment that significantly limited his physical or mental ability to work. If not, the applicant was denied benefits. If so, the examiners asked if the impairment "met or equaled" the medical conditions listed in the guidelines. If it did, the person received benefits. If it did not, the process continued, and the examiners asked if the impairment prevented the applicant from meeting the demands of past relevant work. To rephrase the question, could the applicant do the sort of work he had been doing before he became disabled? Those who failed to pass this test of occupational disability would not receive benefits. (An exception was made in the case of blind applicants over the age of fifty-five.) Finally, the examiners asked if the impairment prevented the applicant from doing other work. If it did, the applicant would receive disability benefits.

The grid employed what was called "residual functional capacity" in combination with other variables to reach a decision on whether an applicant should receive disability benefits. If, for example, a person's maximum sustained work capacity was limited to sedentary work and he was fifty to fifty-four years old, had less than a high school education, and had no skilled work experience, then he was considered disabled. But if his previous employment experience included skilled work, then he was not disabled. The grid contained rules for every possibility.

The appearance of the grid gave the disability insurance program a resemblance to the workers' compensation program. At one time Altmeyer and Falk had made fun of workers' compensation for its rigid use of schedules that equated an impairment and disability. Now disability insurance had its own published list of impairments, its own schedule. It also had its own set of rigidly applied rules, just as workers' compensation did. Both programs began with a desire to estimate a disabled person's wage loss and then abandoned the approach in favor of the convenience of a list of impairments that automatically qualified a person as permanently disabled.

The similarities did not end there. States made disability determinations in both programs, decisions that often varied from state to state. When applicants were turned down, they often engaged in litigation. Courts had considerable influence over both programs.

In some ways, the rules of disability insurance encouraged more lengthy proceedings even than those in workers' compensation. Workers' compensation always kept the window of compromise open, as a worker had the option of striking a deal out of court. He could bargain over the amount of his benefit and the degree of his disability. The Social Security Disability Insurance program did not offer this flexibility. There was no possibility for compromise: A worker won and got full benefits or lost and got no benefits. The process of appeal could never be short-circuited, except by awarding benefits to the applicant.

Perhaps the most surprising thing is that, unlike the workers' compensation administrators, the founders of disability insurance knew at the outset what problems they needed to avoid — notably, inconsistency and litigation. Yet they were unable to do so because the program contained state, federal, and judicial elements over which they were able to exert little control. The effort to administer a program with these disparate levels made disability insurance more like workers' compensation than its founders intended. The problems of disability policy were transferred from one generation to another.

4. The continuing debate over Social Security Disability Insurance

Since both generations of income-maintenance disability programs developed similar problems, it would be natural to assume that reform measures have centered on reducing litigation and making policy consistent from place to place. As rehabilitation measures have improved and the capabilities of the handicapped have become more widely recognized, it would seem appropriate for policymakers to concentrate on helping the handicapped to work rather than on granting them retirement. Such assumptions, however, run contrary to fact. Instead, nearly all of the political discussion in the Carter and Reagan years has highlighted disability insurance, which has held a hypnotic effect over the rest of disability policy, to the exclusion of nearly everything else. Litigation and inconsistency remain pressing concerns, and rehabilitation is as elusive a goal as ever, despite the passage of significant disability legislation in 1980 and 1984.

Since 1956, the disability insurance program has undergone many changes, as the stories of Homer Philips and Linda Ross indicate.

Homer Philips, a resident of Johnstown, Pennsylvania, developed polio at the age of nineteen. Because he had been working – both part-time after school and full-time following graduation, in a lumber mill – he qualified for disability insurance. He became the youngest person ever to qualify since his illness occurred shortly after the 1960 amendments eliminated the age requirement from the disability insurance program. Although polio left him severely paralyzed, Philips was determined to return to the labor force. The Pennsylvania rehabilitation department trained him for a new job, and Philips was able to take advantage of a twelve-month trial work period in which he resumed working but was allowed to continue receiving disability benefits.[1]

Linda Ross, a woman with a college education and a high intelligence quotient, entered the disability insurance rolls in 1977. Considered a manic depressive, she was, at the time, hospitalized in Philadelphia's Thomas Jefferson Hospital. She was awarded a retroactive lump-sum payment and an ongoing monthly check of $330. Ross remained on the rolls until June 1982. At that time, helped by psycho-tropic drugs, she was dropped from the program on the grounds that she was able to work. "I was forced to go on welfare and even then could not afford to pay my rent. That's why I had to foresake the modicum of independence I was achieving through therapy and ask my ex-husband for cash to make the rent," Ross wrote a year later in an Op Ed article that appeared in the *New York Times*. Soon Ross faced the prospect of becoming one of the homeless people attempting to survive on the city streets.[2]

Philips's case is straightforward. He encountered misfortune in the form of illness, and the Social Security Disability Insurance program stepped forward to protect him. It did so in a way that undermined neither his morale nor his initiative. Ross's case reveals the complexity of disability and the policy dilemmas of disability insurance. She fell in and out of disability and bitterly resented being cut off, despite her apparent intelligence and her ability to present her case articulately. In a sense, the story of the development of disability insurance is that it began helping people like Homer Philips only to encounter people like Linda Ross.

Between 1956 and 1972, the disability insurance program enjoyed strong congressional support and, as a consequence, the scope of the program expanded considerably. Amendments in 1958 added benefits for a disabled worker's dependents; amendments in 1960 ended the requirement that a worker had to be fifty years old to qualify for disability insurance; amendments in 1965 liberalized the definition of disability; and amendments in 1972 allowed recipients of disability insurance to qualify for medicare.

Senator Vance Hartke, speaking on the Senate floor in 1960 in terms typical of the rhetoric that accompanied the expansion of disability insurance, stated: "This follows once again the great American experience of self-reliance, of permitting an individual to pay into an insurance fund from which he may benefit when he retires or when he becomes disabled and is no longer capable of working."

Hartke's speech might be contrasted with one that HEW Secretary Joseph Califano made in April 1978. "This program has drifted into crisis. . . . The social security disability program is in urgent need of fundamental reassessment and overhaul," said Califano, who called the program a "caricature of bureaucratic complexity."[3]

To rectify the situation, the Carter administration passed comprehensive disability reform legislation in 1980. First, it changed the formulas that determined the amount of disability benefits an individual would receive. Specifically, it lowered the percentage of an individual's income that disability benefits replaced and, in so doing, reduced the incentive for someone to enter the disability rolls. This part of the legislation marked a response to the rise in the rolls that occurred between 1960 and 1978. In 1960, for example, the program awarded benefits to 179,419 workers, and in 1975 it added 591,995 workers to the rolls.

Second, it made it easier for a disability insurance beneficiary to work. As handicapped rights advocate Frank Bowe stated, he wanted the disabled "to walk off the rolls." In order to produce this result, the amendments allowed a handicapped person to continue receiving medicare for up to four years, after he returned to work. The law also permitted workers to deduct the expense of attendant care from their earnings; only after that deduction would the Social Security Administration decide if a worker earned too much to continue on the disability rolls.[4]

Even though the number of people on the disability rolls fell from 4.9 million in 1978 to 3.8 million in 1984, the 1980 law produced a political crisis of titanic proportions. Although the program appeared to be under control – during Reagan's first administration, program costs remained relatively constant, hovering around $17 billion – Senator Carl Levin reflected considerable public concern when he opened a congressional hearing by stating, "Today we are investigating a system that is in a shambles." The senator referred to the Reagan administration's effort to prune the disability rolls by removing people like Linda Ross. These efforts caused the states to refuse to process disability cases, the administrative law judges to sue the government, and Congress to pass a new disability law in 1984 that prohibited the removal of beneficiaries from the disability rolls unless their medical conditions had improved.[5]

As the words used to describe the program demonstrate, it has passed through several stages, beginning with "self-reliance" in 1960, followed by a period of "crisis" during the 1970s, and one of "shambles" in the 1980s. Paradoxically, although the number of congressional committees and policymakers interested in disability policy and the problems of disability insurance has increased during the 1970s and 1980s, the range of their concerns has actually narrowed. There is no longer a consensus concerning the beneficial nature of the program and the need for it to expand, and the nation is no closer to the creation of a comprehensive disability policy than it was during the days of this consensus. Two major disability crises have passed without any effort at comprehensive reform of the nation's disability policy.

The social security consensus

The essence of the consensus that governed the first twelve years of the disability insurance program was that the Social Security Administration delivered substantial benefits to people like Homer Philips at little political cost. Once Congress passed the measure, senators and congressmen reaped the gratitude of the beneficiaries. The political costs involved in defying the insurance industry and the American Medical Association in order to pass the program soon evaporated. Since the AMA and insurance industry opposition had not been a matter of immediate economic gain or loss, neither made a serious effort to repeal disability insurance.

The fact that the Social Security Administration ran the disability insurance program competently, with a sense of political and economic responsibility, eased congressional approval of expansion of the program. Congressional inquiries met prompt response. Senator Robert Byrd of West Virginia, for example, took a personal interest in many cases, as he represented an area where many unemployed coal miners sought disability benefits. After an administrative law judge reached a decision, the senator expected to be informed by letter. "Since Senator Byrd follows up in every case in which he expresses an interest," wrote one Social Security supervisor to an administrative law judge, "we have requested that hearing examiners in your area advise Senator Byrd of the final action by means of the letter." At the same time, strict controls did not imply favoritism; the program remained within the strict letter of the law.[6]

Congress also relied on the responsible estimates of the costs of expanding disability insurance prepared by the actuaries in the Social Security Administration. Robert Myers, the chief actuary, knew the details of social security better than anyone. A Republican, he did not share the enthusiasm of his colleagues for expanded social welfare programs, but he prided himself on being scrupulously accurate and fair. Only if Myers decided the program could afford a particular change, would the tax committees in Congress recommend it.

The Social Security Administration had a not-so-secret agenda for the expansion of disability insurance. It wanted disability benefits to be as generous as old age benefits (including benefits for dependents and health insurance), and it wanted these benefits to be available to all qualified workers, regardless of age.

There would have been no consensus or expansion of disability insurance, however, if Congress had not shared the Social Security Administration's goals. The fact that the Democrats controlled Congress from 1956 to 1972 furthered this alliance. When constituents complained about the program's shortcomings, these congressmen would ask the Social Security Administration to write legislation that would enable Congress to remedy the situation. For instance, in the summer of 1958, Representative John E. Henderson wrote to Social Security commissioner Charles Schottland to complain on behalf of his constituents of the delays in processing disability cases and of the low percentage of applicants being approved for benefits. Representative Carl Perkins (Kentucky) spoke on the floor of the House of the "thousands on thousands" of applications that had not been approved. In response to these complaints, the Social Security Administration worked with Wilbur Mills of the Ways and Means Committee to produce amendments, in 1958, that slightly eased eligibility requirements and provided benefits for the dependents of disabled workers.[7] Before the Social Security Administration sent its proposals to Mills, Myers analyzed them and decided the system could afford them.

The push for the 1960 amendments, which removed the requirement that recipients of disability insurance be at least fifty years old, clearly revealed the consensus on the beneficial nature of social security. First, career employees of the Social Security Administration persuaded the Eisenhower administration to put the removal of the age requirement on the legislative agenda. In order to do so, Robert Ball and other Social Security officials enlisted the support of Arthur Flemming, secretary of Health, Education, and Welfare. Flemming endorsed the removal of the age barrier at a staff meeting in the fall of 1959. The Bureau of the Budget raised a tentative objection to the proposal on the grounds of cost, but lost the internal debate within the Eisenhower administration. When the Bureau of the Budget officials questioned Ball about the proposals, he "snowed them under with lengthy answers to short questions," according to one Social Security official.[8]

Second, the Social Security Administration worked with Congress to create interest in the removal of the age requirement provision. Late in 1959, an ad hoc subcommittee of the Ways and Means Committee held the first in a long series of oversight hearings and investigations on the administration of the disability insurance program. Although the real purpose of the hearing was to divert the public's attention from the politically controversial issue of extending social security to cover health insurance for the elderly, the Social Security Administration managed to use the hearings as a means of advancing its campaign to eliminate the age-fifty requirement in disability insurance.

As the staff director of the subcommittee recalled, "The fix was in to eliminate age fifty from the beginning." William L. Mitchell, then the commissioner of Social Security, told the subcommittee that there were no "administrative obstacles in the way of improving the protection afforded by eliminating the age requirement." When the hearings concluded, Harrison introduced a bill to eliminate the age requirement.[9]

The proposal made sense to the members of the Ways and Means Committee. As Arthur Hess of the Social Security Administration later recalled, the members of the committee sat, "sort of looking at each other and saying, well, there's no logic to age 50. Whatever made anyone think that had any sense to it!" In the spring of 1960, Flemming appeared before the committee and announced his support for the removal of the age requirement, noting that he was "very glad" the change could be made without increasing the social security payroll taxes. Not only was the measure endorsed by Ways and Means, it became a bipartisan proposal.[10]

When the proposal to eliminate the restrictions of disability benefits to those fifty or older appeared on the House floor, it was bathed in the light of consensus. Medicare stood on the cutting edge of political controversy; disability insurance was already established, past controversy. The House debated the bill prepared by the Committee on Ways and Means under a closed rule that permitted no amendments to be made from the floor. The House and Senate passed the measure overwhelmingly; the collaboration between Congress and the Social Security Administration to expand Disability Insurance had worked.

This collaboration persisted through the early years of the program. Although controversies arose from time to time – one point at issue, for example, was whether to make the definition of disability more lenient for the blind or to tighten it in response to court rulings like

Judge Friendly's in the Kerner case – most disability bills enjoyed bipartisan support. Health insurance in 1964 and 1965, welfare reform in 1969, all contained within Omnibus Social Security bills, generated considerable controversy. These controversies seldom strayed into the area of disability insurance. During the first twenty years of disability insurance, it occasioned few dissenting votes.

The end of the consensus

What shattered the calm? No single cause was responsible. In part, changes in the social security program itself and changes in the structure of Congress brought the consensus to an end in the middle of the 1970s.

As a mature program, social security cost more in the 1970s than it had before, if for no other reason than the fact that a greater percentage of retired people were covered than ever before. Social security also cost more because the benefits were more generous. In 1972, Congress legislated the largest single benefit increase in the program's history, and then, out of a sense of political desperation, the Republicans decided to put benefit increases on a more scientific basis and index them to the rate of inflation. The rate of inflation rose in the 1970s and carried social security benefits along with it. At the same time, average wages and employment rates failed to increase as rapidly as expected. As a result, the social security program had less money coming in and more going out than anticipated.

Disability insurance expenditures rose at an even greater rate than did the cost of other social security benefits. This rise has never been fully explained but seems related to one of the paradoxes of modern times: at the same time that health conditions have been improving, disability has been increasing. Economists have pointed to the generosity of disability benefits and changes in the labor market as possible explanations. Between 1969 and 1978, for example, the number of men between forty-five and sixty-four who reported themselves unable to work increased from 72 per thousand to 101 per thousand. By 1977, the "nonparticipation rate" of males aged forty-five to fifty-four in the labor force had increased from 3.5 when disability insurance was passed in 1956 to a high of 8.8. This phenomenon occurred in other countries as well. One explanation was that because of slower economic growth in the 1970s, competition in the labor force became keener and employers substituted younger (or female) workers for older, impaired workers. A slow economy and a rise in unemployment shook some of the older and impaired workers out of the labor force and onto the disability rolls.[11] The disability rolls were, in fact, composed of people who were on the average older than the rest of the population.

Features peculiar to disability insurance also accounted for the rise. Employment rates affected the other components of social security indirectly, since a person needed to be of retirement age to collect benefits. In disability insurance, the waiting period was only six months from the onset of the disability. Disability insurance therefore picked up the effects of unemployment much more quickly than did old age insurance.

Whatever the explanation, disability insurance became visibly out of control. Adverse publicity began to appear in the press, and policymakers, such as Joseph Califano, pointed out that the growth of entitlement programs such as disability left little in the federal budget for the government to accomplish other goals. As a result, Congress no longer embraced the program so tightly and the consensus began to dissipate.

Two other considerations figured in Congress's disenchantment with disability insurance. First, the disability insurance program, like the social security system itself, was near completion. The items that still remained on the agenda of the Ways and Means Committee staff and of the Social Security Administration concerned administrative reforms such as disciplining the state disability determination units. These reforms would engender more controversy and produce fewer political payoffs than previous reforms. One question raised for example, was how much political credit would the congressman who pushed for federalization of the disability determination process receive?

Second, the fragmentation of power within Congress made consensus more difficult to obtain. Wilbur Mills had run the Ways and Means Committee without permanent subcommittees. After Mills left Congress in 1975, it became mandatory for all House committees to have subcommittees. A subcommittee on social security, chaired by Representative James Burke of Massachusetts and then Jake Pickle of Texas, devised legislation for disability insurance; another subcommittee, under the charge of Representative James Corman of California, oversaw the Supplemental Security Income program.

A final, more general explanation for the end of the consensus on social security has to do with the difficult policy choices that congressmen were required to make. The discussions that preceded the 1980 amendments to the Social Security Act reflected those difficulties. By the time Califano singled out disability insurance for special attention, the "replacement rate" argument enjoyed a wide currency. This line of reasoning began with the observation that generous disability benefits replaced a high percentage of a person's income. Since a person lost only a little income by going on the disability rolls, he had a great incentive to retire on disability. Why should he wait if he could retire with a generous pension? Because fewer people waited for their old age pensions, the disability rolls expanded.

Certain features of the disability insurance program lent plausibility to this "replacement rate" argument. Disability insurance benefits were tax exempt and therefore, as actuary John Miller explained, "50 percent of salary in the form of disability benefits may well equal 65 percent or more of gross earnings after tax." The disability beneficiary also would no longer incur expenses related to work.[12]

Since disability benefits also tended to be higher than old age benefits, many people who retired early received more money than those who waited to retire. Furthermore, since young people on disability had a greater chance of having young children than older people on retirement, these younger disability beneficiaries often received higher benefits as a result of the allowances for dependents. Technical features in the computation of benefits also favored the young. Faced with the prospect of paying benefits to older workers on the basis of their average wages, Social Security personnel had introduced the concept of "dropout years" in the days before benefits were indexed to the rate of inflation. A worker could have his five worst years dropped from the calculations, causing his average earnings and his social security benefit to rise. In the case of younger workers seeking disability benefits, the feature meant that benefits were often based on a very few years of relatively recent earnings. In an inflationary economy, recent earnings tended to be higher earnings, even given the tendency of a person's earnings to rise over the course of his working lifetime. Because of these factors, average monthly benefits to disabled people exceeded monthly benefits to elderly people. In the 1970s, the average differential grew from twelve to fifty dollars.[13]

Whether a young permanently disabled individual deserved more than a healthy elderly person was just one of the questions that the social welfare system posed. A more difficult policy question was how to reduce people's incentives to enter the disability rolls without hurting those who belonged on the rolls. Policymakers needed to make disability benefits less attractive to those who could work, without at the same time harming people who genuinely could not work.

When the Social Security system began, such dilemmas never arose; they were the product of an older, more mature social welfare system with which policymakers contended in the 1970s. In the 1930s, people accepted social welfare benefits only as a last resort, and the low level of the benefits and the stringent conditions for receiving them made welfare an unacceptable choice for anyone who had a chance to work.

Between the 1930s and the 1970s, benefits became more generous and social welfare programs grew in an incremental and unrelated way, to reach more of the eligible population. Created and operated in isolation from each other, they grew in an uncoordinated manner. Different programs awarded benefits to the same people; the same policy mechanisms that allowed the programs to grow also inhibited the coordination of programs. As a consequence, disability insurance benefits accounted for only 40 percent of the total cash income of families receiving disability benefits in 1979.[14]

Policymakers had to consider how to coordinate disability benefits and how to cut back on some of the programs. This politics of subtraction was difficult not only from a technical point of view but also from a political point of view.

The Carter years

Jimmy Carter inherited a disability insurance program in disarray. The number of beneficiaries was rising; requests for hearings before administrative law judges were rising; the cost of the program was rising fastest of all. The actuaries predicted that if no remedial action was taken, the deficit in the disability insurance program would reach $16.4 billion in 1987. Although short-run problems could be handled by transferring money from other parts of social security to disability insurance, the decline in administrative standards and the high replacement rates threatened to fuel an endless expansion of disability insurance, dragging it into progressively greater debt.[15]

Jimmy Burke, a veteran congressman from Massachusetts who headed the newly formed Subcommittee on Social Security, had already begun to investigate the disability insurance program. By 1976, he had produced a trial reform bill that proposed measures to give disability beneficiaries greater work incentives and suggested that disability benefit levels not exceed those received by people retiring at age sixty-five.[16] Far from increasing benefits in the usual manner, the bill represented a sharp break from social security tradition. Indeed, with its emphasis on work incentives, it bore a closer resemblance to a welfare bill than to a social security amendment.

By 1977, when Burke introduced a new version of his disability bill, Carter himself had received a briefing on the disability insurance program. The first priority of the Carter administration, however, was to put the entire social security system on more solid financial footing, and in 1977 Congress passed comprehensive legislation that, among other things, increased the amount of money going into the disability insurance trust fund. With the social security financial crisis under immediate control, the focus turned again to the unresolved, and growing, problems in the disability insurance program.

In 1978, Burke issued a revised disability bill that would put a cap on disability benefits by lowering the percentage of a worker's wages that these benefits would replace and by establishing a maximum level of benefits that a family could receive. For example, a family, no matter how large or how poor, could receive only 150 percent of a disabled worker's benefits. Burke also proposed changes in the method of computing disability benefits. In Burke's proposal, a person twenty-eight years old or younger would not be allowed to drop out any years in the computation of his average wages; a person forty-five years old or older would be allowed to drop out the traditional five years.[17] Despite the profusion of technical details, Burke's bill held the potential to halt the growth of social security and to change the terms of what had traditionally been viewed as a compact between generations.

It was a mark of how seriously Congress viewed the crisis in disability insurance that Burke's proposal made headway through the subcommittee, which reported out the bill in September 1978. With the election approaching, the full Ways and Means Committee decided not to enter what was sure to be a difficult and emotional debate over social security. However, Burke had laid the important political groundwork for a change in the disability insurance program, which the 96th Congress, convening in January 1979, could use as a point of departure in its considerations of disability insurance.

Because of Burke's ill health, Jake Pickle, who had been in Congress since 1963 and on the Ways and Means Committee since 1975, took over the Subcommittee on Social Security. For the first time since its enactment, disability insurance stood at the head of the legislative agenda. No wonder, then, that Social Security commissioner Stan Ross claimed that Pickle "wanted to make his name with disability insurance."[18]

Early in 1979, Pickle cosponsored a bill similar to Burke's previous bill with William Archer, another Texan and the ranking Republican on the subcommittee. The Carter administration also introduced a bill, which, although it differed in a number of details, followed the broad outline of the Pickle–Archer bill.[19]

At this point, a consensus appeared to be developing on disability insurance. Everyone, said Pickle's staffer Janice Gregory, understood the argument about replacement rates. It did not seem fair to allow a family to receive more after disability than it had earned before disability. Despite this apparent agreement, the Pickle bill led to a major political conflict between the Carter administration and those who had started the disability program and helped Congress to expand it. Representing the administration's position were HEW secretary Joseph Califano, HEW under secretary Hale Champion, and Social Security commissioner Stan Ross; the principal spokesmen for the other side were former Social Security commissioner Robert Ball, former HEW secretary Wilbur Cohen, and former AFL–CIO lobbyist Nelson Cruikshank. The fact that all of these men were Democrats (Cruikshank even served in Carter's White House) only intensified the conflict. Both sides thought the other misrepresented the facts; both viewed the other side as arrogant. It made for bad feelings. Califano referred to Cohen, Ball, and Cruikshank as the "high priests" of social security; Cohen called Califano the worst secretary in the history of the department.

Within the Carter administration, Califano spent most of his time on welfare reform and put Champion in charge of disability insurance and other social security issues. As much as anything else, Califano's priority followed the president's. The nuances of welfare reform fascinated Carter, and, in his enthusiasm, the president had a tendency, in Champion's words, "to treat everyone like staff," a condition that rankled Califano, who did not wish to attend to the details of welfare reform. On the other hand, Califano's decision to remove himself from disability insurance legislation reflected his own interest in what Ross calls "social programs" and his relative lack of interest in such a technical subject as social security. Besides, Califano trusted Champion and Ross with social security since Champion had a background in state finance ("a mere accountant," countered one of the high priests) and Ross was a former tax lawyer ("a disaster as social security commissioner," according to the social security loyalists).

So it was Champion and Ross who set out to reform disability insurance, relying for assistance on two types of experts available in the Carter administration. Henry Aaron, a Brookings staffer and one of the nation's leading authorities on social welfare policy, led a cadre of economists from his position as assistant secretary of Health, Education, and Welfare. Champion and Ross also solicited the advice of lawyers whom Califano hired to staff the Office of the Secretary; among them was Dan Marcus, a young attorney from the Washington firm of Cutler–Pickering. The economists analyzed the replacement rate, and the lawyers inquired into the program's administrative structure.

The Carter lawyers and economists set out to rationalize the program; the people who had created the program and worked to expand it watched with concern. One source of conflict was disagreement over the future of the program. Ball believed that in the 1990s the social security program would enjoy a period of surplus and that as legislators sought to patch up temporary, short-run problems, nothing should be done to lessen the program's adequacy. The Carter administration, worried more about short-run predictions that the disability insurance program would soon run out of money.

Another source of conflict was that to the Carter administration, social security was just one of a number of costly entitlement programs that limited the ability of the president to manage the economy, solve social problems, and achieve other national goals. Champion regarded efforts to trim entitlement programs as inevitable, and thought it important that compassionate people do the trimming. The social security loyalists were outraged at the idea of treating social security as just another program that could be subject to political tradeoff.

Wilbur Cohen later remarked that he knew something was wrong when Carter signed the 1977 amendments. "He just walked in the room and signed the law, no ceremonies, no pens," Cohen complained.

In the struggle that followed, the Carter administration forged an alliance with the Committee on Ways and Means. Ross and Champion sold the ideas of a cap on benefits and a change in the computation of disability benefits first to the members of the Subcommittee on Social Security, which held hearings in February and March 1979, and then to the House Ways and Means Committee, which approved the legislation by April 1979.

Because Cohen, Ball, and Cruikshank opposed the cap on family benefits and the change in the computation of average earnings, they prevailed on Richard Bolling, the head of the Rules Committee and a friend of Ball's, to keep the legislation from reaching the floor of the House until they could mobilize opposition. Bolling bottled up the bill in his committee until September 1979. In the meantime, a Supplemental Security Income bill, which included provisions designed to encourage recipients to work and which involved none of the disputes related to social security, passed the House of Representatives in June.

The battle over disability insurance now reached its climax. The supporters of the Pickle–Carter administration bill suffered a setback when Carter fired Califano in the summer of 1979. Patricia Roberts Harris, Califano's replacement, was not a strong supporter of the bill. As Ross remembers, Harris said, "disability is killing us," and tried to get him to drop the bill. Ross replied that he had already talked with Senators Long and Dole about the bill; things had gone too far. So much work had been done on the bill, however, that ultimately Harris let Ross continue, but, she said "It's yours, not mine."[20]

Cohen, meanwhile, mobilized the friends of social security into a coalition to fight the administration's legislation. He called the organization Save Our Security (SOS), and it included such important figures in the development of social security as Wilbur Mills, Arthur Flemming, and Robert Ball. Here then was a fine historical irony: An organization of program founders and supporters mobilized to protect the program against the proposals of a supposedly sympathetic administration.

While SOS urged senior citizens to write their congressmen in opposition to the legislation, members of the Subcommittee on Social Security conducted what one staff member called a "whip operation" to get it passed. Each subcommittee member took it upon himself to talk with other members of Congress about the bill in an effort to push it through.[21]

What was so controversial about the bill? To the liberals, the bill, with its cap on family benefits and its new way of computing average wages, smacked of a cutback in social security. As the AFL–CIO stated, "If anything, disability benefits should be raised, not lowered." The supporters of the bill emphasized its thrust toward rehabilitation. The House Ways and Means Committee's report on the bill stated that high replacement rates had produced "major disincentives in attempting rehabilitation." This bill would, in fact, expand the program and create incentives for beneficiaries to return to the labor force (for example, through provisions that allowed a disabled worker reentering the labor force to keep his medicare benefits longer).[22]

There did exist a broad area of agreement between the SOS-liberal faction and the Carter administration–congressional committee faction on the need for improvement in the way in which the disability insurance program was administered. In the words of the House Ways and Means report, the proposed legislation sought to "ensure uniform treatment of all claimants and to improve the quality of the decision-making." In this manner certain aspects of the bill related to the period before the disability crisis, when reform had concentrated on procedural and administrative matters in addition to benefit levels. Features in the bill such as the requirement that states reexamine each "non-permanently" disabled beneficiary (a person who might be expected to recover but whose disability qualified him for eligibility because it was expected to last for twelve months) at least once every three years occasioned no comment or controversy.[23]

On September 6, 1979, the House of Representatives debated HR 3236, the disability bill. On the House floor, Jake Pickle and Claude Pepper (D.-Florida) engaged in a dialogue encompassing the major points of contention. It was a disagreement between friends, between fellow Democrats, even between fellow southern Democrats.

Pickle warned his colleagues that the bill contained two controversial sections: the cap and the provision that changed the computation of the earnings levels on which benefits were based. "I will tell my colleagues," he said, that "either now or later these recommendations or something more serious are going to be passed. . . . The American people are going to demand that we not give benefits larger than they were receiving predisability." Pickle argued that his committee did not want to cut benefits; it wanted to provide the disabled with work incentives. He quoted a handicapped person who said that "disability may be permanent but unemployability is not." "Unfortunately," said Pickle, "the current system does not recognize this and insists on adding the tragedy of uselessness to the tragedy of ill health."[24]

Pepper scoffed at the work incentive argument, claiming that Pickle and others like him refused to believe that the recipients of disability insurance were in fact disabled. They acted as though people had to make a choice between disability and work when, in fact they lack the physical ability to make the choice, he argued. The disabled, he stated, were not chiselers. Besides, he continued, disability benefits did not permit beneficiaries to lead "glamorous" lives, although the authors of the bill "would have us believe that the beneficiaries are living off the fat of the land at the expense of the American taxpayer." The effect of the bill, he summarized, was only to reduce benefits to the disabled. Furthermore, in the past, Pepper concluded, social security had been an "ironclad intergenerational compact." The bill threatened to change the rules of the game for the next beneficiaries.[25]

In the end, the replacement rate argument and pressure from the administration persuaded the congressmen to vote for the bill, which passed 235 to 162. Compared to the votes on other social security legislation, it was an exceptionally close vote.[26]

By December 5, 1979, the bill reached the floor of the Senate, where the debate was similar to that in the House. Edward Kennedy played Pepper's role; Senators Dole and Long, both of whom served on the Finance Committee, took over for Pickle.

Kennedy, on the verge of challenging Carter for the Democratic presidential nomination, called the measure "watershed legislation" that would create a precedent for cutting back on social security. "If social security protection toward which people have paid can be so suddenly taken away, what protections are safe?" Kennedy asked. He ridiculed the rehabilitation argument: "Part of the reasoning behind the benefit cuts in HR 3236," he said, "is that if totally disabled people are given lower benefits, they will try harder to get work. That is using buckshot to kill a mosquito."[27]

Dole, himself handicapped, spoke eloquently on the conflict between rehabilitation and income maintenance in the nation's disability policy. "With a little imagination and creative thought handicapped per-

sons can lead active lives and find employment suitable to their skills,"
Dole said. Dole claimed that the system provided no middle ground;
"one must be either completely dependent on public welfare or totally self-sufficient." Forced to make the choice, many handicapped
people accepted dependence. One reason for this choice, he said, was
the fear of losing medical benefits. To expect a handicapped person to
find an entry-level job "at a salary high enough to cover his attendant
care and medical expenses" was unrealistic, Dole argued. The proposed legislation made it possible for a person to progress a step at a
time, without losing medicare coverage.[28]

After the debate, the Senate passed the measure by a vote of 87 to
1. However, the debate over disability reform and the legislative process continued. A conference committee was convened on March 27,
1980, to reconcile the Senate and House versions of the bill. Not until
May 29, 1980, did the Senate pass the conference committee's bill. On
June 9, 1980, Carter, deep in the midst of the presidential campaign,
signed the legislation into law.[29]

The debate that culminated in the 1980 amendments revolved around
two main points: People should not make more money on disability
than they did while working, and younger workers should not receive
more than older workers. The technical translation of the first point
was the cap on family benefits, and the technical translation of the
second point was the change in the dropout years. Two other areas of
concern, the provision of work incentives for people on the rolls and
improvements in the federal–state administrative system for disability,
brought little comment.

The debate and the entire policymaking process that framed the
proposals for debate showed the narrow range of the discussion. Con-
centrating only on the technical details of disability insurance, policymakers never considered broader reform of disability policy. For example, rehabilitation, addressed in the debate through expanded
medicare coverage, might also have been advanced by other reforms,
such as removing architectural barriers. Establishing such linkages
proved beyond the capability of a policy process that was nearly paralyzed by the difficulties of attempting any sort of cut in social security
benefits. Indeed, it was the social security program, and not disability
policy, that was uppermost in the minds of congressmen when they
voted for the 1980 disability amendments.

If congressmen had been able to think about disability policy rather than social security, they might have changed the all-or-nothing nature of disability benefits and made the choice of going on the rolls a little easier. An interim status might have allowed a person to obtain temporary help and begin a program of rehabilitation. Instead, the policymakers tried to counter the expansion of the rolls with potentially lower benefits for new applicants, which put the "deserving" applicants at a disadvantage. The work-incentive features helped to create incentives for rehabilitation, but they did little to prevent a person from going on the rolls in the first place, and they were no substitute for a broader consideration of the barriers to employing the handicapped.

The politicians were not so reflective. Although Carter lost the 1980 election, he left office with the satisfaction of having reformed the disability insurance program in a way that would save rather than cost money. Despite the opposition of Democrats who had supported him in the 1976 election, Carter signed a bill into law that he and his advisors believed would prevent another run on the disability rolls.

The Reagan years

Ronald Reagan inherited a recently reformed and financially healthy disability insurance program. As Reagan prepared to take office n 1980, the number of new disability awards, which had reached a peak of 592,000 in 1975, were expected to drop to 390,000. The number of workers on the disability rolls appeared to be stable, having leveled off at about 2,837,432 in 1977; a month after Reagan took office, the number stood at 2,854,519. The program cost more but only because inflation continued to drive up the average benefit a worker and his family received. For the first time in many years, the program appeared to be under control.[30]

Despite this apparent financial stability and administrative control, disability insurance became the most volatile social welfare issue Reagan had to deal with during his first term, with the exception of the near bankruptcy of the social security program. Neither the cap on benefits nor the change in computing benefits caused the trouble. A noncontroversial feature of the 1980 law produced the worst crisis in the history of the disability insurance program and one of the worst in the entire history of social security: The reason for the controversy was the mandated review of a disability beneficiary's status once every three years to ascertain whether he remained disabled.

The need for such a provision appeared obvious, and the efforts to create such a provision reflected persistence on the part of the Social Security subcommittee staff. On numerous occasions, the staff pointed out that very few people on the rolls were ever reexamined. So, largely at the suggestion of the staff, Congress passed a provision in 1980 that mandated " continuing disability investigations." As a practical matter, the staff realized that it would take time for the states to acquire the necessary personnel for these investigations, and so the new requirements were to be phased in over three years.[31]

It was not a completely new idea. The "diary" system, which almost everyone admitted was inadequate, was already in place. According to the diary system, if a person was on the disability rolls because of any one of seventeen listed impairments (such as functional psychotic disorders or tuberculosis), his file was flagged or "diaried" to be examined at periodic intervals. In fact, though, few cases were checked. During the 1970s, despite the rapid growth in the program, the number of investigations conducted never topped 200,000 a year. Of the people who came onto the disability rolls during the 1970s, 72–82 percent were never looked at again. For example, of 2.7 million disabled workers in 1977, only 165,000 were investigated.[32]

Between 1969 and 1976, the Social Security Administration required that before a disability beneficiary could be removed from the rolls, specific documentation showing that his condition had improved be filed. In 1974 and 1975, the years of quick decisions made by a harassed bureaucracy, the states probably made many errors in admitting people to the disability rolls. Although the Social Security Administration recognized this fact, it also recognized how difficult it was to prove that a person's condition had improved. As a result, it advised the states not to pursue aggressively a policy of trying to remove people from the rolls. One former Social Security field officer confided that he used to tell people on the disability insurance rolls that they would receive benefits for life.[33]

At the end of the decade, auditors from the Social Security Administration's Office of Assessment and policy analysts from the General Accounting Office (GAO) explored the question of how many people then on the disability rolls belonged there. The GAO questioned the validity of a quality control system that failed to review 80 percent of the cases. The Social Security Administration officials worried about trust fund money being spent improperly on the nondisabled; they knew that removing them from the rolls could save a great deal of money.[34]

Since this exercise occurred during a presidential election year, the Social Security Administration was reluctant to show GAO officials its figures. Fred Schutzman, the Social Security Administration official in charge, waited until after the election before confirming the results of the disability insurance pilot study: Perhaps 20 percent of the caseload did not meet the eligibility standard in April 1979; Social Security could have paid more than $2 billion a year to people who were not eligible. The GAO used these data in a report it was preparing on the way the Social Security Administration monitored its disability caseload.[35]

The GAO draft report cautioned that, although 20 percent of the people on the rolls perhaps should not have been there, the termination rates from an effort to remove them would not be that high. Even if the states threw 20 percent of the caseload off the rolls, many of those people would appeal the decision and stand a good chance of having it overturned. Before all these cases could be reviewed, state disability examiners would have to be trained; a failure to staff the effort properly would lead to the same sort of abuses that had created the problem in the first place. Despite these cautionary notes, the GAO concluded that the Social Security Administration should target more money on the disability insurance caseload in fiscal 1981, singling out people who were supposed to be reexamined but never were, particularly those who came onto the rolls in 1974–5.[36]

By the time the GAO had finished a draft of its report and was getting ready to circulate it, the Reagan administration was preparing to take over the government. The GAO draft report fell into the hands of Reagan transition team members David Swope and John Svahn, who later became key Health and Human Services officials in the Reagan administration. "This was a gift," said Paul Simmons, who became Svahn's chief deputy.[37]

It was the perfect gift for the occasion. Just like the outgoing Carter administration, the Reagan administration wanted to check the growth of entitlements and reduce federal spending. As a means of reaching this goal, Reagan was known to favor the strategy of separating peo-

ple entitled to benefits from those not entitled. Reagan and his associates called this process "purifying" the rolls, referring to the methods
of reducing welfare fraud they had instituted in California. In the social security program, which dominated the social welfare budget, this
strategy was, however, hard to execute since entitlement to old age
benefits depended mainly on a person being a certain age. As a result,
the program contained few welfare "cheats"; indeed, that characteristic of the program accounted for its political success. Furthermore,
many people spoke of "inexorable" demographic patterns that automatically raised the costs of entitlement programs. The GAO report
was therefore particularly welcome since it offered a means of saving
social security dollars and saving them quickly. If the administration
could "purify" the disability insurance rolls, it stood to save money in
the 1981 fiscal budget.

When the GAO report made its public appearance in March 1981,
it received a great deal of attention. It appeared to fit the administration's plans to reduce the budget neatly. Even though the administration was in the euphoria of its first days, and even though the consensus
on social security had long since eroded, challenging the social security
program remained risky. If the Reagan administration decided to pursue the strategy of removing those who should not have been on the
disability rolls, it could expect adverse political reaction.

In this case, two mitigating circumstances cushioned the impact.
First, the administration could claim to be implementing the recommendations of the nonpartisan General Accounting Office. Second,
although removing people from the disability rolls required no special
congressional legislation, congressional sanction appeared to be contained in the 1980 amendments, which held that every "nonperma-
nently disabled" person should be reviewed every three years.

A follow-up study conducted by the Social Security Administration,
now intent on weeding out corruption, showed an even greater percentage of the caseload to be ineligible for benefits. The new study, of
those on the rolls in July and September 1980, concluded that 26 percent – more than one-quarter of the caseload – should not have been
on the disability rolls.[38]

In the excitement caused by these findings and in the confusion that
accompanied the presidential transition, the Reagan administration
lost sight of the subtleties of disability determination. Administration
officials spoke of error rates as though a clear distinction could be

made between the disabled and the nondisabled. They failed to assess how many of those removed from the rolls would appeal the decisions and win, even though the GAO report clearly cautioned about this point.

Because the Social Security career employees, more skilled at administration than politics, tried to anticipate the desires of the new administration, they, too, lost sight of the true nature of the disability insurance program. Rhoda Greenberg, who headed the disability insurance program at the time of the transition, suggested that the Social Security Administration failed to realize that "there was a big difference in saying no to someone already on the rolls, compared to saying no to someone not yet on the rolls." "All they knew there was 2 billion dollars to be saved," commented another career employee, and once the effort to save this money began, it was "gargantuan, difficult to stop." As Paul Simmons, who served as an assistant commissioner of Social Security in the Reagan administration, put it, "Here was billions of dollars that was available and social security was going to go bankrupt. . . . The bureaucracy said: 'let's please the boys.' "[39]

Although some of the Social Security bureaucrats wanted to "please the boys" in the Reagan administration, the boys, not the bureaucrats, made a decision early in 1981. In March, Reagan's Office of Management and Budget reported that as a result of "bad management . . . as many as 584,000 beneficiaries who do not meet SSA's eligibility criteria may be receiving benefits." Taking its cue from the GAO report, the Office of Management and Budget estimated the potential savings of removing these beneficiaries from the rolls at $2 billion a year. In the budget figures, the administration estimated savings of $50 million as early as fiscal 1981 and $1.1 billion in fiscal 1986.[40] Reagan administration officials decided that instead of waiting until 1982 to begin the process of investigating people on the disabililty rolls, as the 1980 law directed, it would start early and also increase the number of people being reviewed.

For the Reagan administration, "purifying" the disability rolls had been a major policy initiative; for the Carter administration, "purifying" the rolls had taken second place to inhibiting their growth and rehabilitating those on the rolls. The Carter administration viewed the investigation of those on the rolls as a good government measure that would not save much money and was distinctly less important than the other provisions of the 1980 law. Neither the Carter administration nor the Committee on Ways and Means expected much of the continuing disability investigations. The conference committee that prepared the 1980 law thought that increased administrative costs would overshadow the potential savings in 1982, when the investigations were scheduled to begin, and yield a net loss of $41 million. Only in 1984 would this feature of the bill save the government money, and even in 1985 the government's savings would be relatively modest, less than $62 million. In contrast, Reagan's Office of Management and Budget estimated savings of $900 million in 1985.[41]

The Social Security Administration geared up for a major assault on the disability rolls. It sent files to the state disability determination units, asking them to decide if the beneficiaries still qualified for benefits. The Social Security Administration hoped to perform 554,000 of these investigations in fiscal 1981, which included 150,000 reviews already scheduled and 400,000 new, so-called accelerated, reviews. During March, April, and May 1981, the Social Security Administration referred 64,000 of these accelerated review cases to the states. The administration selected younger beneficiaries for whom the potential savings were quite high as well as those whose cases had been decided between 1973 and 1975, the years of the black lung and SSI onslaught.[42]

As the reviews got under way, the Social Security Administration became more optimistic about the amount of money that could be saved. Originally, for example, the administration estimated a saving of half a billion dollars in fiscal 1983; by April of 1982, it envisoned savings of $730 million. As a result, the administration scheduled even more investigations. By fall 1984, the administration had reviewed about 1.2 million disability beneficiaries and informed about 490,000 of them that they would lose their benefits.[43]

Many terminated beneficiaries appealed, and many were successful. At least 200,000 of the approximately 490,000 people whose benefits had been terminated had their benefits restored. Certain groups, such as the mentally ill whose conditions fluctuated from day to day, enjoyed particular success in the appeals process. By August 1982, for example, the Social Security Administration had terminated 31,700 people with mental impairments. Of those, 13,400 requested a reconsideration. Although the states sustained the decisions in 76 percent of the cases, the administrative law judges reversed 91 percent of the mental impairment cases that reached their hearing rooms.[44]

Horror stories

Soon horror stories began to appear in the press about those who had been removed from the disability rolls. In September 1981, Jack Anderson reported that in tightening the requirements for eligibility for the disability program, the administration was creating a bureaucratic nightmare. "Reagan's money managers have been scrutinizing the federal budget with eyes as cold as the marble around them," he wrote. "Tales of tragedy have reached my office from all sections of the country." Anderson then told the story of Helen Mary Carlton, a fifty-four-year-old Detroit woman who was denied benefits, even though she had undergone triple heart bypass surgery, and then died.[45]

There was press coverage from New York City to Los Angeles on others who had lost their lives after being cut from the disability rolls. The *Wall Street Journal* reported on a Vietnam war veteran whose jaw was wired shut and who had lost a leg and two fingers; part of his stomach was gone. Although he had been on the disability rolls for seven years, he was cut off. By the time the Social Security Administration restored his benefits, he was dead. The *Los Angeles Times* reported that eleven people died in 1982 as a result of being cut from the disability rolls.[46]

Condemnations of the cutbacks appeared in papers with national circulations and in local papers. In May 1982, the *New York Times* ran a front-page story criticizing the administration's actions with this lead: "In the last seven months, the Reagan administration has ended disability insurance for more than 106,000 families, including some who are almost certainly entitled to them."[47] In an article entitled "Social Security Cutbacks Border on Terrorization," the Fort Smith, Arkansas, *Southwest Times Record* reported that "it borders on terrorizing those least able to defend themselves, stripping them of dignity, creating additional anxiety for heart and lung patients, forcing them onto the welfare rolls, and forgetting they even exist."[48] Whether cosmopolitan or provincial, the newspapers invited the reader into a world of bureaucratic indifference and made readers think about President Reagan's commitment to maintain the safety net and to protect the nation's dependent citizens.

Each city, it seemed, had its horror story. The *Detroit News*, for example, reported the case of Frank Harrison Williams, who suffered from a bad back. According to the article, this was "not just [a] plain old bad back." It was "too many foggy, pain-killing, mind-altering pills every single day bad. . . . Screaming at the bedroom ceiling at 3 o'clock in the morning bad." But it was not bad enough to stay on the disability rolls in the Reagan administration.[49] The *Birmingham News* reported the case of Frederick Lee Henderson from Bessemer, Alabama. He had been involved in an accident in which his car had been hit by a train. He spent nine months in a coma following the accident and then remained in a wheel chair. His doctor described him as "pretty much totally bedridden." According to his wife, "a newborn baby could work if my husband could work." Yet he was bumped off the disability rolls by the Reagan administration.[50]

One story, that of Roy P. Benavidez, moved Reagan to intervene personally. Benavidez, a migrant worker, had served in Vietnam and had rescued eight of his fellow Green Berets who had been trapped under enemy fire. In recognition, Reagan had awarded him the Medal of Honor for "extremely valorous actions in the face of overwhelming odds." When Reagan gave Benavidez the medal, Benavidez was already on disability insurance. In the disability reviews, however, this heroic Hispanic war veteran and father of three was declared no longer eligible for disability benefits. He had fallen through the safety net, and that rankled the president. Paul Simmons put out a statement: "The President is, indeed, personally concerned about this one. He does know the man, and he wants to make sure he doesn't fall through the cracks." Meanwhile, Benavidez issued his own statement: "After seven years, they seem to think that the wounds have healed and that I can work. What is wrong with these people? I would work if I could, but no one will hire me because no insurance company will insure me."[51] Benavidez's case got put on the fast track, and soon an administrative law judge declared that he was eligible and would continue to receive his benefits.[52]

A television program broadcast in 1984 as part of the PBS *Frontline* series was typical of journalistic coverage of disability reviews. The program referred constantly to the contract between the Social Security Administration and the American worker. Then, it showed pictures of a mentally retarded person testifying before Senator John Heinz. Unfortunately, many questions were never raised. Had the retarded person ever worked? Was he eligible for social security or only for Supplemental Security Income? The program also televised an administrative law judge's hearing. "Only Congress can make a law. If you change it by interpreting it too strictly, you're changing the law," said the administrative law judge. Yet the program failed to explain the provisions of the 1980 law, much less what constituted a strict interpretation of it.[53]

Although dramatic, the stories, as reported in the popular press and on television, simplified a highly complex matter almost to the point of being deceptive. The stories largely ignored the appeals process, during which, by law, continued benefits were guaranteed; they failed to report if a person's case was under appeal or, in some cases, that his benefits had been restored. The stories often did not portray accurately the severity of the disability standard contained in the law, nor did they make it clear that the standard was not invented by the Reagan administration. Finally, the stories made no mention of the other disability benefits, such as veterans benefits, that the person may have been receiving.

In a sense, the Social Security Administration had itself to blame for the criticism its removal of people from the disability rolls generated. Employing inspirational stories, such as that of Homer Philips, to inform the public about the program, it had never done a good job in communicating the program's complexities. As a result, when the horror stories appeared, they violated the public's image of broad coverage against the risks of disability.

The political response

The press reports stimulated congressmen to take political action. A great number of congressional committees and subcommittees became involved in the process of correcting the abuses caused by the disability reviews; the staffs of the Ways and Means and Finance Committees and of the Social Security Administration no longer dominated disability policy discussions as they had in the 1960s and even the 1970s. Where once the Social Security Administration developed legislation from a well-defined agenda, it now reacted to events as much as it controlled them.

New experts, particularly legal aid advocates, now influenced congressional consideration of disability insurance. The legal aid advocates were valuable to the congressmen because they brought to the attention, first of the local press and then of congregational committee staffs, the horror stories that could be dramatized in Congress. Jonathan Stein, who worked for legal aid in Philadelphia, for example, provided material to Senator Heinz and his staff; Kathleen Grover, a lawyer in Portland, Maine, worked with Senator Cohen and his staff.[54]

The legal aid advocates believed it to be a basic right of a disability insurance applicant to have a lawyer, despite all the effort that had gone into lessening the amount of litigation in disability programs. Michael Pritchard of the Arkansas legal aid program stated that the Social Security Administration no longer adequately protected the applicant's rights. He said that he found it necessary to perform work that the state disability determination offices were supposed to do, such as making sure that the applicant got an in-depth physical examination, "gathering the evidence, talking to members of the family, and then bringing all of this together for a hearing."[55] To the legal aid advocates, disability insurance was a matter of equity, and in congressional testimony and in newspaper interviews they highlighted injustices done to individuals.

Testimony of this nature contrasted with that of Social Security officials, who discussed disability insurance in terms of large numbers and abstract concepts. Where Social Security officials talked about such things as the percentage of covered payroll, the legal aid advocates always used the case study. The vivid testimony of the legal aid advocates about the suffering individuals endured because of the disability reviews invited congressmen to forget their concern with such troubling issues as the volatile costs of the disability insurance system and to redress the injustices. Congress accepted this invitation eagerly.

The case studies of the legal aid advocates surfaced first in such committees as the Governmental Affairs Committee and the Special Committee on Aging, not the traditional Social Security committees. As the Senate Committee on Finance struggled with the social security financing question in the spring of 1982, the Subcommittee on Oversight of the Governmental Affairs Committee, which enjoyed a mandate to investigate a wide range of problems within government, decided first to write a report and then to hold a hearing on the continuing disability investigations. Although the Senate committee was relatively old (it had been one of Senator Joseph McCarthy's forums), the subcommittee, created in 1979, was comparatively new. Five senators and four staff members worked on the subcommittee, yet two senators, William Cohen (Maine) and Carl Levin (Michigan), used it as a personal vehicle and controlled the staff.

When the disability stories broke, both Cohen and Levin, who anticipated difficult elections in 1984, recognized the disability issue as an important one, as one that could plausibly be termed a problem in government management, and as one with a potential political payoff. Levin, who, like his colleagues, had discovered the problem through his constituency mail, brought the problem to Cohen's attention. Cohen checked with his local offices and learned of horror stories in Maine. Confronted with what staffer Linda Gustitus called a "direct assault on constituents," free to investigate problems as disparate as the role of the administrative law judge and the management of the synthetic fuels corporation, Cohen and Levin decided to hold a hearing in the spring of 1982.[56]

Ethel A. Kage of Reed City, Michigan, appeared before the subcommittee on May 25, 1982. She testified that her husband had worked on a survey crew, traveling all over the state of Michigan; even after he lost the sight of his left eye, he kept working. Then, she reported, he had a stroke that left him with tunnel vision so that he was unable to drive. At the age of forty-two, she continued, he went on disability. "When we received the Notice of Review," she said, "it was quite a shocking affair." She had arrived home, she testified, to find her husband very agitated. "He thought everything, you know, was going down the drain, that the plug had been pulled out. He didn't know how we would survive. . . . We were on for seven years and never any indication." On Thanksgiving evening, she stated, her husband got sick, and he died the next day, the victim of two massive heart attacks.[57]

Mrs. Kage made good testimony for Levin and Cohen. The subcommittee staffers called the testimony "riveting." A congressional staffer for the Senate Special Committee on Aging reported to his boss that the testimony was "damaging" to the administration.[58]

Levin and Cohen now felt entitled to play a part in the legislative process that would correct the problems their subcommittee had exposed. Thus a subcommittee created twenty-three years after the passage of disability insurance, which had never been involved in social security policy before, entered the arena of disability policymaking. In this way, as well, a staff came cold to the technical world of social security and offered suggestions for reform.

Levin and Cohen's success in attracting so much attention brought competition, from other congressmen and other committees. Before comprehensive legislation was passed, Congress held twenty-seven hearings, in locations across the country. The result was nothing less than a rediscovery of disability insurance by Congress. Not since 1956, and perhaps not even then, had the program been so thoroughly examined.

Senator Jim Sasser, for example, became involved in the spring of 1982 after he had received a letter from a woman in the Tennessee disability determination office that alleged the existence of a quota. The woman charged that the administration was forcing the state of Tennessee to take people off the disability rolls. Although neither the existence of a quota nor the authenticity of the letter were ever proved, the senator's staff used the letter to political advantage. A staff member advised Sasser, who served on the Senate Budget Committee, to confront Secretary Richard Schweiker during a meeting: "A television crew from *Sixty Minutes* is supposed to cover this hearing . . . there is a good chance that if you ask Mr. Schweiker about the problems of the new accelerated review procedure you might get good press. . . . Disability is a good political issue. . . . Few dispute the need for a program which purports to care for those who cannot care for themselves due to a disabling condition. Therefore, I believe that the political risks are minimal."[59] Indeed, Sasser's involvement with the disability issue aided his reelection effort.

Senator John Heinz of Pennsylvania became involved in the disability issue after reading a story in the *Philadelphia Inquirer* about a woman named Kathleen McGovern who committed suicide when she discovered she had been terminated from the disability rolls. Heinz said that the story "got to him."[60] Heinz's staff supported his involvement in reevaluating the disability reviews. "There is growing media interest in this problem," they told him, "because the human interest stories are compelling." Advising him that neither Pickle in the House nor Dole and Long in the Senate wanted to deal with the matter, since Pickle was "largely responsible for the current disability process" and Dole and Long wanted to wait for a specific bill from the House before taking action, they urged him to work with Cohen and Levin on disability legislation.[61]

Heinz served on the Senate Finance Committee and chaired the Senate Special Committee on Aging, and he brought up the issue of disability reviews before both of these committees. When the Finance Committee finally held hearings on the continuing disability reviews in late summer 1982, Heinz made a statement about Kathleen Mc-Govern. The Special Committee on Aging had already issued a special report on disability insurance.[62]

In the spring of 1983, the Special Committee on Aging examined the special problems of the mentally disabled in the disability review process. Heinz believed that the mentally disabled presented the "clearest example of abuse and catastrophe."[63] In part this catastrophe resulted from a conflict between the goals of disability and mental health policy.

To protect the public against an explosion in the disability rolls, disability insurance relied on a strict definition of disability; mental health policy was based on the concept of deinstitutionalization, removing people from the state asylums and putting them in the community. Once in the community, however, the mentally ill required income support, since many could not hold steady jobs. Although the logical sources of this support were disability insurance and Supplemental Security Income, these programs applied the same tough standards to the mentally ill as they did to everyone else. As a consequence, many of the mentally ill and retarded became cut off from state institutions on the one hand and from welfare and social insurance payments on the other.

Furthermore, the process of disability determination for the mentally ill posed considerable problems. (The earliest drafts of the disability insurance legislation excluded the mentally ill from the program.) With the introduction of psychotropic drugs, the conditions of those with mental problems (such as Linda Ross) could be stabilized, yet often their conditions fluctuated widely over time, from manic to depressive. An applicant or beneficiary might see the disability examiner just as his condition was passing through the normal range. Thus even though his prognosis might be poor, he would appear to be normal. Further, as the Government Accounting Office told the Senate Committee on Aging, the disability examiners had difficulty obtaining a complete medical file, one that would compensate for the pendulum effect. The very nature of the illness might prevent a person from giving an accurate personal history; the stigma of it made many people want to appear normal, even through this violated their own self-interest.

In addition, the Social Security Administration maintained particularly tough standards to govern the mentally impaired's eligibility for the disability insurance program. A schizophrenic, for example, needed to demonstrate "marked restriction of daily activities and constriction of interest and seriously impaired ability to relate to other people."[64] Those capable of watching television might not meet the standard of a "marked restriction of daily activities." One medical consultant noted that it was "practically impossible to meet the listings ... for any individual whose thought processes are not completely disorganized, is not blatantly psychotic, or is not having a psychiatric emergency requiring immediate hospitalization."[65]

The continuing disability investigations made an already difficult problem much worse. Since the greatest savings would result from purifying the disability rolls of its younger beneficiaries, for whom expenses would otherwise mount over the course of their lifetimes, the administration singled out young people for disability reviews. Many of these younger beneficiaries were on the rolls because of a mental disability. Therefore the mentally disabled were disproportionately represented in the disability reviews, a fact that did not escape the attention of the legal aid advocates, the press, or Senator Heinz.

Martin Gladstone, whose anchor to mental stability was built on psychotropic drugs, counseling, and close daily supervision, found a letter in his mailbox that told him he was off the rolls. For thirteen years he had lived in a state hospital; now he would be expected to survive in the community, without the support of disability insurance or Supplemental Security Income. A mental health worker worried that the "deinstitutionalization movement will disintegrate" and that people like Gladstone would disappear into "the netherworld of street life."[66]

With so much congressional attention focused on disability insurance, it was almost as if the congressmen were adding a new level of appeal to the disability insurance determination process. If a person pressed his case far enough, it could end up in the halls of Congress, where the members would conduct their own hearings according to their own rules. Disability policy discourse, once characterized by dry statistics on covered payrolls and average indexed monthly earnings, now took on a newer, more accessible, and more strident form of rhetoric. Senator Levin, for example, kicked off a congressional hearing by stating: "Today we are investigating a system that is in shambles. ... For every weed that social security is plucking, it is crushing two flowers, if the reversal rate by administrative law judges is any indication."[67]

In this spirit, Senator David Pryor of Arkansas questioned Anna Lee McNoel during a hearing held in Fort Smith, Arkansas, conducted jointly by the Special Committee on Aging and a subcommittee of the Committee on Government Affairs. McNoel was forty-eight years old, with a sixth-grade education. She was painfully thin, eighty-eight pounds, with chronic anemia and severe digestive problems. "What did the social security worker say that you could do, Mrs. McNoel?" Senator Pryor asked. "They said I could do secretarial work." "Have you ever had secretarial training of any nature?" "No." "And you went through the sixth grade, as I understand?" "That's correct," replied McNoel.[68]

The horror stories and the ensuing congressional investigations pointed to the existence of a real problem: People who belonged on the disability insurance rolls were being removed from them with tragic results. Even Reagan administration officials began to realize they had made a mistake by summer 1982. "We should have had a lot more safety-valves, more probes of small groups of people," said Pat Owens, a career employee of the Social Security Administration who ran the disability program for most of Reagan's first term. Paul Simmons, who took a very hard line on the issue, confided that it "might have been better to grandfather in the people who were on the rolls illegally and begin with a clean broom on the problem."[69]

A general feeling surfaced that Congress would have to respond with new disability legislation. Until the Benavidez case arose in late spring 1983, the administration hoped to solve the problem administratively or to work with the Ways and Means Committee on a piece of moderate legislation. The administration tried to pin the blame on Congress for passing the 1980 law. "It is not Reagan's cut-off," complained Social Security Commissioner John Svahn to the *New York Times,* "it is a Congressionally mandated crackdown on eligibility." Svahn's rationale simply would not wash, however. Despite the relatively recent 1980 amendments, Congress could not put disability insurance behind it.[70]

The courts' response

As continuing disability investigations became the central object first of disability policy and then after a 1983 law disposed of the financing crisis of social security policy, the administrative law judges, who viewed the removal of beneficiaries from the disability rolls as a direct rebuke of their work, rebelled. The administrative law judges perceived themselves as holding the line against injustice. Many on the disability rolls got there, after all, only through the intervention of an administrative law judge; now, with their benefits threatened, many could remain on the rolls only with the judge's help. Francis O'Byrne expressed the exasperation of his colleagues when he talked of the mentally impaired. "There are mentally impaired people whose vocabulary is perfect, who can write well, but when we see them they're nude and spitting on the floor," he said. "If they didn't have the administrative law judges, we wouldn't have a chance," said Anna McNoel.[71]

With so many cases under investigation, however, the sheer volume of the requests for hearings defeated efforts of the administrative law judges to handle them. In 1981, the year in which requests for hearings hit a new high of 281,737, a backlog of 128,764 cases remained at the end of the year.[72]

The results of a study, mandated by the 1980 law, increased the tensions that were building between the Reagan administration and the administrative law judges. It compared the decisions reached on 3,600 disability cases by the administrative law judges who heard the cases; by the Office of Assessment at the Social Security Administration, which used the standards applied by the states; and by the Appeals Council, which used the standards that applied to the administrative law judges. The results showed just how much these standards differed. The administrative law judges granted disability benefits in 64 percent of the cases; the Appeals Council would have allowed benefits in 48 percent of the cases; the Office of Assessment would have permitted disability payments in only 13 percent of the cases.[73]

In the midst of these developments, the Social Security Administration decided to improve the training of its administrative law judges. New judges, being hired to deal with the large number of cases, received what one official described as a better foundation in the law. More experienced judges were asked to take refresher courses. To the administrative law judges, the training initiatives carried the connotation of discipline; they felt as though they were being reprimanded for not making the correct decisions, for allowing too many people to receive disability benefits.[74]

Faced with what the administrative law judges perceived as so many provocations, they did what came naturally: they sued the government. The Association of Administrative Law Judges, composed of 540 administrative law judges, filed a suit in which it charged that the Social Security Administration targeted judges with high reversal rates for harassment. This harassment included the retraining (which the association called "reeducation") as well as more overt forms of "punishment" such as reducing secretarial help. The association regarded the administration's management initiatives as leading toward quotas. It charged that the administration regarded judges who approved disability benefits in 45 to 55 percent of their cases as unacceptable. To show how serious it was about the suit, it retained Elliot Richardson, the former cabinet officer and a highly respected legal counsel, as its lawyer.[75]

The politics of disability insurance now featured a publicized rift between the judges who heard appealed cases and the government agency that managed the entire process. The issues under debate soon found their way into congressional deliberations on disability insurance. When John Svahn sought confirmation as under secretary of Health and Human Services early in 1983, Senator Pryor asked him whether the administration had given the justices quotas. He also confronted Svahn with a memorandum that reportedly made reducing the reversal rate from 57.3 percent in 1982 to 45.2 percent in 1984 an agency goal. Svahn denied the existence of a quota or directive, and Paul Simmons said that the figures merely represented the rate of approvals if good legal procedures were used and if the judges made no mistakes.[76]

The administrative law judges found themselves pressed not only by the Social Security Administration from below but also by the federal courts from above. As Judge O'Byrne expressed it: "I was a lawyer for a long time before I became a Judge, and I am very nervous about ignoring orders of Courts."[77]

Friction between the Social Security Administration and the courts, always apparent, increased as the disability reviews proceeded. In two decisions, for example, a Ninth Circuit court held in 1982 that the Social Security Administration had to show that a beneficiary's medical condition had improved before it could take away his disability benefits. The issues arose because many believed that those who did not qualify for disability benefits were nonetheless permitted to receive them between 1973 and 1975, when standards declined under the pressure of implementing SSI and black lung. When the states reviewed these cases in 1981–3, they used the prevailing disability standards that were, without a doubt, tougher than those applied earlier. That raised the question of whether a person whose condition had not improved could be removed from the rolls. The Social Security Administration thought it could do so, but many of the courts, such as the one in the Ninth Circuit, disagreed.

Another controversial matter concerned what the lawyers called "nonacquiescence." Although the Social Security Administration paid benefits to beneficiaries who successfully appealed decisions to remove them from the disability rolls, it did not change its policies to reflect court decisions reversing the removals. That meant, in theory, that each beneficiary threatened with removal from the disability rolls would have to bring his case before the court in order to receive relief. The judges objected to this challenge of their authority, as Judge McMillan of the Eighth Circuit made clear when he wrote, "I have no wish to invite a confrontation with the Secretary. Yet if the Secretary persists in pursuing her nonacquiescence in this circuit's decisions, I will seek to bring contempt proceedings against the Secretary."[78]

The treatment of the mentally ill also occasioned considerable controversy. In May 1982, for example, the Mental Health Association of Minnesota brought a class action suit against the Social Security Administration charging that the mentally disabled had been unfairly removed from the disability rolls. A Minnesota district court judge decided that the Social Security Administration had created a new eligibility standard for the mentally ill, which he called "arbitrary, capricious, irrational, and an abuse of discretion." The basis for this decision was that if a mentally disabled person failed to qualify for disability insurance on physical grounds alone, his vocational capabilities were never examined. Yet the law required an applicant's residual functional capacity to be considered and the rules in the "grid" to be applied. As this decision applied to an entire class of individuals, it required that the states reexamine cases in which beneficiaries may have been illegally removed from the disability rolls.

On January 11, 1984, District Judge Jack B. Weinstein ruled that the Social Security Administration had implemented "a fixed clandestine policy against those with mental illness." In his opinion, the Social Security Administration had relied on "bureaucratic instructions rather than individual assessments" and had overruled "the medical opinions of its own consulting physicians." With the ruling in hand, the New

York State attorney general began proceedings against the Social Security Administration for contempt.[79]

By August 1984, even the Social Security Administration conceded that "there is a crisis in SSA's litigation process," caused by the sheer volume of cases and the critical attitude of the court toward the Social Security Administration. "As a consequence," an internal Social Security Administration study noted, "the agency's credibility before the courts is at an all-time low." The number of court cases indicated a failure of public administration. In the summer of 1984, 50,000 Social Security cases were pending in federal courts, as well as 125 disability class actions. The Social Security Administration expected the number of new court cases to reach 28,000 in fiscal 1984.[80]

The state's response

If the administrative law judges and the courts, which enjoyed relative independence, felt squeezed by contradictory pressures in the disability system, the states were subject to even more pressure. The state disability determination services, after all, were the agencies of government expected to remove people from the rolls. The disability reviews, the congressional hearings, the public statements by the administrative law judges, and the court decisions made the states uncomfortable. This discomfort eventually led to an unprecedented state revolt against the Social Security Administration.

During the height of the publicity about the harm done by the disability investigations, the press talked with many state officials who seemed eager to disassociate themselves from the review process. They did not like being the bearer of bad news. Robert C. Cohen, the Wisconsin director of that state's disability service, sent a letter to the Chicago regional office of the Social Security Administration that made its way into the papers. Far from loyally following the administration's orders, Cohen criticized the disability reviews, saying, among other things, that the federal government's attitude toward the mentally ill was "deny, deny, deny."[81]

Just like the administrative law judges, the state officials accused the Social Security Administration of imposing a quota system. Setting a target for the number of beneficiaries to be removed violated the image of impartial justice that the program had always maintained. That is why the anonymous letter that Senator Jim Sasser received created such a stir. "We are now in fact meeting a quota system, to satisfy the administration higher ups and keep our jobs," the letter, allegedly from a state disability worker, said. "I am a Christian person and do not believe in this." Although the existence of a quota system was never proved, the issue raised a furor.[82]

The states had every reason to disapprove of the continuing disability investigations. In the first place, denying benefits was inherently unpleasant and potentially dangerous. In Michigan, where the state offices were cutting benefits in the middle of a severe recession, the state found it necessary for its disability examiners to work under bulletproof glass.[83]

In the second place, the states regarded the continuing disability investigations as repeating work they had already done, since many beneficiaries were on the rolls only after having been denied benefits by the states and having appealed their cases to administrative law judges. In effect, the continuing disability investigations caused both the states and the applicants to retrace their steps.

In the third place, removing people from disability insurance put financial pressure on the states. A disabled person could receive social insurance benefits through the disability insurance program or welfare benefits through the Supplemental Security Income program, both funded by the federal government. Although the rules governing who qualified differed between the two programs, the programs used the same definition of disability. If a person was thrown off the disability insurance program because he did not meet the definition of disability, that meant he also could not qualify for Supplemental Security Income. If a beneficiary was thrown off the disability insurance rolls, therefore, his safety net consisted of general assistance, a welfare program for all poor people, paid for entirely by the states. From a state's perspective, dropping someone from the disability rolls decreased the amount of federal dollars coming into the state and increased the strain on the state budget.

The continuing disability reviews forced people to go off disability insurance or Supplemental Security Income and accept general assistance. In the state of New York, after a lag of three to four months, those dropped from the disability rolls appeared on the general assistance rolls. Mayor Edward Koch and Council President Carol Bellamy said that if only a quarter of the people removed from the disability rolls in 1982 received general assistance, then the state's cost would be $10.6 million. In Maryland, a study of early retirement revealed that nearly a third of the people who lost their disability insurance eventually received general assistance at a cost of $2.3 million in 1984.[84]

Whatever the reasons, a full-scale revolt of the states occurred in the summer of 1983. On May 9, 1983, Massachusetts Governor Michael Dukakis told his disability determination service not to terminate anyone from the disability rolls unless that person's condition had improved. On July 22, 1983, the social services commissioner of the state of New York acted on his own initiative to suspend terminations from the disability rolls pending the establishment of a medical improvement standard to govern such cases. As these actions demonstrated, the administration had begun to lose control of the disability determination process. The states simply refused to review cases and to terminate benefits.[85] What began as an isolated phenomenon soon grew into a national movement.

The unified state revolt took a significant step on August 2, 1983, at a meeting of the National Governors' Association at which the governors, many of whom knew little about their disability determination services, discussed the disability program. They passed a resolution in favor of legislation pending in Congress to force the administration to follow a medical improvement standard and to discontinue its nonacquiescence policy toward court rulings. The association therefore became allied with the movement to change the disability determination process.[86]

Having passed the resolution, the governors went home and many suspended the disability reviews in their states. Governor Richard Celeste of Ohio, for example, issued a proclamation on October 11, 1983, ordering "cessation of all adverse determinations of continuing disability determinations" for 150 days.[87] Michigan's Governor Blanchard received advice from two of his cabinet officers that reminded him of the political and legal ramifications. Senator Levin, noted the cabinet officers, already had written the governor "implicitly encouraging action." Michigan, they added, was under court order "to . . . reinstate mentally impaired claimants." So Michigan joined the revolt. A severe strain developed on the federal–state partnership in disability determination as each day brought a new story about a state refusing to handle disability reviews. Governor George Wallace of Alabama ordered the Alabama disability determination agency to stop processing Continuing Disability Review (CDR) terminations on September 19; Governor Charles Robb of Virginia issued a similar order on September 28, and so on through more than half of the states, until Governor Mark White of Texas acted in March 1984.[88]

The ironies mounted. The states entered the disability insurance program as a break on federal generosity. Now they rebelled against the federal government for being too stingy and not paying enough benefits. The same people who once complained that the federal government did not have enough control over the states now argued it had far too much.

Problems that had plagued the disability determination system from its inception now became apparent to all. The administrative law judges, who operated under different standards than the states, were now threatening to sue the Social Security Administration for forcing them to follow the same standards as the states. The states were engaged in a pitched battle with the Social Security Administration because their interests did not coincide. The courts continued to intervene in the process in an ad hoc way, creating an epidemic of litigation in a program already plagued with far too much litigation. Congress, for its part, highlighted the injustices of the continuing disability reviews in hearing after hearing. The disability insurance program, thrown into crisis during the 1970s, neared a state of chaos in the 1980s.

Passage of the 1984 law

With so much controversy surrounding the disability program and with so many interests and political actors to accommodate, Congress took more than two years to pass legislation in response to the continuing disability investigations. It passed several interim laws before President Reagan signed Public Law 98-460 in October 1984. Senators Long and Dole of the Finance Committee, Congressman Pickle of the House Ways and Means Committee, and Senators Heinz, Cohen, and Levin all played significant roles in the process. Those new to disability policymaking, such as Cohen and Levin, clashed with those long involved; the administration continued to shift its position as the situation changed; and the House leaders reversed their position at a significant point in the debate. In addition, factors totally unrelated to disability – the financing crisis in social security itself – played a role in prolonging and complicating the debate by taking the time of congressional committees and by focusing attention on the financial solvency of the entire program.

With all of this political maneuvering, continuity between the 1980 and 1984 reforms was almost totally lost. Passage of the 1984 law became a short-sighted political exercise rather than part of a comprehensive effort to reform disability policy, despite the time that the process consumed.

The process began, as social security bills always do, in the House of Representatives where, if anyone was invested in the 1980 amendments, it was Congressman Jake Pickle, the chairman of the Subcommittee on Social Security of the Committee on Ways and Means. As Stan Ross had mentioned, Pickle wanted to make his name with the 1980 amendments, and to a large extent he succeeded. With Dan Rostenkowski, described by one staffer as "not a substance person," in charge of the Ways and Means Committee, Pickle enjoyed more influence over social security than ever. Only Representative Pepper challenged Pickle's preeminence, and Pepper concentrated on old age insurance rather than on disability.

Pickle let go of the 1980 amendments very reluctantly. As the horror stories mounted in 1982, however, it became clear that he had to do something. By May, he had a relatively modest bill. As if to underscore the continuity of this bill with social security tradition, it carried the names of Pickle and Archer, the majority and minority leaders of the subcommittee, respectively. In developing the bill, Pickle relied on the advice of Fred Arner, the staffer most responsible for previous disability insurance legislation.[89]

The bill itself was as noteworthy for what it did not contain as for what it did. It made no mention of medical improvement standards, which were at the heart of the political discussions that would lead to the 1984 law. At issue was whether the administration could remove someone from the disability rolls whose condition was the same as when he went on the rolls. The question centered on whether the secretary should have to prove that a beneficiary's medical condition had improved before his benefits could be terminated. Many, including Senators Long and Dole, believed that such a "medical improvement standard" would be costly to implement. The Social Security Administration estimated that the medical improvement standard could cost as much as $1.9 billion between fiscal years 1984 and 1988.[90]

Instead of legislating on the question of a medical improvement standard, the Pickle bill would have permitted a terminated disability beneficiary to continue to receive disability insurance and medicare benefits for six months after termination or until a state reconsideration decision had been made. The bill also would have prohibited submitting new evidence after this reconsideration decision was made, in effect closing the record at the reconsideration level. Finally, the bill would have asked the secretary of Health and Human Services to promulgate uniform standards to be used at each level of adjudication.[91]

Pickle's bill never made it very far. As Janice Gregory, Pickle's staffer, put it, there was "a slow and steady realization that the bill would not be sufficient." Because it did not mention medical improvement standards, many groups, such as the Save Our Security coalition, opposed it. Legal advocates disliked the provision closing the record at the reconsideration level, since it would put greater reliance for gathering the facts in the hands of the state disability determination services and less reliance on lawyers. In the face of this opposition, the measure simply died. Fred Arner, who had, in the words of some veteran program observers, been "beaten up by the disability groups," left Pickle's staff.[92]

By the beginning of 1983, Pickle started over. This time he carefully met with disability groups such as the Association of Retarded Citizens. "We're trying to see what these groups want and to see if we can accommodate them," Pickle said.[93]

For a time Pickle tried to include the administration in the negotiations. Then came the Benavidez affair and the administration's June 1983 efforts to end the crisis by means of administrative actions: As many as 200,000 disability beneficiaries were declared permanently disabled and thus exempt from the review; the Social Security Administration would move toward a random selection of cases for review and, as a result, more beneficiaries would remain on the rolls; and the administration would propose legislation to make sure that the beneficiaries reviewed kept their benefits until they received a face-to-face hearing at the reconsideration level. These initiatives angered Pickle, who resented the administration's efforts to solve the problem without consulting him. According to Gregory, Pickle decided that if the "administration wanted it that way, we'll pass our own bill."[94]

In September 1983, Pickle presented a new and far different bill. This one included a medical improvement standard. Under its terms, benefits would continue for those beneficiaries whose medical conditions had not improved, provided they remained out of the labor market or earned less than the level of substantial gainful activity. The only exceptions concerned original determinations that were in error or obtained by fraud, individuals who benefited from medical technology or vocational therapy, or cases in which new evidence showed an impairment was not as disabling as it was originally thought to be. Other features of the bill, such as a provision that the administration needed to apply federal circuit court decisions uniformly through that circuit, also indicated a break with his earlier bill.[95]

Pickle earned high marks from the disability groups. The Association of Retarded Citizens, for example, noted that Pickle "did a superb job of developing social security disability legislation with bi-partisan support."[96]

With Pickle's mind made up, attention shifted to Senators Dole and Long, the Republican chairman of the Finance Committee, and the ranking Democrat and former chairman. Practical politicians who knew the value of compromise, they also regarded themselves as custodians of the disability insurance trust fund. Questions of a beneficiary's fair treatment troubled them and the potential costs of disability reform worried them most of all.[97]

Long, who, with the passing of years, believed ardently that disability insurance was his program, one for which he had a special responsibility, worried particularly that beneficiaries who could engage in substantial gainful activity would remain on the rolls because the Social Security Administration would be unable to prove their conditions had improved. (A case file, for example, might be lost. That would make it impossible to reconstruct the original decision.) He felt strongly enough about the program to assert his political power to block consideration of reform bills that contained a medical improvement standard, which would add to program expenditures.

When Long debated the issue, he gave what veteran disability program watchers called *the* speech. He liked to include personal anecdotes, and this time he told of his maid, who had cancer, received disability benefits, and continued to work on the side. Long emphasized that the law did not condone the actions of his maid. Congress wanted a tough disability standard. The disability reviews emphasized the toughness of that standard and Congress should not back off from them, even in the face of strong political pressure. As indicated by this presentation, Long became a powerful force on the side of retaining the disability reviews.[98]

Dole and Long regarded the administration as a natural ally in the effort to defeat a medical improvement standard, yet they discovered, as Pickle had, that the administration was unreliable. The administration's position varied widely during the long debate. In general, it preferred to take administrative actions (over which it had control) rather than work with Congress on new legislation. The stock administration line held that the problems with the disability reviews were administrative, not statutory. On the administration's own initiative, for example, it created a special interview between local Social Security officers and disability beneficiaries whose cases were being reviewed. The administration hoped this interview would both lessen confusion about the reviews and weed out the obviously disabled from the review process.[99]

Although the Reagan administration took these steps willingly and also experimented at various times with a moratorium on disability reviews, it drew the line at medical improvement standards. A medical improvement standard might keep the soft undercore of disability recipients who entered the rolls in the mid-1970s on the rolls, because it would be difficult to prove that their conditions had improved. If a person entered the disability rolls by mistake, he could remain there for life. The administration also feared the effect on the program of a double standard. A person applying for benefits for the first time would be subject to the tough current standards; a person being reviewed would be judged by the medical improvement standard.[100]

The administration's uncertain position weakened Dole and Long in the negotiations with insurgents Levin, Cohen, and Heinz. As early as spring 1982, Levin and Cohen had introduced legislation that would have instituted a medical improvement standard and they remained committed to the concept through the long debate.[101]

Cohen and Levin shared the spotlight with Heinz, who adopted the cause of the mentally ill. Heinz referred to the disability reviews as "a holocaust against the mentally impaired." In the summer of 1983, Heinz succeeded in getting the Senate to pass a measure that would have suspended reviews of the mentally impaired until the secretary of the Department of Health and Human Services revised the criteria that applied to them. Attached to an appropriations bill, the measure died in conference. "The Heinz bill should not be mourned," commented an advocate from the American Psychiatric Association. "It served and served well as a substantial impetus for the recent activity in the House Ways and Means Committee."[102]

The House of Representatives experienced fewer conflicts, and in the fall of 1983 the House leadership attached Pickle's disability bill to a tax reform bill, a political gambit that failed. When the tax reform bill was defeated, the disability measure died. By this time, however, the popularity of the measure was undisputed. Pickle tried again in March 1984, and this time he succeeded in getting the measure through the House.

Although the Senate quickly passed its version of a disability reform bill on May 22, 1984, the process leading to the 1984 law did not end until September, when a conference committee finally worked through the complicated provisions of the House and Senate bills. The conference committee functioned as a direct negotiation between Senator Dole and Representative Pickle. The differences between the House and Senate bills included the wording of the medical improvement standard, the emphasis to be placed on pain and multiple impairments, and the way in which the Social Security Administration should follow the decisions of the federal court.[103]

By the time the bills reached the conference stage, both the House and the Senate, with the reluctant acquiescence of Long, accepted the idea of a medical improvement standard. The arguments now centered on how the medical improvement standard would be applied and how the disability insurance trust fund would be protected against large expenditures.

As for this last matter, Long had managed to insert something called the COLA-Fail Safe provision into the Senate version of the bill. According to this provision, if the disability trust fund fell below a given level, the cost-of-living increases for disability beneficiaries would be scaled back to make up the difference. Old age beneficiaries but not disability beneficiaries would get cost-of-living adjustments, an unprecedented development for social security. The Senate passed the measure out of deference to Long, but, attacked by Pickle and by social security loyalists like Robert Ball, it died in conference.[104]

The issue of a medical improvement standard remained lively. The House bill stated that disability benefits could be terminated only if there was "substantial evidence" that the beneficiary could work as a result of medical improvement, technological advance, vocational therapy, or new diagnostic techniques, *or* the earlier eligibility determination was "clearly erroneous and fraudulently obtained." The Senate bill, which differed substantially, did not contain this last phrase, as staffers believed that it would be nearly impossible to prove that an earlier eligibility determination was erroneous or fraudulent.[105]

The Senate and the House also disagreed on where the burden of proof should lie. Senate conferees thought the beneficiary should prove that his medical condition had not improved rather than requiring the government to prove that it had. When an applicant sought disability insurance, he had to show that he was disabled. In disability review cases, though, the courts had shifted the burden of proof back to the secretary, who had to show that a beneficiary's condition had improved in order to excise him from the disability rolls. The House bill agreed with the approach of the courts. The Senate bill, however, required the beneficiary to state (and the evidence to show) that his medical condition was the same as or worse than it was before. A beneficiary who should not have been on the rolls in the first place could still remain there since his medical condition might be the same, unless there was a "demonstrated substantial reason to believe a prior decision was . . . erroneous."[106]

The conference committee chose the House approach to medical improvement, although it deleted the language about the prior decision being "clearly erroneous" and called for substantial evidence showing that the prior decision was in error. The conferees believed that they had struck a balance between allowing a medical improvement standard that automatically permitted a beneficiary to retain his benefits and allowing a standard that could be used in an arbitrary manner to remove people from the rolls.[107]

Although the House won the argument over a medical improvement standard, the Senate won on nonacquiescence. The House sought to compel the Social Security Administration to appeal the disability decisions with which the administration disagreed to the Supreme Court. The Senate bill required only that the secretary report to Congress on why the Social Security Administration did not choose to follow a court ruling beyond the immediate case. The conferees asked only that the Social Security Administration make "every" effort to appeal decisions to the Supreme Court or, alternatively, to ask Congress for a legislative remedy.[108]

In this convoluted and highly technical manner, the new law effectively undid the provisions in the 1980 law that required a person with a nonpermanent impairment to be reviewed every three years. Once on the rolls (and the standards for getting on the rolls continued to be very tough), a beneficiary now had a much better chance of staying there. Reforming the program by removing beneficiaries from the rolls was removed as a realistic policy option.

Although billed as a reform, therefore, the 1984 law stopped the longer-run reform process cold. Concern had shifted from containing the future costs of the system to protecting the present rights of the disabled. Where once policy highlighted the growth of the rolls, it now centered on protecting the rights of people already on the rolls. Where once the economics of replacement rates predominated, the legal issue of entitlement now held sway. Where once the disparate components of the disability insurance policy system were a source of despair, they were now viewed as a check on the arbitrary actions of the Social Security Administration. Where once reform sought to streamline disability determination, more bureaucracy was now added to the system through such measures as face-to-face reconsideration hearings.

The points of the 1980 reform, such as the need to remove people from the rolls, produced counterpoints in the 1984 reform, such as the need to protect people on the rolls. In the process, the nature and direction of the reform of the disability insurance program changed. Perhaps the most significant casualty of the change in focus was neglecting the earlier effort to get beneficiaries to walk off the disability rolls. The 1980 law had attempted to create incentives for handicapped individuals to work; in the struggle over the 1984 legislation, few mentioned these incentives. Instead, the legal issues such as the burden of proof in establishing medical improvement or closing the record at the reconsideration level became all-consuming and exercised a hypnotic effect over disability policy. As a result, the congressmen made the tickets out of the labor force more secure without considering the effects of their actions on handicapped individuals who wanted tickets into the labor force.

And so the disability insurance program plunged from the era of awarding benefits to Homer Philips to the era of taking benefits away from Linda Ross. The consensus that enabled the program to be integrated into the rest of social security was only a memory by 1984. No longer did congressmen have the satisfaction of letting the tax committees handle the details of the program and of voting a handsome expansion of the program as an election approached. Where once congressmen could do political favors for their disabled constituents, they now engaged in damage control.

So, also, as the discussion of disability insurance grew to embrace so many congressmen and so many members of the general public, the discussion of broader issues in disability policy narrowed. The Governmental Affairs Committee and the Special Committee on Aging turned their attention to disability policy only to become mired in the technical and legal issues that surrounded disability insurance in the 1980s.

In the end, disability insurance became a more secure entitlement for those who managed to get it; the coordination of programs and the reform of the disability system remained as elusive as ever.

II. The corrective response

Two generations of income-maintenance programs – workers' compensation and Social Security Disability Insurance – form the core of America's public policy toward disability. Both of these programs, in the words of Robert Haveman and two of his fellow economists, represent ameliorative responses to disability. By raising people's incomes, they seek to ease the financial burden that physical and mental impairments impose on people. They do nothing about the impairments themselves.

Haveman and his collaborators contrast ameliorative responses to disability with corrective responses. Programs that embody the corrective response seek to improve the productivity of the handicapped or to change the economic environment in which they function. In other words, corrective responses represent efforts to overcome impairments or make them less of a handicap to the affected worker.[1]

The corrective strategy has an obvious appeal. Whereas ameliorative responses consist of transfers of money from the able-bodied to the impaired, which will continue unabated throughout the impaired person's life, corrective responses resemble investments. Transfers involve politically controversial efforts to redistribute income; investments imply that no long-term redistribution of income will be necessary. Investments hold the promise of saving the government money and of returning money to society in the form of an impaired person's productivity. Beyond these political concerns, the corrective response allows the handicapped to achieve independence instead of remaining dependent on the government.

In America, the corrective response takes the specific forms of the vocational rehabilitation program, independent living programs, and civil rights and architectural barrier laws. Vocational rehabilitation permits a handicapped individual to meet with a counselor who may authorize a wide range of educational and medical services to make the individual employable. Independent living programs establish local independent living centers that serve as a focal point for the distribution of services designed to make the handicapped able to live independently in the community, such as wheelchair repair and attendant referral. Civil rights and architectural barrier laws mark legislative efforts to reduce discrimination against the handicapped and to make locations physically accessible to the handicapped.

Just as there are two generations of income-maintenance programs that comprise the nation's ameliorative response to disability, so two generations of programs contribute to the corrective response. Vocational rehabilitation, a product of the 1920s with substantial modifications in the 1940s and 1950s, belongs to the first generation. Civil rights laws, architectural barrier laws, and independent living programs, all products of the late 1960s and early 1970s, represent the second generation.

The corrective responses play a distinctly secondary role in America's public policy toward disability. The ameliorative response consumes many more public dollars and attracts much more attention from Congress than does the corrective approach. Although vocational rehabilitation, America's major corrective disability program, now costs well over a billion dollars a year in federal money alone, the Social Security Disability Insurance program costs at least seventeen times more. The predominance of income maintenance over rehabilitation, of ameliorative over corrective responses, of cash over services, and of withdrawal of the handicapped from the labor force over their independence raises fundamental public policy questions. Is it possible to rehabilitate people on the disability rolls? Can we separate those who should retire from those who should be encouraged to work? Can we deliver the right kinds of services that will allow a person his or her independence without subjecting the public sector to prohibitive costs?

The tensions between the ameliorative and corrective responses to disability and between the older and newer programs that comprise the corrective approach are examined in the pages that follow.

5. Vocational rehabilitation

By rehabilitation I mean giving people the chance and the challenge to develop their own resources, inner and outer, to become as independent and responsible as possible. I mean giving people the chance and the challenge to make the most of their talents and their lives and to find personal satisfaction and fulfillment through participation to live their lives with some measure of dignity.

John Gardner[1]

Cutting loose

The vocational rehabilitation program began in 1920, its purpose to provide for the "vocational rehabilitation of persons disabled in industry or in any legitimate occupation."[2]

As the program got under way, the vocational rehabilitation offices expected to receive the bulk of their cases from the state workers' compensation program, which shared a common outlook on the nature of disability. Both programs equated disability with an inability to work in one's customary occupation.

Despite the similar outlook on disability, the programs proved incompatible. One reason was that, on both the state and federal levels, the programs were isolated from one another. More than bureaucratic politics separated the two programs. Differences existed in the programs' basic objectives, in the ways in which the programs were administered, in the methods used to serve their beneficiaries, and in the beneficiaries themselves.

At the state level, workers' compensation programs remained close to the "labor" bureaucracy, and vocational rehabilitation became linked to the education bureaucracy. State industrial commissions or departments of labor ran workers' compensation programs. Wages, hours, and safe working conditions were the typical concerns of such agencies. Vocational rehabilitation, on the other hand, which was considered a training operation, fell into the domain of the chief state school officer, who spent most of his time on public schools and vocational education programs. It made the vocational rehabilitation program, according to one federal official in 1950, "a virtual stepchild [left] to struggle along for funds as best as it can."[3]

At the federal level, state workers' compensation administrators depended on the Department of Labor to guard their interests. Vocational rehabilitation was tied to the education bureaucracy. It began under the control of the independent Federal Board for Vocational Education, then came under the tutelage of the Department of the Interior, moved to what ultimately became the Department of Health, Education, and Welfare, and finally, after much congressional debate, became a charter member of the cabinet-level Department of Education.

With this bureaucratic distance between the two programs, misunderstandings arose that often developed into bitter political fights, as in the case of vocational rehabilitation officials and the labor unions. More concerned about maintaining close relations with such private charitable groups as the National Tuberculosis Association and the American Hearing Association, the vocational rehabilitation programs, according to one federal official, failed to "sell" labor in the years between 1920 and 1950. The unions, struggling to become major American institutions, resented this lack of attention. When the Department of Labor seized upon the idea of transferring vocational rehabilitation to the Department of Labor, the unions eagerly went along.[4]

The debate over the transfer generated enough emotion in the early 1950s to disrupt permanently any chance for a working relationship between vocational rehabilitation and workers' compensation. One internal vocational rehabilitation memorandum noted that the "unification of rehabilitation and workers' compensation [in the Department of Labor] would be a real step toward the weakening and disintegration of the rehabilitation program." Attempting to explain why rehabilitation administrators felt so strongly about this matter, the federal director of the vocational rehabilitation program noted in 1954 that organized labor believed that "employment is the primary purpose of vocational rehabilitation"; by 1954, the vocational rehabilitation administrators considered the program's activities to be so different from those of an employment agency that they dismissed the argument of the labor movement out of hand.[5]

The disabled, vocational rehabilitation administrators argued, required much more than the services of an employment agency; they required the medical and psychosocial services that the vocational rehabilitation program had learned how to provide. In this regard vocational rehabilitation counselors resembled social workers who attended to the needs of the poor. Just as social workers believed that the poor had far more problems than a lack of money, so vocational rehabilitation counselors saw the needs of the handicapped as multifaceted and complex. Therefore, they and their program administrators regarded organized labor's concerns as dangerously old-fashioned and not in the best interests of the handicapped, and they resisted efforts to link workers' compensation and vocational rehabilitation. The organized labor movement countered that the activities affecting employment were the responsibilities of the Department of Labor, and that therefore the program should be administered by the Department of Labor.

Beneath the surface of this political dispute lay a difference in program objectives that stemmed from the fiscal base of each program. Vocational rehabilitation spent only government money, and its administrators realized that the program was engaged in a competition for funds in Washington and in the state legislatures. Winning this competition required gaining the greatest return on program appropriations, so the counselors learned to concentrate on cases where job placement was a real possibility. Certain types of disability, combined with a "certain type of mentality and temperament," made the chances of success so slight that the state agency could not warrant spending its time on these "low promise" cases. For example, elderly people, past the normal working age, were "futile to consider . . . a possibility for retraining." The general rule was that a person had to want to engage in rehabilitation, and if he was not "responsive from the first," he should be labeled "infeasible" and denied services.[6] Since workers' compensation benefits came from insurance premiums paid by private employers, that program operated under different types of constraints. Although workers' compensation had its limitations – for example, it was unable to compensate industrial diseases – it never excluded people because of the severity of their disability or because they lacked motivation to get another job. These differences meant that the programs quickly developed a largely separate clientele, even though Congress had envisioned the programs as working together.

Separate clientele meant separate methods of operation. Workers' compensation used many legal and medical tests to determine the degree of a person's disability. Vocational rehabilitation developed psychological tests designed to indicate a person's potential. The early years of the vocational rehabilitation program coincided with a formative period in the use of these psychological tests as a tool of vocational placement as well as with the rise of psychiatric social work. Eager to use the latest technology, the program allied itself with these "scientific" methods. That put vocational rehabilitation on its way to developing a distinctive approach toward disability, even in its first decade of existence, and left little room for a constructive relationship between it and workers' compensation.

For example, a man who suffered from a hand injury came to the vocational rehabilitation agency and said he wanted a white-collar job, something like bookkeeping or office work. Although he appeared intelligent, when the agency checked his educational background it found that he had failed to reach the eighth grade. To clear up any doubts, the state director gave the man some tests, and science reached a verdict: The man had "a mentality too low for continuous bookwork and mental work. The man was accordingly trained in a manual line."[7]

Another critical difference between the two programs was that workers' compensation, which aimed for financial settlement of damages caused by occupational conditions, disparaged the very concept of rehabilitation. Workers' compensation, created before rehabilitation reached its true potential, made a separation between a worker's occupational and nonoccupational problems. As the leaders of rehabilitation explored the links between psychology and a worker's performance, they began to realize the importance of examining what Dr. Howard Rusk, who was a pioneering figure in rehabilitation medicine, liked to call the "whole man." Their objective was to reintegrate the worker into the community and the labor force, and they believed that it was impossible to separate a worker's occupational and nonoccupational problems and still reach that objective. Workers' compensation administrators reacted with suspicion to these notions, regarding rehabilitation as a costly and uncertain operation that asked the employer to solve problems he had not created. Accordingly, the administrators took pains to advise workers not to take steps, such as rehabilitation, that might reduce their settlements, and rehabilitation became a low priority within the workers' compensation agencies.[8]

As a result of all of these differences, no effective links existed between the two programs. That left disability policy in a bind. Consider the problems of a worker injured in an industrial accident that made him severely disabled. He might be too severely disabled to become a client of the vocational rehabilitation agency and receive training for a new occupation. Bad communication between the two state agencies might make it hard for the injured worker even to hear about vocational rehabilitation. Forced to rely on the workers' compensation agency, the worker would discover that that agency made few provisions for rehabilitation, preferring to concentrate on reaching a financial settlement with the worker. In this way, rehabilitation was shunted aside, and monetary benefits predominated.

One result of the failed relationship between vocational rehabilitation and workers' compensation is that today many state industrial commissions and private insurers turn to private rehabilitation providers rather than state rehabilitation programs when an injured worker wants and needs rehabilitation. For example, the director of the vocational rehabilitation program in a large midwestern state says that the state workers' compensation program "dips in and out of services," so that only about 6 percent of his caseload originates from workers' compensation cases. The director of the Virginia rehabilitation program concedes that private rehabilitation may produce "quicker results."[9]

Rehabilitation and social security

Despite evidence of the failed effort to rehabilitate workers' compensation clients, Congress hoped that when the social security disability freeze and disability insurance programs were initiated in 1954 and 1956, respectively, they would take on the constructive employment emphasis that characterized vocational rehabilitation. For example, if a person applied for his social security pension on the basis of disability, he would automatically be put in touch with the vocational rehabilitation program. Instead of receiving a government pension for the rest of his life, the applicant might instead have an opportunity to improve his condition and get a job.

Historically, vocational rehabilitation and social security were already connected. When the depression hit, the handicapped suffered severe unemployment in the newly compressed economy, and the vocational rehabilitation counselors, having difficulty securing jobs for their rehabilitated clients, worried about the program's future. As a means of gaining appropriations, federal vocational rehabilitation officials urged that vocational rehabilitation be mentioned in the Social Security Act of 1935. The authors of the act held no strong opinions on vocational rehabilitation, which played such a minor role among social programs that it was almost invisible. Arthur Altmeyer told the rehabilitation representatives that if Senator Robert Wagner or Congressman "Muley" Doughton asked about rehabilitation appropriations, "we would indicate that we were not opposed." With this lukewarm endorsement, vocational rehabilitation was written into the Social Security Act.[10]

By the 1950s, vocational rehabilitation had achieved some prominence, so that it seemed more natural to link it with the new Social Security Disability Insurance program. From the beginning, however, Congress put the states in a bind by sending them a mixed message. In 1954, Congress told the states that it wished to use the disability freeze program as a means of encouraging rehabilitation; in 1956, Congress asked the states to help administer a disability insurance program limited to people aged fifty or older. Everyone agreed that of all the barriers to rehabilitation, old age and severe impairment were the most difficult to overcome. Congress sent the states nothing but old people with severe impairments (people who were, by all practical measures, well beyond rehabilitation) and expected the states to achieve large numbers of rehabilitations.

The state vocational rehabilitation agencies looked to the Social Security Administration for help in making disability determinations and in managing the large number of people that would now come into contact with the agency. The Social Security Administration questioned whether the states would be able to make disability determinations and entertained the idea of running the disability insurance program itself. Arthur Hess, the Social Security official in charge of the disability program, admitted, "We had a social security program which to that time was a hundred percent, straightline federal operation. There were few if any people . . . who were philosophically conditioned to working with a state program. . . . All through the first years in the disability program we had repeated reactions from our field and regional people and from many of the central office people that we ought to get the state agencies out of the picture just as quickly as possible." Hess convinced these people to respect the wishes of

Congress, which had devised a delicate compromise on disability insurance, and to work with the rehabilitation agencies despite what one Social Security administrator termed a "negative attitude" on the agency's part.[11]

In the early years of the program, the federal rehabilitation office continued to insist that a rehabilitation counselor see each disability insurance applicant. It was expected that most of the applicants would be rejected for disability insurance because they were not severely disabled enough and that they would receive rehabilitation services instead. The directors of the state programs, already overwhelmed with trying to implement the disability determination process, did not share this optimistic view. Even under the best of conditions, their programs could not accommodate the numbers of people who were applying for disability insurance. The state directors therefore hoped to work out an arrangement by which certain applicants would be screened from further consideration for rehabilitation services. Accordingly, the agency would not have to reject as many people for services and would save some of the counselors' valuable time.

The Social Security Administration proved more than happy to oblige. Working closely with the state directors, Arthur Hess and his associates developed procedures to refer only motivated disability applicants from the determination process to the state vocational rehabilitation programs. In 1959, the Social Security Administration came to an agreement with the Office of Vocational Rehabilitation that the vocational rehabilitation program would not have to deal with disability applicants who were over the age of fifty-five, bedridden, institutionalized, mentally ill with negative prognosis, or who had an impairment that was worsening.[12]

Thus, as early as 1959, the state disability determination units ceased being recruiting stations for the vocational rehabilitation program. That also happened to be the year that Congress held hearings on the operation of the new Social Security Disability Insurance program, at which Social Security official Robert Ball testified on the link between rehabilitation and disability benefits. When asked by Congressman Burr Harrison how many disability insurance applicants had actually been rehabilitated, Ball admitted that the number was small. It turned out that less than one thousand potential disability beneficiaries out of perhaps 1.5 million referrals had been rehabilitated.[13]

In the fall of 1963, Ball, now commissioner of Social Security, reported on vocational rehabilitation in the same negative terms. During fiscal 1963, the vocational rehabilitation agencies interviewed 456,000 disability applicants for possible rehabilitation, out of which they accepted 48,800. That same year, the vocational rehabilitation agencies completed work on 10,200 cases referred from the social security program, of which they managed to rehabilitate successfully only 5,600.[14] Ball's testimony made vocational rehabilitation look like a long funnel: Social Security poured nearly half a million clients into the wide end; about five thousand of those clients (1 percent) trickled out the other end.

Undeterred by the statistics or by compelling historical evidence, Congress in 1965 offered the states money from the social security trust fund for rehabilitating disability insurance applicants. When the Supplemental Security Income program began in 1974, Congress moved under the comfortable cover of precedent to spend more money, this time from the general revenues, to rehabilitate welfare recipients. The notion of rehabilitating people who wanted workers' compensation, social security, or welfare glided from generation to generation along a track greased with political promise, untempered by experience.

The numbers in 1978 looked only a little better than they had in 1963. In fiscal 1978, the state vocational rehabilitation agencies served 154,541 social security and federal welfare beneficiaries. They rehabilitated 12,268 people at an average cost of $7,976. As a result of rehabilitation, 6,346 people left the benefit rolls.[15]

By this time, many regarded the effort to rehabilitate disability benefits with some suspicion, and they began to scrutinize it more closely. Representative James Burke of Massachusetts, who chaired the Subcommittee on Social Security of the House Ways and Means Committee, suggested that the practice of giving money to the states to rehabilitate social security beneficiaries be changed. As matters stood, the states received money, more than $100 million in fiscal 1981 for the 226,035 beneficiaries deemed to be eligible, without regard to the outcome of the expenditures. In other words, the states spent the money without any further accountability.[16]

During the Carter years, the General Accounting Office, the Office of Management and Budget, and the Department of Health, Education, and Welfare all proposed changes in the process. One idea was to pay the states only when they made a successful rehabilitation; another was to take administrative control away from the rehabilitation bureaucracy and give it to the Social Security bureaucracy. Congress proved reluctant to disturb the existing arrangement, however, and no changes were made.[17]

The Reagan administration moved more quickly. The Reagan administration held no brief for the rehabilitation agencies; indeed, it hoped to fold rehabilitation into a social services block grant. In a typically forthright article, David Stockman wrote in 1975 that "explicitly service-oriented programs [such as vocational rehabilitation] that fall under the social spending umbrella have yet to demonstrate any effectiveness and are most notable for their almost random distribution of benefits among a tiny fraction of the formally entitled population." In August 1981, as part of the Omnibus Budget Reconciliation Act, the Reagan administration followed Stockman's advice and changed the system of rehabilitating social security beneficiaries.[18]

Under the new system, only after a beneficiary accomplished nine continuous months of employment at a rate of pay specified by the Social Security Administration would a state vocational rehabilitation agency be reimbursed with federal money. The law allowed private rehabilitation agencies to participate in the effort and gave the commissioner of Social Security the authority to determine whether it was rehabilitation or simply the passage of time that allowed the person to return to work. The Social Security Administration estimated that this new, stringent program would cost $3.5 million (or less than 3 percent of the previous program) in 1982. Creation of this program meant that policymakers had tempered their expectations about rehabilitation applicants for disability insurance.[19]

As already pointed out, America has two generations of income-maintenance programs, and neither has established a successful relationship with the vocational rehabilitation program. Income maintenance continues to predominate over rehabilitation in disability policy.

Costs versus benefits

Despite this failed relationship, vocational rehabilitation has developed into a billion-dollar-a-year federal commitment. It has, in effect, discovered a group of the handicapped that are not served by the other programs and created a means of preparing them for employment. What are the elements in the program's history that have led to its success?

People do not regard vocational rehabilitation as a welfare program, and that is one reason for its success. Vocational rehabilitation officials portray rehabilitation as the antithesis of welfare. Where welfare fosters dependence, rehabilitation promotes independence. Welfare represents a net cost to society; vocational rehabilitation is an investment in society's future. Vocational rehabilitation, in other words, holds the same promise as do the other forms of social services that have so often been directed at the poor in an effort to end the welfare "mess."

To measure the costs of dependency and as a means of illustrating the distinction between rehabilitation and welfare, program officials seized upon a crude form of cost–benefit analysis that first appeared in the 1920s and became one of the program's trademarks. Since the cost–benefit analysis showed that the program returned more to society than it cost, the officials argued that the program paid for itself and therefore deserved public support. Here was a program, they contended, that turned potential welfare recipients into taxpayers.

The cost–benefit rhetoric of vocational rehabilitation persisted from the era of Warren Harding to the time of Ronald Reagan. Ovetta Culp Hobby, President Eisenhower's secretary of Health, Education, and Welfare, defended the program in 1953 by claiming that it cost $600 a year to maintain someone on public assistance but only $560 to rehabilitate the average person into gainful employment. Further, for each dollar the government contributed to vocational rehabilitation, it received $10 in federal taxes alone. In 1952 the federal government spent $19.7 million on rehabilitation and rehabilitated 64,000 people. Within a year, these people paid more than $10 million in federal income taxes, and within a few more years they repaid the government's investment ten times over. Hobby concluded that vocational rehabilitation was a better buy than "the most golden of gilt-edged stocks. I have used this argument because all too often the layman . . . thinks of this program as only a Good Samaritan program . . . but it's also a very practical Samaritan endeavor and deserves respect."[20]

Hobby's Democratic predecessors had spoken in exactly the same way about the program. In 1949, Oscar Ewing, who headed the Federal Security Agency for President Truman and was fiercely in favor of passage of national health insurance, noted that in the past year the program had rehabilitated more than 53,000 disabled men and women who had increased their earnings from approximately $18 million earned in "unsuitable" jobs to $86 million "derived from suitable employment." This group would pay $5 million in federal taxes. Furthermore, "they will continue paying Federal and state taxes, rather than consuming them."[21]

The cost–benefit argument became a potent political weapon for the vocational rehabilitation program. When Congress threatened to cut federal money for vocational rehabilitation in 1953, the director of the program argued that such a cut would mean a loss of more than $1 million in federal taxes and an increase of more than half a million dollars in welfare costs. It also would prevent handicapped people who would otherwise be clients of the program from earning $10 million in their first year of employment after rehabilitation.[22]

Nearly twenty years later, a congressional report noted that vocational rehabilitation returned more money than it cost: "Conservative estimates of the ratio of benefits to costs have ranged between 8:1 and 35:1." The agency's annual report for fiscal 1981 made the same claims, estimating a return of ten dollars for every one dollar spent on the program and substantial savings in public assistance costs.[23]

As economists got better at cost–benefit analysis, however, more questions arose about the validity of the vocational rehabilitation figures, which gave a scientific gloss to a humanitarian enterprise. The impressive displays of the program's effectiveness, which assessed the average returns to the program, missed the real issue: on average the returns might be high, but such a finding failed to show the return on a particular client. Nor did it make clear whether investing another dollar in the program would return more than a dollar to society. According to the economists, decisions should be based on the effectiveness of what might be called the discretionary dollar – not the first dollar or an average of all the dollars, but the very last or "marginal" dollar spent.

Other questions arose about the cost–benefit analysis. How, for example, could it be determined whether the gains in a person's income after rehabilitation stemmed from the rehabilitation? They might have come from an improvement in the economy. In conducting their cost–benefit analyses, the vocational rehabilitation programs assigned the value of zero to a beneficiary's prerehabilitation wages and took all the credit for the wages he earned after rehabilitation. For an educated person, who might well have secured a job without the agency's help, this evaluation overstated the benefits of the program. In addition, negative events needed to be taken into account: An economic downturn might cut a person's working life short, particularly if the person suffered from a lingering impairment; people became ill; people decided to retire; and people got fired. Far from taking these effects into account, the officials simply assumed that a rehabilitated worker would remain at the job until retirement. In so doing, they overstated the benefit. In addition, the officials understated the costs of rehabilitation because they never attempted to answer the hypothetical question that the economists posed: What would a person have done with his time if he had not gone to see the rehabilitation counselor and what would the counselor have done with his time if that client had not come to see him?[24]

Although the cost–benefit analyses looked rigorous and sounded impressive, program officials never intended them to be analytic tools of policy analysis. Rather than analysis, it would be more appropriate to label the cost–benefit studies as demonstrations or illustrations. As such, the cost–benefit studies resembled the case histories that were another early staple of program literature, such as *Courage Facing Handicaps,* written in the 1920s to "give a picture of the new hope that vocational rehabilitation brings and to provide a storehouse of inspiration."[25]

To gather the evidence for these case studies and the cost–benefit demonstrations, the agency had to exercise close control over cases and had to be able to capture the results in statistical form. The agency accomplished these objectives by designing an elaborate series of status codes that described a client's progress through the agency and listed the services he received. In today's program, for example, a referral elicits the code 00; when an application is acknowledged, the code changes to 02. When the beneficiary receives counseling, he has a 14 status; when he undertakes trial employment, he progresses to a 22 status. When a person ends his association with the agency, his case receives a final or closure code.[26]

The objective of this elaborate exercise is to get as many "26s" (people successfully placed in employment) as possible. The search for the 26 drives the vocational rehabilitation program. The agency, therefore, does best by not spending money on cases in which the probability of reaching status 26, of placing someone in employment for sixty days, is low; the more "28s" (people who receive services but do not end up with a job), the more money that the agency wastes. The more money it wastes, the lower the average returns on the program and the worse the results of the cost–benefit analysis.

The program's operating statistics show the success of this effort. In 1960, the program spent about $80 million; in 1973, on the eve of the passage of a major new rehabilitation law, the program spent about $730 million. In thirteen years, the program grew by more than 800 percent, well above the growth of federal expenditures, the gross national product, or the rate of inflation. Between the 1920s and the 1970s, the average annual number of successful closures rose from 4,338 to 300,000. Beginning in 1971, the rehabilitation caseload contained more than one million people.[27]

Over the years, then, program supporters have successfully employed a large or macro argument for the expansion of vocational rehabilitation based on statistics that show the program returns more to society than it costs; they also have produced a considerable volume of micro, anecdotal, or case study evidence that illustrates its effectiveness and the correctness of its approach to the problem of disability.

The fragmented response to vocational rehabilitation

Another reason for the program's success has nothing to do with distinguishing the program from welfare and everything to do with politics – in particular, with accommodating the interests of congressmen and of interest groups such as the blind or disabled veterans.

The influence of politics may be seen in projects that concentrate their benefits in a particular congressional district. When President Reagan signed a rehabilitation law on February 22, 1984, for instance, he authorized the director of the National Institute of Handicapped Research to establish a research and training center for the Pacific Basin in the Rehabilitation Hospital in Hawaii. The proposal originated in the Senate, and the House acceded to it in conference. The conference committee included Hawaii's Senator Spark Matsunaga.[28]

Special interest politics of this sort tend to rest on a division among impairments, as well as on the strategic dispersal of the centers' locations. For example, grants are awarded to spinal cord injury centers, centers for rheumatoid arthritis, or centers for the treatment of epilepsy. Like the other pillars of the rehabilitation program's success, this one has a long history supporting it that is well illustrated by the way that private charities fund searches for the cure of particular impairments – the March of Dimes, a primary example, illustrates the focus on an impairment, polio in this case, and the appeal of cure over care – rather than disability in general. Such a strategy has an obvious disadvantage in that it tends to exclude people with serious yet politically unpopular impairments, and for this reason it has created some concern on the part of rehabilitation officials. One vocational rehabilitation official has complained that various groups work "in little side bills" and advocate "special activities," leaving the basic rehabilitation program with few defenders. Handicapped activists also decry the tendency of rehabilitation, both public and private, to be organized around impairments and in that way to emphasize differences among the handicapped. Nonetheless, the political benefits of fragmentation, that is, increased appropriations, outweigh its social costs; the practice continues.[29]

Special treatment for the blind is a classic example of fragmentation in vocational rehabilitation and in disability policy generally. When Congress holds rehabilitation hearings, it often hears first from representatives of the blind. In fact, because of divisions within the blind community, there are usually two spokesmen for the blind, one representing the National Federation for the Blind and another representing the American Foundation for the Blind, Incorporated. This special attention stems from regulations governing the vocational rehabilitation program that have always allowed the states to maintain separate rehabilitation facilities for the blind. Today, thirty-two states avail themselves of this option. No other group has this privilege.[30]

The reasons for the special treatment of the blind are not clear. Possibly it is because the unimpaired can easily imagine and sympathize with their plight; unlike mental illness, for example, the state of blindness involves little stigma. Possibly it is because blindness has existed since the beginning of history, so that the blind have had more time to secure a place for themselves as legitimate objects of aid from the state. The very fact that their impairment is less disabling than others gives the blind advantages in political organization.

Whatever the reasons, the blind enjoy special privileges in the American social welfare system. The blind have always held the status of the "worthy" poor. The Social Security Act specified that only the blind and no other physically impaired group should qualify for welfare. The blind also benefit from special legislation that does not apply to other handicapped groups. For example, the Randolph–Sheppard Act, passed in 1936, provides employment opportunities for the handicapped to work as vendors in snack bars or to operate newstands in federal buildings. The disability freeze made it easier for a blind person to have his benefits frozen than for a person with any other type of impairment. In this spirit, all parts of the vocational rehabilitation program, even the most recent, have given the blind preferential treatment. A recent change in the rehabilitation law, for example, enacted special measures to benefit "older blind individuals."[31]

Special privileges also accrue to veterans who have privileged access to rehabilitation services. Civilians have one vocational rehabilitation program, veterans have others. This split between veterans and civilians runs throughout the American social welfare system. In general, veterans are entitled to more generous benefits and their programs are older and better established than civilian programs.

Rehabilitation was no exception to the pattern. The veterans' rehabilitation program preceded the civilian program and offered its participants more generous terms. In the summer of 1918, Congress passed the Soldiers Rehabilitation Act and empowered the Federal Board for Vocational Education to rehabilitate disabled veterans. Returning soldiers who joined the rehabilitation program received special training allowances, which were so attractive that many entered the rehabilitation program just to receive the money, and others lengthened their training period. Before the program ended, it spent nearly $650 million, with which it managed to rehabilitate only about 10 percent of the 329,000 veterans who participated.[32]

When World War II arrived, President Roosevelt made an effort to introduce a unified rehabilitation program for civilians and veterans. He sent a special message to Congress to make his intentions clear. Because veterans groups thought they deserved preferential treatment, they pressed for a special program for those injured in military service. An observer visiting Washington at the end of 1942 said that the bills then before Congress "seemed to be heading in different directions," with one putting veterans' rehabilitation in the Veterans Administration and the other proposing a unified rehabilitation service, along the lines suggested by Roosevelt. By the spring of 1943 the veterans had secured passage of their bill, which retained the distinctions between veterans and civilians. "I have certainly raised no contest," wrote an official of the civilian program in a letter to his counterpart in the Veterans Administration. He realized that even President Roosevelt could not match the political muscle of the veterans' groups. So World War II ended, as had World War I, with an agreement to maintain separate rehabilitation programs.[33]

In the postwar period, however, the civilian and the veterans' programs flourished. During World War II, for example, the civilian program was allowed to spend federal money to purchase medical care, and the federal share in the program grew beyond the traditional 50 percent. Not challenging the special privileges of veterans appeared to pay dividends, and the veterans' program also grew during the war and postwar years. In 1962, for example, Congress broadened the program to embrace veterans who served in peacetime.[34]

Professionalization

Even as vocational rehabilitation program administrators played politics, they strove to bring a professional ethic and approach to the rehabilitation process. They called rehabilitation "an individualized process." Since rehabilitation had no "production line," it demanded professional counselors who could oversee each individual case. Professionalization of the program's counselors and of its services became another factor in the program's success, which, like the other factors, was apparent quite early in the program's history.[35]

The desire to make rehabilitation counselors into professionals permeated the program from its beginnings. "Effective placement," said W. R. Tippet of Milwaukee in an address before the National Civilian Rehabilitation Conference of 1925, is "not an amateur job." Others urged that rehabilitation be conducted in a professional atmosphere. "One cannot [work] in a dirty, noisy office where the men stand at a desk with a line of applicants trailing off behind them," an early analyst of the program wrote. Effective rehabilitation demanded an attractive office, "very much like the office of the better type of physician."[36]

Despite these aspirations, the states at first treated rehabilitation counselors as they did their other employees. "In some of the states, political considerations have outweighed professional qualifications," lamented a federal official. A 1938 field report from a federal agent in Illinois illustrated just how poor some of the state rehabilitation programs were. "In view of the fact that there is no supervisor in charge of the program . . . although the need is urgent for improvement . . . it will not be wise to attempt anything this year."[37]

Spurred by the example of the National Institutes of Health and by competition from the Department of Labor, federal officials in the late 1940s contemplated creating special rehabilitation fellowships and training courses. Better-trained counselors would be more professional, and they would bring credit to the program by dealing more responsibly and effectively with the problems of the handicapped. Nothing much happened, however. Even by 1949, vocational rehabilitation remained almost invisible. For example, Senator Chapman received a letter from a widowed woman with five children, including a handicapped son, which stated, "If I should be unable to work, or die, I do not know what would happen to my handicapped son." One of Chapman's staffers, searching for a federal program that would help the woman, called a friend in the Federal Security Administration. Only then did they discover vocational rehabilitation.[38]

To remedy this situation, Oscar Ewing, the Federal Security Administrator, chose Mary Switzer to head, and invigorate, the vocational rehabilitation program in 1950. Switzer had served as a staff assistant to Ewing and his predecessors in the 1930s and 1940s, participating in the establishment of the social security program and the creation of medical research and hospital construction programs. Through these efforts and her many contacts with the leaders of the medical profession, Switzer had developed respect for a professional approach to social programs. She believed that to perfect rehabilitation counselors required the same tools as those given to the doctors: advanced training, and research grants from the federal government. She set out to improve the program along those lines.

Switzer cajoled the Eisenhower administration into sponsoring major new vocational rehabilitation legislation in 1954 to put the program on a professional basis. The legislation initiated new types of federal grants to establish professional training programs in universities, to subsidize research on rehabilitation methods, and to enable counselors to attend the new programs at public expense. As early as fiscal 1955, the program had initiated more than 1,000 traineeships.[39]

With Switzer firmly in control, the training programs continued to grow. By 1965, about forty colleges or universities offered graduate degrees in rehabilitation counseling; by 1980, the number approached one hundred. The vocational rehabilitation budget for training stood at $30.5 million in 1984; universities received an additional $15.4 million in federal funds for rehabilitation research and training centers.[40]

The education and training programs relied on federally sponsored traineeships to attract students and on federal grants to cover operating expenses. These programs produced so many trained counselors that a master's degree in rehabilitation counseling became a prerequisite for entering the profession. The 1954 law, therefore, elevated rehabilitation counseling to a profession that had been defined, created, and paid for by the federal government.[41]

This process of professionalization fed upon itself. Vocational rehabilitation counselors used their degrees as barriers to keep others, whom they perceived as less desirable, out of the program. In their eyes, the program became the profession. By 1976, the profession contained as many as 19,000 members, nearly three-quarters of whom worked for the state–federal vocational rehabilitation program.

All of this educational activity led to a specialized rehabilitation literature, as academics in rehabilitation counseling and rehabilitation psychology perceived the need for journals in which to distribute their findings to their colleagues. Two researchers have identified 1,413 documents relating to rehabilitation counselors that were written between 1958 and 1968; they have discovered more than 2,000 references to rehabilitation counseling and service delivery. The sheer bulk of this literature, much of it written by people with doctorates in rehabilitation, served to make the study of rehabilitation a legitimate academic enterprise.[42]

Viewed in this context of the program's history, the growth of the professional literature helped to improve the quality of rehabilitation counseling and to protect against the abuses of the program's early years. Judged in its modern context, the literature can be faulted for its self-serving quality. For example, the leading textbook in the field reports that "extensive research strongly indicates a need for rehabilitation counselors trained at the master's degree level" and "clients served by . . . professionally prepared rehabilitation counselors are more satisfied with the services they receive." These satisfied clients "maintain a suitable level of vocational adjustment at follow-up." The self-interest makes an outside observer skeptical of the research, and that, in turn, raises questions about the inherent value of professionalization.[43]

The modern conception of the rehabilitation counselor illustrates the strengths and weaknesses of the professional approach. As a recipient of postgraduate education, the rehabilitation counselor is now expected to perform many specialized functions. He serves as a "record keeper, administrative supervisor, correspondent, budget analyst, program evaluator, consultant, job developer, and public relations expert." He finds cases, determines eligibility, selects the right mix of services, and places clients in jobs. The counselor's success in carrying out these responsibilities, according to authority George Wright, depends upon his "professional abilities coupled with planning, coordinating, and managing skills."[44]

Perhaps the most important of these various counselor skills is marketing. Rehabilitation counselors must market the program among health and welfare institutions and draw clients from the web of public and private health and education organizations. "If we just hung out a shingle, almost no one would line up for our services," says Peter Griswold of the Michigan vocational rehabilitation program. Once clients arrive, the counselor engages in a second type of marketing that involves preparing clients for the labor market. In this highly professional role, the counselor scrutinizes their motivation, goals, and "overall self-concept." To accomplish this difficult task, the counselor acts as psychologist, economist, and educator as he interprets the client's employment history, his interpersonal relations, his educational history, and his "cultural, social, and home background."[45]

Because the rehabilitation counselors have such wide-ranging responsibilities, they wield a great deal of power over the client and over the program. This discretion on the part of the counselors distinguishes vocational rehabilitation from other disability programs such as workers' compensation or disability insurance. As the director of the Maryland vocational program notes, rehabilitation is not "an entitlement." Clients can be turned away by the counselor. To ensure that the counselors make the right decisions it is necessary to institute "hard-nosed management . . . to train the hell out of your staff and to give them latitude." This latitude has been used to fill the agency's rolls with motivated clients who, by achieving success in the labor market, also bring the agency success. Counselor discretion, which is legitimized by the counselor's professional training, becomes the point at which the elements in the agency's success are joined: the strict control over cases and the wide range of the counselor's responsibility.[46]

One last aspect of the program's operation requires elaboration. As one supervisor of the California program notes, "Nothing much happens to [the clients] here." The vocational rehabilitation program only conducts relatively brief interviews in its own offices; otherwise it buys services from other agencies. Since 1943, the program has had congressional funding to purchase not only training for its clients but also medical care. As an agency that buys things from public and private practitioners, the vocational rehabilitation program enjoys the popularity that comes to any enterprise that spreads its money around. Local trade schools, universities, and hospitals all have reasons to support the program.[47]

Each of these elements – cost–benefit analysis, case studies, an accommodation to the politics of disability, the creation of a self-sustaining professional culture, and the ability to purchase services from other agencies – has helped to define the program. Each of these things reinforces the natural appeal of the program as a source of hope rather than a cause of dependency. Each of these things causes people to excuse the bungled relations between the vocational rehabilitation program and workers' compensation and the failed efforts to link vocational rehabilitation and the Social Security Disability Insurance program. Each of these things has helped the program to win increased appropriations and wider responsibilities.

By 1965, for example, the federal government assumed a uniform share of 75 percent of the program's costs. In 1967 and in 1968 Congress passed major new legislation that not only hung new ornaments on the program, such as grants for the construction of rehabilitation facilities, but also increased the federal share in the program to 80 percent (in 1968). The laws also brought new participants into the rehabilitation process. In 1968, for example, Congress established a new program of vocational evaluation and work adjustment to serve the disadvantaged in addition to the physically disabled. The vocational rehabilitation program had, at least for the moment, transcended its original purpose, which was solely to rehabilitate workers' compensation clients, and become a major social program.[48]

A turn for the worse

By the early 1970s, the vocational rehabilitation program, like other social welfare programs, reached a time of transition. In a few years, social welfare expenditures would peak and begin a gradual decline. The program never did better than the 361,000 rehabilitations it achieved in 1974. By 1982, this number had fallen to 226,924. Applications for vocational rehabilitation and acceptance rates also began a downward trend. In 1975, for example, 885,737 people applied to the program and 534,491 (63.8 percent) were accepted. By contrast, in 1982, only 564,443 people applied, and the acceptance rate fell to 56.1 percent. The program managed to rehabilitate only 216,231 people in 1983; this was a drop of 4.7 percent from the previous year and the lowest number of rehabilitations in the past fifteen years.[49]

What had happened? The crisis in rehabilitation had its roots both in general developments that affected nearly all social welfare programs and in circumstances that were particular to the vocational rehabilitation program. The optimism of the 1960s had given way to the realism and pessimism of the mid-1970s.

One condemnation of the 1960s or Great Society approach that proved so favorable for vocational rehabilitation and other social welfare programs was that it involved "throwing money" at problems without considering the fundamental barriers to advancement in American society. By the mid-1970s, for example, it no longer looked as though blacks and other disadvantaged groups could be transformed by government programs into members of the middle class. Failure of the economy to grow as rapidly as before limited the number of new jobs available and put pressure on the federal budget. The dramatic entrance of women and the members of the baby-boom generation into the labor force exacerbated the problem. The disadvantaged turned increasingly to social welfare programs for help only to discover that the nation no longer believed it could afford to support a growing welfare establishment and still make good on its other obligations. Defense and relatively protected entitlement programs such as social security laid claim to diminishing federal funds. Vocational rehabilitation, not an open-ended entitlement in the federal or state budget, was far more vulnerable to budget constraints than were the other disability programs such as workers' compensation and disability insurance.

Further, people began to question the efficacy of counseling and training as a tool of social reform. A number of influential social commentators, who believed that money was a far more effective tool of social advancement than counseling or training, urged the government to "cash out" the service programs.[50] As a program that relied heavily on counseling and training, vocational rehabilitation was a prime target for "cashing out."

Although Congress never went that far, it failed to increase appropriations to match the inflation rate, and, in a direct rebuke of the program, it withdrew the social security subsidy in 1981. The real value of federal funds spent on vocational rehabilitation declined by 31 percent between 1974 and 1982. In fiscal 1981, vocational rehabilitation program expenditures had included $87,050,000 to rehabilitate the beneficiaries of disability insurance and $37 million to rehabilitate welfare beneficiaries. In 1982 this money disappeared.[51]

More than any other factor, however, a 1973 congressional mandate to serve the severely disabled accounted for the decline in the vocational rehabilitation program. The origins of this mandate revealed the complexity of disability policymaking.

Because of the calculus of success that program administrators had created, rehabilitation counselors had always favored those with mild as opposed to those with more severe impairments in selecting their caseloads. As the handicapped became more visible in the 1960s, the exclusion of the severely handicapped from the vocational rehabilitation program became more noticeable. Handicapped students at Berkeley expressed grievances felt by many when they argued that the vocational rehabilitation program screened out applicants who were not "obvious winners" on demographic or educational grounds. The agency called this practice screening out the undermotivated, but the handicapped regarded it as skimming the cream off the top of the applicant pool or "creaming." The handicapped also objected to the way in which counselors consigned them to low-paying or low-status jobs.

The vocational rehabilitation agency, in its defense, noted the limitations placed on it by federal and state regulations. Rehabilitating someone with a severe disability such as paraplegia cost ten times as much and took three times as long as working with the average case, but netted the agency no greater reward than any other case. Why should the agency take on the tough cases when so many people wanted the agency's services, and success came faster, easier, and in greater proportions when those most in need were excluded from the program or taken only in very limited numbers?[52]

At the same time that the severely disabled were criticizing the vocational rehabilitation program from outside the rehabilitation establishment, members of the establishment, such as the state administrators active in the National Rehabilitation Association, were criticizing the program from within. At issue was the lumping of the vocational rehabilitation program with the welfare bureaucracy. Few of the rehabilitation administrators wished to be viewed as part of the "welfare mess" of the 1970s.

What had happened was that in 1967 the program took what its supporters later realized was a wrong turn when Secretary of Health, Education, and Welfare John Gardner created the Social and Rehabilitation Service, uniting welfare, vocational rehabilitation, and other social services into one large federal agency, under the direction of Mary Switzer, within his department. Gardner wanted to bring the positive approach of rehabilitation to the problems of welfare dependency. This unification soon strained the rehabilitation program as, more and more, the rise in the welfare rolls became a problem for vocational rehabilitation to solve. State program leaders would have preferred to keep their customary distance from a problem that was so close to the nation's surface. After Mary Switzer died at the end of 1971, another problem developed. Without Switzer, vocational rehabilitation was no longer considered the central program within the Social and Rehabilitation Service and it became buried within a large bureaucracy.[53]

When Congress turned to the matter of reauthorizing the vocational rehabilitation program in the early 1970s, it faced a difficult situation. Because of the changed social welfare climate, it could not simply add special provisions for the severely disabled to the program without cutting other parts of the program and thereby incurring the anger of constituents and interest groups affected by the cuts. Furthermore, election year politics in 1972 and the showdown between the president and Congress in the Watergate years had boosted what had been a quiet debate among government agencies, congressional committees, and private interest groups into a media event. Vocational rehabilitation made the newspapers and Walter Cronkite.

Congressman John Brademas from South Bend, Indiana, took the lead in developing a new rehabilitation bill. By October 1972, he and Senators Jennings Randolph and Alan Cranston had negotiated a bill, quickly passed by their colleagues, that made three major changes in the vocational rehabilitation program. It removed the program from the Social and Rehabilitation Service and created a Rehabilitation Services Administration within the Department of Health, Education, and Welfare. It mandated that priority be given to the severely disabled, rather than to the mildly impaired or the culturally disadvantaged. It started a new program of independent living services. Unlike the traditional program, independent living services prepared a severely handicapped person for a life in the community, not necessarily for a job.

Then, in a stunning break with vocational rehabilitation tradition, which held that presidents never interfere with "do-good" legislation such as vocational rehabilitation, Richard Nixon, with an election approaching, vetoed the bill. In March 1973, however, the new Congress passed a rehabilitation bill that amounted to a copy of the old bill, with only the level of the appropriations changed. By this time, the media had begun to portray the bill as a challenge to the Nixon administration over the level of federal spending. Congress picked vocational rehabilitation as the object of this challenge because of its political appeal. As one congressman put it, "After all, there can't be too many folks who want to go on record as opposing aid to the crippled."[54]

Nixon vetoed the bill, setting up a dramatic showdown. On April 3, 1973, the Senate failed to override the veto by a 60–39 vote. Beaten but not defeated, Congress produced yet another vocational rehabilitation bill, passed in August and signed by the president in September 1973.

The protracted process yielded a bill that signaled a major change in vocational rehabilitation. For the first time, the law emphasized serving the severely disabled. As a House committee stated, "additional emphasis should be placed on the vocational rehabilitation of the severely disabled, rather than those individuals who can readily be placed in employment." With this language, Congress and the program's supporters hoped to ease the program from the 1960s, when it had drifted toward serving people "handicapped in the social sense . . . rather than . . . physically or mentally," into the 1970s. The change was traditional in its emphasis on the physically handicapped but radical in its recognition of a new group among the physically handicapped. Senator Alan Cranston explained the bill as an attempt "to eliminate the creaming and shift the focus to harder cases."[55]

The act attempted to build a degree of accountability into the program's outreach to the severely disabled. As a condition of the receipt of benefits, the states were required to submit plans that described methods to be used to expand and improve services to those with the most severe handicaps. If more people applied to the program than the program could serve, the state vocational rehabilitation agencies had to show the order of selection and to prove that the severely handicapped came first in the line.

Just who qualified as severely disabled? In typical congressional fashion, the law left the general concept vague and included many specific examples. The general concept of severe disability was a disability so serious as to limit substantially a person's ability to function in his family and community. The law specifically mentioned, among many impairments, amputation, blindness, cancer, cystic fibrosis, deafness, heart disease, hemiplegia, mental retardation, mental illness, multiple sclerosis, muscular dystrophy, neurological disorder, and paraplegia.[56]

Until the final version, the bill included provisions for independent living services. Independent living referred to a new outcome for the rehabilitation process, no longer a job, but rather increased self-reliance. Getting someone out of an institution and into the community might qualify. The new outcome made particular sense when applied to the severely disabled, a group for whom employment might not be a realistic goal.[57]

Nixon disagreed strongly enough to have vetoed the bill twice. Independent living, he believed, smacked of the false promises of the 1960s that made it so difficult to keep the budget in balance. He said that this provision would divert the program from its vocational objectives and "seriously jeopardize" the goals of the program.[58]

Even without independent living, the 1973 vocational rehabilitation law significantly altered the program. By the late 1970s, those identified as severely disabled accounted for more than half of the vocational rehabilitation caseload. In the state of Michigan, for example, 53.8 percent of those served and 49 percent of those rehabilitated during fiscal year 1982 were listed as severely disabled. This new focus on the severely disabled removed one of the vocational rehabilitation agency's traditional safety valves – that is, its ability to take easy cases, generate impressive results, and, as a result, justify increased appropriations. Coupled with the decline in appropriations in "real," uninflated dollars, the focus on the severely disabled helped to bring about the decline in the success rate of vocational rehabilitation.[59]

A new approach

The 1973 law fundamentally changed the relationship between the disabled and the vocational rehabilitation counselors. The program's clients have now become its consumers. The handicapped enter the program, look at the samples that the counselors have to offer, and then decide which of the program's services they will consume. This change challenges the traditional professional conception of rehabilitation. Counselors no longer practice what some authorities, such as Professor Joseph Stubbins, call the clinical model of rehabilitation. Analogies between rehabilitation and medicine, advanced so heroically by Switzer, no longer have the same validity. To use Stubbins's words, the counselor no longer "dominates" the client; instead, the counselor consults the handicapped, and together they formulate a course of action.[60]

To ensure that every handicapped individual had "an opportunity to participate in the decision making," the 1973 law mandated the use of an individualized written rehabilitation plan, signed by the counselor and the client. This piece of paper served as the consumer's warranty.[61]

Congress also initiated client-assistance programs that established ombudsmen in the rehabilitation agencies to protect the rights of the consumer. Although begun as discretionary projects, these client-assistance programs became mandatory in 1984. A state with no client-assistance program forfeited its right to federal rehabilitation funds. Furthermore, these programs were required to be independent of the vocational rehabilitation program itself. Many states turned to the advocacy groups that developed to protect the rights of the mentally retarded to staff their client-assistance projects. In this manner, the client-assistance programs also became a source of legal advice that a disgruntled client could use to pursue his grievance through the courts.[62]

Individual written rehabilitation plans have become legal documents that contain claims that can be enforced in a court of law. These plans, which list services that the client must receive, are written in extremely explicit language. In Virginia, for example, the counselor and the client sign a document that says that "the vocational goal listed above is in keeping with your stated preferences . . . we have jointly concluded that employment opportunities are good in this field." If the client is dissatisfied, he knows that "he will be granted a fair hearing before the chief executive of the department or his designate." These plans, coupled with the client-assistance program, have created a new way of conducting rehabilitation, since the counselor no longer has total discretion over the client.[63]

Although many rehabilitation officials praise the written rehabilitation plans – "beautiful," is one agency director's comment – the new way of conducting rehabilitation exposes conflicts between the handicapped and the professional rehabilitation counselors, as the annals of the client-assistance program illustrate.[64] Some of the recorded complaints are to be expected in a large bureaucratic organization: The agency's secretary does a bad job of taking phone messages, and the clients cannot contact the counselor. Other complaints get to the heart of the conflict.

In February 1983, a woman began a course in automechanics under the auspices of the Michigan rehabilitation program. A month later, she agreed to transfer to the printing curriculum. She quickly grew unhappy and requested another shot at automobile mechanics. Her automobile mechanics instructor said that she lacked the ability to perform the basic functions of mechanics. Furthermore, because the woman suffered from a "borderline personality," agency officials thought that she might have a learning disability. The agency also recognized the importance of gender to the case. "It should be noted," according to the case narrative, "that the student in question is female and it is not clear to what extent this played a factor in her being terminated from the program. Very few women have entered the automechanics program and none have successfully completed it." How did the agency even begin to discern the boundary between ability and expectation, intrinsic barriers of personality and extrinsic walls of prejudice?

The same type of problem can arise at many levels. Another client, for example, wants to study philosophy only to be told that this does not represent a realistic vocational goal. The client, who has cerebral palsy, has made his way through college and now he wants a master's degree or possibly a doctorate in philosophy in order to teach. The agency has already paid to send this client to college and there are few openings for philosophy professors. Philosophy professors lecture, and people with cerebral palsy often have trouble speaking. This client's speech is impaired. "This impairment would most certainly hinder him in attempting to lecture."[65]

It might take a philosopher to untangle the many issues raised by this case. Does the agency have a right to limit a person's potential career because it wants a return from the money it has already invested? Do handicapped people have the same right to be unemployed philosophers as do able-bodied people? Why should a person with cerebral palsy receive special financial assistance to attend graduate school when other, able-bodied students do not receive this special help? If there is disagreement over the answers to these questions, what rights does the handicapped person have? Should he be allowed to use the client-assistance program to sue the government at the government's own expense? Do students have a right to be taught by a professor whose speech is unimparied? Does a university have the right not to hire someone who suffers from a speech impediment? Should the vocational rehabilitation agency become an advocate for this person and by extension open the way for others with the same impairment to enjoy the full rights of employment, or is it inappropriate for the agency to question the decisions of the labor market?

As these questions reveal, the potential for conflict between the handicapped community and the vocational rehabilitation program remains high. Counselors value their professional autonomy, and the handicapped community increasingly believes it possesses inherent rights. The process of psychological adjustment is antithetical to the concept of civil rights. The counselors and the handicapped often disagree over where the limitations of the handicapped end and the failures of society begin.[66]

Only the shared goal of employment mutes the conflict. The disabled individual hopes to gain valuable services from the program and, ultimately, a job. The counselor will be judged on the number of jobs he manages to obtain for his clients. The shared desire for a 26 closure unites the professionals and the handicapped.

In the 1950s and 1960s, the program could point to its tradition of success and avoid discussion of these difficult matters. That is no longer possible. Declining numbers of rehabilitations make the program's inherent conflicts more visible and more difficult to resolve. Today, the conflict between the program and the severely handicapped and the relationship of independent living to vocational rehabilitation occupy prominent places on the program's agenda. Not until program administrators resolve these issues will the program crisis come to an end.

Policymakers no longer lament the failure to blend workers' compensation and vocational rehabilitation, nor do they discuss links between vocational rehabilitation and social security disability insurance. That discussion appears to be over, relegated to history. Income maintenance predominates over rehabilitation as an approach to disability policy; no one seriously thinks the situation will change soon.

Ironically, the resurgence of conservatism has placed an emphasis on the inherent value of work and its superiority to government transfer payments as a solution to social problems. In other times, the vocational rehabilitation program might have benefited from this resurgence and become a center of the effort to substitute work for welfare among the handicapped. The focus on serving the severely disabled and the conflicts between professional autonomy and the civil rights of the handicapped have inhibited the program enough to prevent it from taking advantage of the situation.

Nonetheless, the federal government continues to spend more than a billion dollars a year on vocational rehabilitation. The vocational rehabilitation program, for all of its dilemmas and missed opportunities, still stands as the major "corrective" American disability program.

6. Toward independence

In 1925, a Detroit automobile manufacturer required employees with amputations to wear artificial limbs, not because the artificial limbs would help them work better but because of his concern "for the working morale of the men." The presence of a handicap made people uncomfortable. As two authorities on rehabilitation noted, "the young man whose hand is off at the wrist may not appear to good advantage; the disability is altogether too apparent to the discriminating employer of labor." The prevailing attitude at the time was that disabilities should be hidden.

Hiding disability to accommodate an able-bodied world applied to school as well as to the workplace. Public schools were not designed to accommodate the handicapped. They contained "long stairs to climb and desks that cannot be accommodated to [a] particular physical disability. . . . In fact, everything about the school is adjusted, and properly so, for the normal physical child." Because it was thought that the schools could not and should not educate the handicapped, the handicapped received education in more "appropriate" settings, such as hospitals. In this manner, a person born with a disability lived a life apart from the nation's mainstream.[1]

From the 1920s to the 1970s, the theme of separation predominated in all of the government's social welfare programs. Income-maintenance programs asked the handicapped to remove themselves from the labor force in order to receive government aid. Although politicians spoke hopefully of using the income-maintenance programs as vehicles to promote rehabilitation, political rhetoric seldom produced tangible gains. Vocational rehabilitation administrators prided themselves on their constructive, nonwelfare-oriented approach to disability, yet their program also asked the handicapped to separate themselves from society's mainstream by requiring them to act as clients in need of special assistance.

If the nation now wishes to end this separation and integrate the handicapped into society, policymakers need to discover another ap-

proach toward disability policy. Here the lessons learned by policymakers in other efforts to achieve integration become relevant. In 1962
welfare administrators announced a major campaign to bring the poor
into the nation's mainstream by providing welfare mothers with social
services. This approach resembled jump-starting a car. Education or
some other service would supply the spark that would cause welfare
recipients to overcome their disadvantages, realize their true potential,
and rise above poverty. After the jump-start, the government's services
would no longer be necessary; the disadvantaged could then take care
of themselves. This approach had the appeal of other "corrective"
responses. It purported to save the government money by cutting down
on the nation's long-term welfare bill. The nation's welfare rates continued to rise, however, even after the introduction of massive amounts
of social services. Little or no money was saved.

In the case of the handicapped, the jump-start approach has even
less chance to succeed. A handicapped person is different from an "able-
bodied person," just as a man is different from a woman. The handicapped person cannot be transformed into an able-bodied person by
vocational rehabilitation or any other government program. A policy
of hiding disabilities only makes for an inferior group of able-bodied
people. That does not mean, however, that handicapped people need
to live inferior lives in segregated facilities any more than blacks or
women must be segregated into inferior jobs or lives. Instead, the possibility exists of lessening the prejudice that stems from the way in
which employers misinterpret differences between the handicapped and
the rest of the population. Furthermore, instead of a jump-start, the
handicapped may need continuous assistance from the government,
but that does not mean that the assistance has to be at the expense of
their participation in the labor force. Instead, this assistance might
enable handicapped people to hold a job or to remain outside a costly
custodial institution.

Such a policy would require a more sophisticated approach to the
corrective response to disability than is embodied by vocational rehabilitation programs and other first-generation disability programs. To
emerge from the political arena, a program would require much more
than a simple appeal to saving welfare costs, for it would posit no
contradiction between being independent and receiving government
aid. In the twenties, the formative years of vocational rehabilitation,
such an approach would not have been politically feasible; at the time,

people viewed government assistance to the handicapped either as an exceptional event that occurred only once or as something limited to a few members of the worthy poor. Since then, however, our views of the government's role in the daily lives of all its citizens have changed, and the federal government's responsibilities have broadened to include the maintenance of people's incomes.

As people have reexamined the government's role and reconsidered the inherent capabilities of the handicapped, blacks, women and other minorities, new types of government programs have come into existence. In the field of disability, these civil rights and independent living programs amount to a second generation of corrective disability programs. This new generation of programs points the way to a major reform of disability policy.

Movement for disability rights

One measure of the way in which the world has changed since 1925 is the emergence of new formal policies toward the handicapped. The National Council on the Handicapped, a new federal agency, issued a National Policy for Persons with Disabilities in August 1983. Although written in general terms, it set a new direction for disability policy. It took as the goals of disability policy the achievement of "maximum life potential, self-reliance, independence, productivity, and equitable mainstream social participation in the most productive and least restrictive environment." It called for replacing "disincentives to employment and to full social involvement" with "a comprehensive system of independence incentives and investments in the productivity of persons with disabilities."[2]

The statement of the National Council on the Handicapped emphasizes that the civil rights of the handicapped are as important as their disability benefits. The approach of the earlier, income-maintenance programs stands in direct contrast. The Social Security Disability Insurance program equates disability with a failure to earn a minimum amount of money and therefore with a readiness for retirement. The very definition of disability connotes dependence on social welfare benefits. Similarly, workers' compensation defines a disabled person as one who has been damaged by an accident, implying that disabled people are flawed. Equitable mainstream participation assumes no contradiction between being handicapped and being employed, between being handicapped and functioning alongside the rest of the world.

The policy statement of the National Council on the Handicapped reflects the influence of a movement that has transformed the way that people think about disability. In place of the old impairment-oriented point of view (as in workers' compensation) or the wage-oriented point of view (as in disability insurance), a new generation of analysts asks policymakers to regard the disabled as an "oppressed minority group." John Gliedman and William Roth persuasively argue that the oppression of the handicapped takes such forms as prejudice and job discrimination. Just as some people react adversely to black people, so the "discovery that someone has epilepsy changes our sense of who he is" and we tend to view him as less capable than we would if he were "normal." As with epilepsy, so with other handicaps: a person becomes his or her handicap and suffers the resulting stigma.[3]

Gliedman and Roth's essential point is that the handicapped do not suffer from inherent deficits or deficiencies so much as society imposes those things on them. They admit that a condition such as blindness imposes obvious limits, yet they also believe that society unconsciously excludes the blind by not accommodating them in the design of buildings, transportation systems, and work requirements, practices, and procedures. Instead of creating an environment accessible to the blind, society segregates the blind and other members of the handicapped minority in special schools or special social programs. Not only does this treatment discriminate against the handicapped, it also restricts their independence by placing considerable authority over their lives in the hands of professional guardians. In this way, professionals dominate the handicapped. Further, the professionals, rather than the handicapped, "interpret the meaning of disability to society at large."[4]

Here is where Gliedman and Roth and others in the disability rights community part company with the intellectual tradition that has sustained America's disability programs such as the vocational rehabilitation program. The leaders of the vocational rehabilitation program regard the professional training of counselors and a professionalized approach toward the handicapped as virtues. Although Gliedman and Roth recognize vocational rehabilitation counselors as sources of "invaluable assistance," they also view them as sources of oppression who force the handicapped to adjust to a society whose very design prevents them from full participation. In a metaphorical sense, the counselors require the handicapped to wear artificial limbs, just as the automobile manufacturer did in the 1920s. They want the handicapped to pass as able-bodied citizens and in this way they perpetuate, even legitimate, the barriers that segregate the handicapped from the rest of society.[5]

Even more than rehabilitation counselors, doctors rob the handicapped of their independence. Most people interact with the medical system for short periods of time during which doctors diagnose, treat, and cure their diseases. The handicapped, by way of contrast, often deal with doctors over long periods of time and come away uncured. Although the disabled often owe their survival to medicine, they become long-term patients, dependent on the doctor but unable to take advantage of his ability to cure. Doctors who liberate others create dependence for the handicapped. Gliedman and Roth note that these "perpetual patients remain 'stuck in time,' citizens of a therapeutic state."[6]

Disability programs rely on professionals to admit applicants, to provide services to them, and to determine the extent of those services. To cite just one example, gaining admission to the disability insurance program requires the certification of a doctor. Constantina Saflios-Rothschild, a sociologist who laid the foundation for Gliedman and Roth's work, argues that behind the emphasis on professionalism in disability policy lies the popular notion that "disability implies biological inferiority." People perceive the handicapped as less intelligent, less able to make the right decisions, and therefore less able to determine their own lives than the nonhandicapped.[7]

Harlan Hahn, a political scientist at the University of Southern California, has traced the development and the policy implications of viewing the disabled as a minority group. He refers to this view as the "minority model." Previously, Hahn states, thinking about the handicapped centered on their functional limitations (the "functional limitations model"), and public policy focused exclusively on the problems of the handicapped individual. The model accepted the environment as a given. The minority model, in contrast, recognizes that the environment itself is subject to policy decisions. According to this view, public policy should not help individuals to cope with the existing environment so much as it should combat prejudice and discrimination and, in so doing, alter that environment. Hahn concludes that the "extension of civil rights" should be the "primary means of resolving the problems of disabled citizens."[8]

An intellectual controversy has developed between the supporters of the minority model, who are primarily political scientists and lawyers, and its opponents, who are mainly economists. Because the minority model tends to ignore costs as a determining factor of public policy, it represents a direct challenge to the way in which economists think about public policy. Because it challenges the conventional wisdom of policy analysis, its recommendations are regarded with suspicion by policymakers.

Handicapped rights evolved at a time when civil rights were not high on society's agenda, a time when economic methodology dominated. The handicapped emerged as a minority group only after the passage of civil rights laws aimed at blacks and women in the middle of the 1960s. Although these earlier civil rights movements provided handicapped leaders with positive role models, the later arrival of handicapped rights put the disabled at a disadvantage. Just when the handicapped discovered themselves as members of a minority and began to work toward the removal of attitudinal and physical barriers, the economists pointed to the costs of removing those barriers. The handicapped responded by speaking of rights that transcended cost considerations: "Economics cannot be the issue around which decisions turn. The Supreme Court has said long ago that civil rights cannot be abrogated simply because of cost factors." In the economists' view, however, costs could not simply be assumed away. More of one thing meant less of another. In the economists' view of the world, costs had to be considered in the securing of rights, regardless of the moral validity of those rights.[9]

Another point of contention arose over the question of choice. The economists argued that the handicapped exercised a degree of choice over accepting disability benefits and, in effect, over whether or not they were disabled. The supporters of the minority model contended that society labeled individuals as handicapped or disabled, and therefore it made little sense to think of disability as a matter of individual choice.[10]

The notion of choice was, in fact, central to the way in which economists analyzed disability policy. To them the most important thing to explain was the sudden rise in costs in disability programs during the 1970s. The fact that disability expenditure continued to rise even as health conditions improved added to the intellectual challenge. The evidence on the rise in costs was abundant and unambiguous. One economist has estimated, that between 1965 and 1975, cash payments to the disabled increased from $9.7 billion (or 1.4 percent of the gross national product) to $33.9 billion (or 2.2 percent of the gross national product). Other industrialized countries experienced similar increases. In the decade between 1968 and 1978, income transfer payments to the disabled grew at an annual rate of 7 percent in the United States, 8.1 percent in Italy, and 11.3 in Holland.[11]

Faced with these data, economists examined the details of disability programs to see how they might affect an individual's behavior. They found large increases in the level of benefits, such as a rise of 82 percent in an average person's social security benefits between 1969 and 1975, and discovered that many people experienced no loss of income when they stopped working and started receiving disability benefits. This discovery, economists believed, marked a start in explaining the rise in disability costs. When high unemployment and the fact that a person could draw benefits from more than one program were factored in, economists thought they had found a convincing explanation for the rise in the disability rolls in the face of improving health conditions. In the jargon of economists, people with severe impairments could "maximize their utility" by going on the disability rolls. Disability insurance gave its beneficiaries as much or more money than they had previously, and it offered them considerably more leisure time.

So the economists argued that disability could be explained in economic terms and worked on refining their analysis. Concerned about the effect of transfer payments on the "labor supply," economists attempted to discover what considerations best explained a person's decision to seek disability payments. Was it low income and a high replacement rate? Was it a lack of education, an inability to compete in the labor market, and consequently a desire to retire? By asking these questions, economists treated disability as a social and economic phenomenon, not simply a medical one.

The intellectual explorations of the economists left a large gap between them and the supporters of the minority model over the question of choice, as indicated by the terms the two groups used. For the economists, the distinction between handicap and disability was critical: Handicap did not imply disability. For the proponents of the minority model, the terms could be used interchangeably. Unlike the economists, who saw the physically impaired in highly individual terms, the proponents of the minority model regarded the handicapped or the disabled as a cohesive group that was united by the fact of prejudice and prepared to mobilize to end that prejudice.

Therefore, compared with earlier civil rights movements, the movement for handicapped rights began with a double disadvantage. It came to life in a time of perceived scarce resources and sensitivity to costly social experiments. It also had to fight the perception that disability was an option that could be easily chosen and that offered substantial benefits for not working.

Evidence of prejudice

Despite these disadvantages, the minority model supplied the intellectual basis for an important social movement during the 1970s. Making the environment accessible to the handicapped offered a constructive alternative to the social welfare programs with which the economists found so many faults. Both economists and those espousing the minority model deplored the tendency of existing programs to force the handicapped into states of dependency.

The facts of discrimination and prejudice against the handicapped, like the increases in program costs, were undeniable. People reacted adversely, for example, to the sight of a blind person walking on the street unattended. Ex-mental patients had difficulty securing employment, facing as much distrust as would an ex-convict. The same could be said of people with cancer or of epileptics. In 1956, the year that disability insurance was passed, seventeen states prohibited an epileptic from marrying.[12]

Although such legal prohibitions gradually diminished, policymakers continued to regard the handicapped as inferior to the able-bodied in fundamental ways. Inside the Ford White House, for example, a staffer noted that the military had no intentions of hiring the handicapped for active military duty: "It would impose a distinct hardship on the military to make a large number of exceptions to physical standards. . . . Warfare has become . . . more technical and less physical. At the present time, however, the services are limited by strength ceilings and are not having any difficulty obtaining volunteers." The implications were clear. People continued to associate the ability to work with uninpaired physical condition and regarded the handicapped as distinctly second-rate.[13]

The president himself associated disability with sickness and infirmity. Running for president in 1976, Gerald Ford gave a radio interview in which he expressed his interest in the problems of the handicapped by referring to his visits to the Mary Free Bed Hospital, a facility for the physically handicapped. "I have always been interested in that facility," said the president, unaware of how his choice of example demeaned the handicapped.[14]

Outside of government the same associations equating handicap with sickness and weakness prevailed. Perhaps the most publicized public event for the handicapped was a fund-raising marathon on behalf of children with muscular dystrophy that occurred each Labor Day. As Evan Kemp, a lawyer who plays an active role in litigation involving the rights of the handicapped, has noted, the telethons projected an image of the handicapped as "pale, wan, and brave, but probably doomed . . . childlike and dependent." The telethons stressed the need to find cures for illnesses and in this manner propagated the stereotype of the handicapped as sick. "As sick people," wrote Kemp, who is himself handicapped, "it follows that we should allow others to take care of all our needs until a cure is found." Kemp argued that "barriers of employment, transportation, housing, and recreation can be more devastating and wasteful of our lives than the diseases from which we suffer."[15]

Print journalism, as well as television, have tended to treat stories about the handicapped as medical items. A *Time* article entitled "Freedom in a Wheelchair" ran in the section of the magazine devoted to medicine. The *New York Times Magazine* carried an article that saw "new hope for the handicapped" in medicine. The article, which noted that one quadriplegic hospitalized in California preferred suicide to her life as a cripple, said that "the grim picture is beginning to brighten, however, thanks to one of the youngest and least well known medical specialities – rehabilitation medicine." The article denigrated the quality of life already achieved by the handicapped and elevated the achievements of medicine. One handicapped journalist, writing in a lively grass-roots publication called the *Disability Rag*, complained that "we are celebrated for the brief time when we intersect with medicine and media in our foray into the places of cure." Afterward, however, the picture changes considerably: Bill Schroeder, artificial heart recipient was a hero; Bill Schroeder, stroke patient, was consigned to the far less glamorous designation of handicapped.[16]

Schroeder and his peers faced an inhospitable environment. Carolyn Earl, a Michigan woman in a wheelchair, tried unsuccessfully to get a room at the Harrison Hotel in Oakland, California. When she attempted to make a reservation, the clerk expressed concern about the hotel's liability in case of fire. The handicapped, in other words, have been treated as sources of liability and thus are considered unsafe. Jim Jeffers, a paraplegic who worked for the Social Security Administration in Baltimore, accepted a temporary assignment in Washington, D.C. He decided to commute by train. In order to board and dismount the train, Jeffers needed not only special assistance to lift his wheelchair from the platform to the train, but also a freight elevator to reach the platform at the train station. A Michigan State student captured the frustration that such treatment, often perceived as special treatment, can cause: "If you ask the faculty if some of these buildings are accessible, they'll say, 'Oh yeah, oh yeah. Sure they are. Why, I saw a wheelchair user being carried up the stairs just yesterday' . . . I have this nasty habit of thinking of handicappers [a Michigan term] as people, not as freight."[17]

Incidents of this sort motivated the *Disability Rag* to editorialize that the physical environment "keeps being designed as though disabled people were better off dead. With no thought ever routinely given to designing things everybody simply can use. Exhorbitant costs for decent wheelchairs. . . . 'special' this. 'Special' that. . . . Of course, disabled people rarely can talk of quality of life. But it has precious little to do with deformity and a great deal to do with society's defects."[18]

Differentiating among disabilities: Some case studies

Although the handicapped came to view themselves as a minority because they experienced the same treatment as other minorities, even the creators of the minority model recognized differences between the handicapped and other minorities. For one thing, people are not necessarily born handicapped, unlike those who are born black or female. Nor do the handicapped give birth to future generations of handicapped or promote a handicapped culture. The lack of this common culture isolated the handicapped from each other, and the isolation was exacerbated by the fact that the handicapped differed greatly among themselves. The concerns of the institutionalized retarded person, the older disabled person, the disabled child, a person on disability insurance, and a wounded veteran were not necessarily the same.

The public policy problem was how to apply the insights contained in the minority model to programs, such as disability insurance, that had already developed strong historical identities, and how to incorporate the insights into new programs. This problem could only be solved by differentiating between two kinds of disabilities: what William Roth called "enfeeblement" or "the loss of powers one once had" and what might be called handicap. Enfeeblement went hand-in-hand with aging. In fact, America's major disability program, disability insurance, which served mainly Americans in their fifties, treated disability as premature enfeeblement. The public policy challenge was to differentiate the handicapped from the enfeebled (the pre-old) and protect the dignity of both groups. The handicapped needed "independence incentives" and civil rights guarantees; the elderly or enfeebled needed protection against loss of income.[19]

The handicapped and the pre-old recipients of disability insurance and other income-maintenance programs differ from one another, yet public policy still does not recognize the difference. A workers' compensation beneficiary may incur a partial disability and return to work in a matter of weeks: The label "handicapped" may not apply. A disability insurance recipient may wish to retire, whereas a handicapped person without a job may feel excluded from the mainstream.

In the hearing room of a Baltimore administrative law judge, a disability insurance claimant appears who has no obvious handicap. He does not suffer the stigma of someone in a wheelchair or someone who has trouble speaking, seeing, or hearing. His history is not one of struggle. He enlisted in the military and rose to the rank of sergeant. Upon retirement from the military, he had no difficulty getting a civilian job. He has maintained enough mental and emotional stability to sustain a marriage for twenty years; his wife sits beside him during the hearing. However, at the age of fifty-five, with a history of ulcers, the man has had a heart attack. He perceives his physical strength to be waning and his mental facilities to be slipping. No longer does he do the yard work, and his wife worries about his ability to drive. After walking only a block, he becomes tired. Endowed with a "good head

for numbers" and a good memory, he can no longer remember telephone numbers; he forgets things. Further, his failings often cause him
to "blow up." This tired, demoralized man wants to retire.[20]

The nation's public and private disability programs serve the man
well. Even if he loses his case, he still will receive a military pension
and disability pay from the company with which he worked after his
military service. The company's insurance carrier, hoping to save money
by shifting part of the costs to the public sector, has provided him with
a lawyer to argue his case before the administrative judge.

Lex Frieden also has applied for disability benefits, yet his situation
is fundamentally different, and illustrates what differentiates the
handicapped from the pre-old. Frieden comes from the northwestern
part of Oklahoma, born and raised in a small town that served as a
commercial center for the surrounding agricultural area. After high
school, he decided to study electrical engineering at Oklahoma State.
For reasons that remain unclear to him, he began to slack off and his
grades slipped. He had always done well in school, both in class and
in social activities, favored by a high intelligence, a comfortable family
income, and a congenial personality that enabled him to get along
with people. When he realized that he might be only an average student and that his life would not be an inevitable triumph, he became
depressed. With Thanksgiving vacation approaching, he brooded about
facing his family's questions about his schoolwork. On the Monday
before Thanksgiving, he stayed up late, drinking. A friend who owned
a Camero convertible joined him, and they decided to go for a ride.
High on drink, driving aggressively, they collided with an oncoming
vehicle. Frieden was trapped in the car, unable to move.

Frieden left the world of higher education for the world of advanced
medicine. He began in the college infirmary, where X rays revealed a
lesion in his spinal cord. He was then transferred to the care of a
neurosurgeon in a large general hospital in Oklahoma City. Heavily
sedated, Frieden drifted through his hospital stay. Eventually, he began to recognize his vulnerablility; he was completely immobilized,
unable even to turn the pages of a book or to feed himself. After he
left the care of the neurosurgeon, Frieden entered a rehabilitation center in Houston. After that, he faced the outside world.

Although paralyzed and confined to a wheelchair for life, Frieden
decided to continue his education. A large Oklahoma university, run
by a charismatic faith healer, rejected him; the dean of admissions

wrote that his presence on campus violated the school's image. Like the doctors, faith healers regarded the handicapped as too visible a sign of failure. Frieden instead entered the University of Tulsa and changed his major to psychology.

At this point in his life, Frieden came into contact with the social welfare system. Vocational rehabilitation paid for his education, even agreeing to send him out of state for a master's degree. Because of the various part-time jobs he had held before he became disabled, Frieden also qualified for disability insurance. As long as he earned less than the amount designated as the "substantial gainful activity" level, he received a monthly check from the federal government.

Frieden and the man at the disability hearing had little in common. Frieden became disabled relatively early in life; the man at the hearing applied for benefits at the age of fifty-five. Frieden, immediately recognizable as handicapped because of his wheelchair and the limited movement in his arms, could not pass as able-bodied. The applicant at the hearing fit more readily into the able-bodied world. Unlike the applicant at the hearing, Frieden was the victim of overt discrimination when he applied to a university. Frieden did not choose to be handicapped; society imposed that label on him. Society also made certain locations inaccessible to him; for example, Frieden required specially modified kitchen and bathroom facilities. Finally, Frieden went on to become executive director of the National Council on the Handicapped and a major figure in the disability rights movement; it can be assumed that, through one means or another, the man at the hearing retired.

Many of Frieden's colleagues in the disability rights movement are relatively young, use a wheelchair to get from place to place, and have a physical rather than a mental impairment. A car accident changed Frieden's status from that of an advantaged, able-bodied person to that of an advantaged member of the handicapped community. Judy Heumann, also an influential figure in the movement, came from another large group of the disabled, referred to as "post-polio."

Judy Heumann does not remember the time before she came down with polio, so in a sense she has always been disabled. She never learned to walk, except by means of a wheelchair. Her German-Jewish, working-class parents tutored her at home until she reached the age of eight, when she entered public school in Brooklyn. She describes her school days at PS 219 and Sheepshead Bay High School as "in and out." She arrived late and left early, allowing little time for extracurricular activities. Her opportunities for such activities came during the summers, when she attended a special camp for handicapped children. There, Heumann says, a hierarchy existed among the handicapped. "The polios were on top," she says.

Heumann attended Long Island University on money from the vocational rehabilitation program. Her college years, between 1965 and 1969, marked a time of emergence for her and for others who would lead the movement for handicapped rights. Colleges became centers of sympathy for the black civil rights movement and of protest against the war in Vietnam, bastions of the baby-boom generation's point of view. Heumann blossomed. She protested against the war; she marched to demand the removal of the chancellor; she became a class officer; she participated in dramatics. Heumann gained attention because of her handicap and because of her forceful and exuberant personality. Before she graduated, she was mentioned in the *New York Daily News* for making "Who's Who among Students in American Universities and Colleges."

The year after her graduation, Heumann became the center of a media event. On April 1, 1970, the *New York Times* broke the story of how Judy Heumann was denied a license to teach in the New York City Public Schools. When she applied, she was informed that she had to pass a physical examination – the standard procedure for applicants. After one examination in January, school board officials requested she return for another. According to Heumann, the doctor asked her insulting questions such as whether she lived apart from her parents because she could not get along with them or whether she wet herself when using the bathroom. A few months later she was denied a license; she had failed the physical exam on the grounds of "paralysis of both lower extremities." Jay D. Greene, chairman of the Board of Examiners, explained that, although Heumann was physically fit, the board worried about her mobility in emergencies. Green said that the board had to balance her desire to work against its responsibility for the safety of the children.

Heumann filed a civil suit against the board in federal court, charging discrimination, and made herself available to the press. "We're not going to let a hypocritical society give us a token education and then bury us," Heumann told the *Daily News,* which ran her story under the headline, "You Can Be President, Not Teacher, with Polio." In time, Heumann received a license to teach, after attracting a great deal of favorable publicity. When the Board of Education passed a resolution opening teaching positions to all orthopedically handicapped persons, the *Daily News* wrote, "Take a Bow, Judy!" All three New York City major newspapers ran sympathetic editorials, the *Daily News* referring to the City Board of Examiners' "big, fat, booboo."[21]

Within a month of her rejection by the Board of Examiners, Heumann helped found a group called "Disabled in Action." This group made its presence felt during the 1972 election when some of its members, angered by President Nixon's veto of the rehabilitation act, demonstrated in New York City. Heumann knew many of the group's members from summer camp. Although other groups, such as the Paralyzed Veterans of America, fought for the rights of the handicapped, Heumann's group was younger and cut across disability categories.

In 1973, Heumann left her job as a New York City teacher for a graduate program in health planning at Berkeley. Her move marked a conscious effort on the part of some members of the handicapped community in Berkeley to unite the east and west coast branches of the disability rights movement. As part of her graduate training, she undertook an internship in Washington, D.C., where she worked with Senator Harrison Williams, who chaired the Labor and Public Welfare Committee, which had a Subcommittee on the Handicapped. She participated in writing a bill that created a major program in special education.[22]

Once again, she attracted attention. On a Sunday evening toward the end of the Christmas-New Year's holiday early in 1975, Heumann went to Kennedy Airport to take a National Airlines flight to Washington, D.C. When she boarded the plane, she was asked to leave since she was traveling unaccompanied and without a medical certificate. When Heumann refused to get off, Port Authority police arrested her. Again, Heumann had been discriminated against because public officials believed her to be a safety hazard. The incident led to a public appeal by Senator Williams to end discrimination against the handicapped on airlines.[23]

At the end of 1975, Heumann returned to Berkeley and played an increasingly prominent role in the disability rights movement. She helped to lead many demonstrations, such as the one at the San Franciso federal building in 1977 that attracted wide notice. By the end of the decade, *Ms. Magazine* called Heumann one of eighty women to watch in the 1980s.

Like Frieden, Heumann made an articulate and energetic spokesperson for handicapped rights. They shared other characteristics as well, such as functional limitations related to mobility, which made them clearly visible as handicapped. They represented a new class of individuals who were impaired yet not afflicted with degenerative diseases. Although not cured by medicine, they were able to take advantage of medical advances. The policies designed to help the man at the administrative law judge hearing were not necessarily appropriate for them.

Frieden and Heumann were both younger than the man at the disability hearing, just as members of the handicapped rights community tend to be younger than people on the disability rolls. The difference in age is significant. Frieden and Heumann grew up in an era of greatly expanding social welfare programs; both received aid from the vocational rehabilitation program, for example. They tended to assume as a matter of course that the government should play a role in disability policy. Further, as leaders of a social movement, Frieden and Heumann followed modern rules. They realized that even as social welfare expenditures increased, it remained difficult to start new programs. The same Congress that could vote a handsome increase in social security benefits, for example, might hesitate to initiate a civil rights program designed to end segregation. Faced with deadlock in the legislature, the leaders of the black civil rights movement had learned how to use the courts and the media as tools to circumvent and pressure Congress. Frieden and Heumann could not have failed to observe such political tactics as they prepared to mobilize the handicapped for change.

In the early 1970s, however, the objectives of this mobilization remained unclear. Since they had no intention of retiring, Frieden and Heumann looked for a government role that extended beyond paying retirement benefits. They found this role in independent living.

Independent living

Both Heumann and Frieden became involved in the creation of new social institutions called centers for independent living. These centers, the most well known of which is the Center for Independent Living in

Berkeley, responded to the needs of handicapped individuals who wished to enter the social and economic mainstream. As such, they reflected the aspirations of a new generation of handicapped individuals who were led by Heumann, Frieden, and Ed Roberts, another major figure in the disability rights movement, and they represented the most important application of the minority model to disability policy.

Roberts's story provides insights into the history of the independent living movement. He is post-polio, like Heumann, and, like Frieden, he was once a relatively privileged member of the able-bodied community. Roberts describes his background in much the same terms as Frieden uses to describe his Oklahoma childhood. Roberts refers to himself as "a likable kid, an athlete," and a person with "leadership abilities."

Roberts came down with polio in 1953 at the age of fourteen. Polio left him with no movement below the neck. He spent most of his teenage years in an iron lung, finishing high school by telephone. Nonetheless, he was able to enroll at a local college and then to earn both an undergraduate and a master's degree from the University of California at Berkeley.[24]

During his student days at Berkeley, Roberts lived in the university's Cowell Hospital, a student by day and a patient by night. Other quadriplegics joined him, and the third floor of Cowell Hospital gradually became less of a hospital and more of a dormitory. By the 1968–69 academic year, a formal Cowell Residence Program came into existence, run by the California department of rehabilitation.

The quadriplegics influenced and were influenced by the Berkeley community. As students, they observed the political give and take of the many groups that set up tables in Sproul Plaza and passed out literature; they listened to rock music, experimented with drugs, and participated in "countercultural" activities. More than most students, however, they were affected by Berkeley's distinctive political activism, since their dormitory-hospital was staffed by orderlies and attendants who were doing public service as an alternative to participating in the Vietnam War. Driving around in motorized wheelchairs, the quadriplegics also became visible to the surrounding community, another of what outsiders took to be Berkeley's freakish sights. In 1970, the quadriplegics formed their own political group, which they called, with tongue in cheek, the "Rolling Quads." The group pressured the university to remove the architectural and physical barriers that made the hilly campus inaccessible to them.

By now, Roberts and the others wanted to move out of the hospital and into the community. In 1972, the group incorporated the Center of Independent Living (CIL). In February 1974, Roberts became the head of CIL and, during an eighteen-month tenure, which ended with his appointment as director of the state vocational rehabilitation program, brought the center to national attention. Heumann maintained a close association with CIL, serving as deputy director from late 1975 to 1982.[25]

Today the center, located several blocks from the university, remains an important outlet for handicapped activism. It has the frenetic feel of the headquarters of a busy not-for-profit organization with an overwhelming sense of purpose. CIL staff members cope with stacks of telephone messages between frequent meetings, creating the impression of Nader's raiders in wheelchairs.

CIL members pride themselves on their distance from hospitals and other institutions. Although the center itself is a formal institution, it attempts to provide services that the handicapped can control on their own terms, and it is dedicated to independence and the transcendence of other institutions. Roberts makes a point of emphasizing that no one lives there.

CIL staff members offer services that include attendant referral, advice on social welfare benefits, information on programs for the blind and the deaf, housing referral, and information on van transportation and wheelchair repair. Each of the services promotes the independence of the handicapped.[26]

Attendant care best exemplifies the services provided at the center. Attendant care referral allows a handicapped person to control a situation that by its very nature exposes the person's dependence on others. Roberts, for example, requires an attendant to unload him from his van and to feed him. The center provides its members with a list of people seeking employment as attendants; the handicapped individual does the actual hiring. Although the possibility exists for abuse of a handicapped person by an attendant, the center believes that the state of independence justifies the risks and that the handicapped person must himself manage the services on which he depends.

Because of the CIL, Berkeley has become what the *New York Times* has called a "mecca for the handicapped."[27] Judy Heumann has spoken of Berkeley's attraction. Her move to Berkeley worried her, but her fears eased when she landed at the airport and was met by a disabled friend who drove a van with a hydraulic lift. She stayed in a home with no architectural barriers and benefited from the assistance of a personal care attendant. She began to live her life on her own terms: She went to sleep when she wanted; she took a shower when she wanted. For the first time, "my handicap did not completely control my life," Heumann said. She believed that coming to Berkeley made her a more mature person; she compared the situation to "being a baby and learning how to grow up and . . . how to take on responsibilities."[28]

With so much attention centered on Berkeley, it is easy to forget that independent living is a national movement. Even before the Cowell Residence Program, there was a program for handicapped students at the University of Illinois at Urbana. Columbus, Ohio, another university town, contains Creative Living, Incorporated, a residential program for para- and quadriplegics with twenty-four-hour, on-call attendant care services. In Houston, a transitional living project, until recently run largely by Frieden himself, attempts to bridge the gap between hospital and community by means of a six-week program that teaches independent living skills. Each of these programs, and many like them, qualifies as an independent living center.[29]

Independent living is a profoundly local movement, bred of the specific needs of individual communities as divergent as Berkeley and Columbus. For all of its heterogeneity, however, it represents a clear alternative to previous disability programs and it has brought the leaders of the disability rights movement together and drawn them into national politics. Heumann, Roberts, Frieden, and others offer independent living as the institutional cornerstone of a new generation of disability policy.

The uniqueness of independent living centers becomes apparent when they are compared with the rehabilitation centers started by doctors at the end of World War II. Both doctors and the founders of the independent living movement considered their approach to disability policy revolutionary. Nor were the two movements dissimilar in their basic objectives: Dr. Howard Rusk, for example, believed in moving medicine beyond pure diagnosis and treatment, and minimizing a patient's period of confinement and bed rest.

Because the doctors and the founders of independent living centers believed so strongly in their ideas, both developed institutions to put them into practice and spread them from coast to coast. In 1945, Rusk received money from philanthropist Bernard Baruch to create a blueprint for a veterans' rehabilitation center. This exercise led him to draw up a similar blueprint containing the "philosophy, aim, and relationships for a civilian rehabilitation center."

Rusk intended the civilian rehabilitation center to bring together a community's resources to treat disability. The center would unite a wide range of services. It would have facilities to accommodate both inpatients and outpatients and would maintain a loose affiliation with the community's general hospital. A physician who specialized in physical medicine would act as the captain and coach for a flexible team of specialists that would include a psychiatrist, a staff of clinical psychologists, both medical and psychiatric social workers, occupational therapists, and craft and physical education instructors. Like the founders of independent living centers, Rusk and Dr. Henry Kessler, another pioneer of rehabilitation medicine, believed they had discovered a community-based model that responded to the needs of many localities.[30]

Although they shared common objectives, the leaders of independent living centers and the founders of rehabilitation centers differed in the use they made of, and the attitude they took toward, professional caretakers. The doctors believed it proper to put the handicapped under medical and other forms of professional supervision. They wanted their rehabilitation centers to be integrated into the community, but they saw nothing wrong with, even encouraged, links between the centers and the community hospital. The Rusk Institute, for example, became part of the New York University–Bellevue teaching hospital. By their very nature, the rehabilitation centers were residential, which meant that to some extent they resembled hospitals.

The leaders of the independent living centers prided themselves on their distance from doctors, and their centers emphasized peer control rather than professional care. Roberts, who seldom goes to a doctor, denigrated the "medical model" and argued that its emphasis on cure was inappropriate to the handicapped. To the people in Berkeley, doctors and the other professionals at the rehabilitation centers, who emphasize medical care and psychological adjustment, represented the antithesis of the self-help philosophy. Different generations have therefore given rise to different institutions as the focal point for disability policy: the medically oriented rehabilitation centers and the "consumer"-oriented independent living centers.

As innovative institutions in disability policy, emphasizing the corrective rather than the ameliorative approach, rehabilitation centers and independent living centers have both become associated with the vocational rehabilitation program. In both cases, however, the leaders of the movements met with resistance when they asked the administrators of the vocational rehabilitation program for financial assistance. When Drs. Rusk and Kessler begged the state rehabilitation administrators to send their clients to the new centers, the administrators dragged their feet, pointing to the expense of the care provided and expressing their fears that a rehabilitated client would still be unable to get a job. Only after Office of Vocational Rehabilitation director Mary Switzer convinced Senator Lister Hill to sponsor amendments to the Hill–Burton hospital construction program in 1954 for building rehabilitation centers did the doctors receive the money they sought.[31]

The vocational rehabilitation administrators also hesitated to endorse the concept of independent living, which posed an even greater challenge to the vocational rehabilitation program. The doctors and vocational rehabilitation counselors shared a common professional outlook on disability; vocational rehabilitation counselors and the leaders of the independent living movement regarded each other as antagonists. Although outsiders viewed the independent living centers as a positive phenomenon, the centers were treated much more cooly in the inner world of rehabilitation.

Despite Switzer's sympathy toward independent living, it took considerable pressure from the handicapped community to put independent living on the legislative agenda of the vocational rehabilitation program. In 1972 and 1973, after repeated skirmishes over legislation to give the severely disabled priority in the vocational rehabilitation program, independent living finally made it to the top of that agenda. Only President Nixon's objections prevented the passage of special grants in the vocational rehabilitation program to fund independent living centers.

Roberts regarded funding for independent living centers as the most important political initiative of the handicapped "consumers," and, along with Heumann, he conducted a national campaign to pass the necessary legislation. When Jimmy Carter entered the White House, this campaign gained momentum. By 1978, the House Committee on Education and Labor was strongly committed to independent living center legislation and, working closely with Roberts and Heumann, it held a hearing on the subject in Berkeley. Roberts testified that independent living centers came from "our experience directly, our experience of trying to survive away from the institution . . . we know these can be duplicated." "I think all of us are in agreement," concluded Heumann, "that what we need is ongoing, permanent funding for independent living programs."[32]

Title VII, passed in 1978, provided authorization for that funding. It contained three parts. The first part made grants to state vocational rehabilitation agencies to help pay for comprehensive independent living services. The second part gave the commissioner of Rehabilitation Services the discretionary power to award money to the states to establish and operate independent living centers, provided handicapped individuals were substantially involved in policy direction. The third part awarded grants for independent living services for older blind individuals. President Carter signed the measure somewhat reluctantly, sympathetic to its contents but wary of its costs. Before signing the bill, he extracted a promise from certain members of Congress to delay appropriating all the money authorized. In fact, only the second part of Title VII was funded on a permanent basis; the first part received funds for the first time only in 1984, and the third part was never funded.[33]

By exposing the differences between the vocational rehabilitation program and independent living, Title VII bred conflicts. In the first place, the notion of disability rights advocacy, central to the independent living movement, made rehabilitation officials uneasy. One goal of the independent living centers was to help a handicapped person secure all the welfare benefits to which he was entitled. Counselors coached people on how to present themselves at the welfare agency and, in the words of one academic expert, attempted to "destigmatize the receipt of welfare." The vocational rehabilitation program, in contrast, was perceived as an alternative to, rather than as a source of expansion of, the welfare rolls. In effect, funding the independent living centers with money from the vocational rehabilitation program was asking the system to finance its challengers.[34]

The leaders of the vocational rehabilitation program and the leaders of independent living had other reasons to distrust any attempt to form an alliance between the two movements. The rehabilitation community was accustomed to mathematically calculated measurement of the results of its efforts, such as employment. Independent living, on the other hand, constituted a vague concept; whether a person succeeded or failed in reaching the goal of independence could not easily be measured. Further, making independent living services available to the severely disabled could be costly and could detract from other goals of the agency. The handicapped community, for its part, feared that vocational rehabilitation counselors would use independent living as an excuse not to find jobs for the severely handicapped. Creating a dichotomy between independence and employment would leave the severely handicapped outside of both the custodial institutions and the labor force; by making it possible for the handicapped to be free to do nothing, it would call the very meaning of independence into question.

If, on the other hand, independent living were to embrace the goal of employment, then independent living centers would become competitors of the traditional vocational rehabilitation program, and independent living would reconceptualize disability policy. Problems formerly assumed to reside in the individual would more often be attributed to the environment; short-term assistance would yield to lifelong associations with independent living centers. The very basis of disability policy would be transformed from the goals of employment or retirement to the more complex objective of what might be called empowerment: the participation of the handicapped in community life. Such a broad-based goal lay well beyond the scope of the vocational rehabilitation program.[35]

Independent living now finds itself in the paradoxical position of depending for its survival on the goodwill of a program with which it has fundamental disagreements that may end in active competition. Nor do the problems end there. Independent living is a concept in flux that includes residential, antiresidential, and transitional models, and it faces an emerging crisis of leadership. The pioneers of the movement are aging or working at the national level; a new group must emerge to take their place. Further, some members of the handicapped community do not identify with the independent living centers, which are geared toward people in wheelchairs or those with spinal cord injuries, post-polio, cerebral palsy, muscular dystrophy, and multiple sclerosis. "Almost every . . . analyst agrees that there is a powerful physical disability orientation," says Donald Galvin, a former director of a state rehabilitation program. Roberts and Heumann have been accused of "living in a white, middle-class dream world" that excludes the poor and the aged.[36]

Nonetheless, independent living represents a fresh approach toward disability policy that squarely faces up to the differences between the handicapped and the rest of the population. The handicapped require special assistance, and the centers help to provide that assistance. Their local orientation helps to channel federal money to the places and services where it can do the most good. Although the centers cannot eliminate bureaucratic barriers across programs, they can act as forces that break those barriers down in individual cases. Local institutions, the centers also stretch from coast to coast, enabling the leaders of the local centers to learn from one another. The fact that the handicapped themselves run the centers minimizes the conflicts between counselors and clients that arise in other programs. True, the centers do not meet everyone's needs, but no government program meets everyone's needs, and the centers must be considered improvements over the traditional vocational rehabilitation program, the first real alternatives to the income-maintenance programs to appear in some time.

Legal guarantees

At the same time that the independent living center became the institutional embodiment of the disability rights movement, Congress passed a series of civil rights laws that applied to the handicapped. The mentally disabled were among the first to benefit from such a law when Congress passed the Developmental Disabilities and Bill of Rights Act in 1975. The act asserted the inherent rights of the developmentally disabled, a group that included the mentally retarded, epileptics, and others with an impairment that manifested itself at birth or in early childhood. Passage of the act followed a series of class-action law suits in which the courts ruled that the mentally retarded in institutions had constitutional rights to treatment, services, and habilitation that "maximize the developmental potential of the person and are provided in the setting that is least restrictive of the person's personal liberty."[37]

The Developmental Disabilities and Bill of Rights Act followed a pattern common to disability-related civil rights legislation. It required the states to provide each developmentally disabled person under their care with a "written individual, habilitation plan." It also required each state to create a legal system to protect the rights of the developmentally disabled. The same procedures applied to the vocational rehabilitation program, with its written rehabilitation plans (initiated in 1973) and its client-assistance program (begun on a nationwide basis in 1984). In both cases, Congress regarded the provision of services to the handicapped as a contractual obligation on the part of the states and provided means for the handicapped to sue the state for breach of contract.[38]

The most publicized of the laws, which guaranteed both a written contract and legal means of appeal, dealt with the education of the handicapped. The law, enacted in 1975, required public schools to write an individualized education plan for each handicapped child. The plan had to include an educational goal and a means of measuring the child's progress toward that goal. In addition, each time the school made a decision that would affect the child's education, it was obligated to provide the child's parents with written notice. Should the parents disagree with the school, they had the right to a "due process hearing," at which, accompanied by counsel if they wished, they could present their own expert witnesses.[39]

Although far-reaching, the laws marked only the start of comprehensive civil rights protection for the handicapped. The early laws applied mainly to children and owed their existence to the political strength of able-bodied parents, rather than to the handicapped themselves. With the development of the disability rights movement, new groups among the handicapped, such as post-polios and paraplegics, became interested in a more comprehensive civil rights law for the handicapped, one that went beyond custodial institutions or special schools and applied to mainstream activities such as employment.

Toward a handicapped rights law

For Roberts and the rest, however, the expansion of centers for independent living remained the priority of the handicapped rights movement well into the 1970s. A comprehensive civil rights law did not emerge as an issue until 1976. In 1974, for example, when President Ford met with a group of handicapped individuals, they talked about the need for a barrier-free society, the desirability of a spokesman for the handicapped in the White House, and the importance of making Washington's Metro accessible to the handicapped. No one mentioned Section 504 of the Rehabilitation Act of 1973.[40]

At the end of 1974, President Ford signed a law that authorized a White House Conference on Handicapped Individuals, which quickly became a vehicle for the discussion of handicapped rights. Intended as an expression of the grass-roots concerns of the handicapped community, the conference fell short of its objectives. It generated an enormous amount of activity, beginning at the state level and culminating in a splashy Washington event held at the beginning of the Carter administration in May 1977. Both the president and Joseph Califano, secretary of Health, Education, and Welfare, addressed the conference, which produced a laundry list of recommendations and findings, not one of which attracted much attention.[41]

A look behind the scenes revealed political maneuvering and public relations packaging of the most cynical variety. Jim Cannon of the White House staff told President Ford that "such White House conferences tend to produce few substantive results while automatically generating pressures for higher funding regardless of need." In the inflation-conscious Ford White House, such a characterization put the conference in the worst possible light. Caspar Weinberger, then secretary of Health, Education, and Welfare, advised the president, "If I felt you really had any discretion in the matter, I would recommend against holding the conference." At first, Ford's advisers hoped the conference would be held in October, before the 1976 election. As Weinberger noted, "Presidential statements and conference-related activities highlighting the President and concern for the handicapped could be advantageous for the Administration in an election year." Besides, Weinberger noted, "the weather is more predictably better in October than during the winter months, thus perhaps facilitating logistics for handicapped participants."[42]

The lower echelons of the Ford administration did little to make the conference an effective vehicle for the advancement of handicapped rights. The White House and conference staffs appeared to regard the conference as a problem of political management. "Should there be a deficiency in any consumer or ethnic category," wrote one staffer, "the White House will correct the deficiency with a limited number of delegates-at-large." The instructions to the delegates were written in language so obscure as to be meaningless. One instruction, for example, attempted to define what was meant by a "good issue" to raise at the conference. "You will probably be able to think of clue words such as monitoring systems, management sensitization . . . interagency co-ordination," the instruction read. Although the White House staff hoped to "suggest a plan of action in clear terms," its instructions to the delegates were anything but clear.[43]

As the White House and the conference staffs played politics with the handicapped, a new organization, created by the handicapped themselves, began to make its presence felt. Organized at a 1974 meeting of the President's Committee on the Employment of the Handicapped, the American Coalition of Citizens with Disabilities (ACCD) held its first formal meeting in 1975. By September 1976, the organization had enough money – largely because of the efforts of Jim Garrett, a longtime associate of Mary Switzer in the vocational rehabilitation program who had taken an interest in ACCD – to open a Washington office. Unlike the local coalitions organized around independent living centers, or single-disability organizations such as the American Foundation for the Blind, the United Cerebral Palsy Association, or the Disabled American Veterans, ACCD concentrated on national concerns and attempted to reach across disabilities.[44]

The success of ACCD in bridging disability groups stood in stark contrast to previous efforts to unite the handicapped. As with the other aspects of disability policy, a generation made a difference. During the 1940s, for instance, at the time when Rusk and his colleagues were formulating plans for rehabilitation centers, a man named Paul Strachan founded the American Federation of the Physically Handicapped. Strachan and the federation helped to start National Employ the Handicapped Week, which led to the President's Committee on National Employ the Handicapped Week (eventually the President's Committee on the Employment of the Handicapped). Strachan also tried to pass a major civil rights law for the handicapped that would have established a federal commission for the physically handicapped as well as several new benefit programs for the handicapped. Strachan called for federal safety engineers to eliminate architectural barriers, an affirmative action plan for hiring the handicapped, and subsidized loans to the handicapped.

Strachan argued that "transportation interests are serviced by the Interstate Commerce Commission, banking interests by the Federal Reserve Board. . . . The handicapped, who have no such services and few real champions are fully entitled to a special agency in their interest." He fought for "more money and less rehabilitation philosophy," claiming that the vocational rehabilitation program led the handicapped "around by the nose whilst developing a caste system that benefits chiefly the so-called rehabilitation experts rather than affording real and needed services to the handicapped themselves." "Who," he asked, "can tell more eloquently than the handicapped what the handicapped need."[45]

Few of the handicapped rallied to Strachan's cause. In the era of rehabilitation centers and professionalization, Strachan was out of step. The future of disability policy, it was thought, lay with the professionals, not the consumers. Strachan would have felt more at home in the 1970s. The role that Strachan hoped to play in uniting the handicapped community would be held by Frank Bowe, the first executive director of ACCD.

Bowe's selection reflected a conscious desire to include the traditional disability categories, such as the deaf, in the national coalition, which was otherwise dominated by the "new" handicapped such as the paraplegics. "I was deaf. Deafness was me," says Bowe in describing his background. Like the other leaders of the movement, Bowe came to his position almost inadvertently.

Despite his handicap, Bowe attended the regular public schools in Lewisburg, Pennsylvania. He understood "maybe two words every day" and was tormented by the other students. Persevering through the school system, he attended college and then Gallaudet, the national college for the deaf in Washington, D.C. There, for the first time, he was with a large number of deaf people. It was an experience that made Bowe sensitive to the abilities of the handicapped and to the natural tendency of the handicapped to isolate themselves in protected settings. He learned sign language at Gallaudet, which greatly facilitated his ability to communicate. From Gallaudet, Bowe continued his studies as a doctoral candidate at New York University, hoping for a "nice, quiet, scholarly life." He came to the attention of Eunice Fiorito, a blind woman active in handicapped affairs in New York City, and she offered him the post of ACCD executive director. Soon he underwent what he describes as his "baptism by fire."[46]

Section 504

What pulled the handicapped together in the 1970s and baptized Bowe was an obscure provision in the 1973 rehabilitation act entitled

Section 504, which has acquired an almost religious aura within the handicapped community. It states: "No otherwise qualified handicapped individual in the United States shall, solely by reason of his handicap, be excluded from participation in, be denied the benefits of, or be subjected to discrimination under any program or activity conducted by an Executive agency or by the United States Postal Service."[47]

Everyone knows where these words come from, but no one is quite sure how they got there. The unmistakable source is Title VI of the Civil Rights Act of 1964, which applied these words to discrimination based on race, color, or national origin. Title IX of the Education Amendments of 1972 uses similar language to prohibit sex discrimination in educational institutions receiving federal financial assistance.[48]

The words drifted into the 1973 rehabilitation law with no special urging on the part of the handicapped and no special interest on the part of Congress. When Senator Hubert Humphrey and Representative Charles Vanik had introduced legislation to extend Title VI to the handicapped early in 1972, they failed to gain much attention. In late August 1972, during the long battle to enact a vocational rehabilitation law, a congressional staff member, no one knows which one, suggested putting a civil rights provision into the vocational rehabilitation law. According to Richard Scotch, who has made the closest study of the matter, the suggestion sent an aide to Senator Jacob Javits to look for the wording of Title VI; when he brought the words back to the meeting, he created Section 504. Even though congressional debate on the rehabilitation law occasioned great publicity, Section 504 received the least possible mention in the committee reports and congressional hearings. It would not be an overstatement to say that Section 504 was enacted into law with no public comment or debate.[49]

The political battle over Section 504 that failed to occur in Congress took place afterward, first centering on who would write the regulations. The Office of Civil Rights in the Department of Health, Education, and Welfare received the assignment over the rehabilitation bureaucracy, ensuring that Section 504 would be regarded as a civil rights law rather than an extension of the vocational rehabilitation program.[50]

As a result, Congress changed the definition of handicapped from the one in the vocational rehabilitation program, which stressed employability, to an individual with a physical or mental impairment that limited one or more life activities, who had a record of such impairment, or who was regarded as having such an impairment. More important, cost played less of a role in the formulation of the regulations than it might otherwise have. Civil rights issues concerned rights, according to the lawyers who interpreted them, that transcended costs.[51]

Argument also arose over which department should take the lead in implementing the regulations. Although the Department of Health, Education, and Welfare was the logical choice, first Weinberger and later David Matthews, both of whom served as secretary of HEW, expressed reluctance to have their agency implement the law. Matthews in particular was eager for the Department of Justice to assume this role. Meanwhile, supporters of handicapped rights feared that the Office of Management and Budget (OMB) might coordinate implementation of the law. "I am deathly afraid that OMB would give too much weight to economic considerations which have a very small place in a program designed to vindicate basic human and legal rights," a lawyer concerned with the rights of the retarded wrote in a letter to Peter Lissy, a domestic council staff member in the White House. In the end, Matthews agreed to accept authority for issuing the regulations on Section 504 and for enforcing them, "which is not to say that he believes he should have such authority," commented one White House staff member.[52]

Matthews's reticence delayed completion of Section 504 regulations and ultimately led to a confrontation between the newly organized ACCD and HEW Secretary Califano. A draft of the regulations had been available early enough for Weinberger to sign before he left HEW in July 1975. When Weinberger failed to act, the matter fell to Matthews, who wanted further analysis of the regulations as well as an inflationary impact statement. That delayed things until the beginning of 1976. Martin Gerry of the Office of Civil Rights submitted the latest draft of the regulations to Matthews in March 1976.

By this time, Section 504 had attracted public notice, as it became clear that implementation would cost a significant amount of money. Political issues had surfaced, such as whether drug addicts and alcoholics came within the scope of the regulations and whether the regulations as applied to the handicapped should be the same as those for blacks and women. Gerry told Senator Harrison Williams (D.-New Jersey) that in matters concerning race or sex one strived for "equal treatment," but "that might not work for the handicapped," for whom "you might have to provide differential treatment in order to provide equal treatment."

These issues made Matthews even more tentative. As a result, instead of regulations, what appeared on May 17, 1976, was a "notice of intent to publish proposed rules." During the summer, a "notice of proposed rulemaking" was published, and the Office of Civil Rights held hearings across the country soliciting comments. By January 1977, the staff of the Office of Civil Rights had revised the regulations once again and submitted what it regarded as final regulations for Matthews's signature. On January 18, 1977, Matthews announced his intention not to sign the regulations. Instead, he sent the regulations back to the Senate Committee on Labor and Public Welfare for its comments. Two days later, Matthews and the regulations ran out of time; Jimmy Carter arrived.[53]

During the 1976 campaign, Carter had announced his intention to sign Section 504. Closer to Washington, however, Carter and Califano, his designated HEW secretary, discovered that ending discrimination with a stroke of the pen would not be so easy. During the transition period, Califano learned that although Senators Jennings Randolph (D.-West Virginia) and Claiborne Pell (D.-Rhode Island), whose support was vital on a broad range of education issues, both wanted the regulations signed, state governors advised him against it, emphasizing, in Califano's words, "cost, cost." Califano hesitated. He later said that the debate needed to "percolate," that it would have been "bad public policy" for him simply to sign regulations drafted by others.[54]

Califano set out to make the regulations his own. In characteristic style, he assigned a group of lawyers the task of reviewing the draft regulations and writing new ones. This action again insulated the regulations from the economists. As Dan Marcus, one of the lawyers in charge of the special task force on Section 504, recalled, civil rights issues were not perceived in economic terms; considerations centered more on who would benefit from the regulations. Carter and Califano both worried about public reaction to civil rights guarantees for alcoholics and homosexuals.[55]

The change in presidential administration affected the regulations very little. What had changed was the position of the ACCD, which became more assertive. Nonetheless, Califano, who believed in the importance of dealing with a leader in sensitive negotiations, saw Bowe as someone he could "talk to." "Bowe made sense," Califano said. Bowe became the point man in the negotiations between Califano and the disabled community. That meant that Bowe, relatively new to the disability rights movement, had to mediate differences among those within the handicapped community so that it could speak with one voice on Section 504. Politically powerful groups like the Association of Retarded Citizens had to be consulted; differences between the east coast and the more militant west coast branches of the disability rights movement had to be smoothed out.[56]

The ACCD board called for Section 504 regulations to be issued in April 1977. On April 3, protesters appeared in front of Califano's house, urging him to sign the regulations that Matthews had left. Two days later, the handicapped staged demonstrations in Califano's office and at the San Francisco headquarters of HEW. Although the Washington demonstrators left within twenty-eight hours, having attracted media coverage, the San Francisco demonstrators, led by Judy Heumann, remained until the regulations were signed.

Although Califano had no desire to give the appearance of caving in to the demonstrators, he called a news conference on April 28 and announced that he would sign the regulations. As Dan Marcus later recalled, the regulations would probably have been signed anyway: Califano simply wanted a decent interval to pass so that the Carter administration could claim credit for them.[57]

If nothing else, the demonstrations changed the appearance of things. The photograph on the front page of the *New York Times* of a demonstrator hugging Heumann confirmed the arrival of the handicapped as a minority group. By demonstrating, the handicapped had made the regulations appear to be the result of their actions, transforming Section 504 into the only major component of public policy toward disability that the disability rights movement could call its own.

In essence, the regulations that Califano signed in April 1977 – which applied to all hospitals, schools, local governments, or other institutions that received funds from the Department of Health, Education, and Welfare – required that all new buildings be barrier-free, that all activities (such as a doctoral program in a university or a recreational facility at a school) be made accessible to the handicapped, that all handicapped children be given a free public education, and that all colleges and universities modify their academic requirements and provide auxiliary aides (such as readers for the blind) to allow the handicapped to participate.

Califano signed the regulations, but as early as 1974 and 1975, John

Wodatch, Martin Gerry, and their staffs at the Office of Civil Rights
had posed the significant questions, and answered them. In a sense,
the work they did in assessing the questions raised by Section 504
resembled the activities of the Social Security officials during the long
planning period that preceded the adoption of the Social Security Disability Insurance program. The answers they left behind in 1977 formed
the basis for the final regulations, which set the pattern for regulations
to follow in relation to the handicapped, such as those applying to
public transportation.

The sequence of questions began with who should be considered
handicapped. In the 1970s, the term "handicapped" proved to be very
elastic, the result of the discovery in the 1960s of various forms of
deprivation, such as cultural deprivation, and of various new diseases,
such as dyslexia. The Wodatch team decided that those suffering from
environmental, cultural, and economic disadvantages would not be
covered by Section 504, nor would those with prison records, the elderly, or homosexuals. Those with physical problems, however, were
covered, even if the problems were only skin deep. Grossly disfigured
persons, dwarfs, or people who limped qualified because they were
"misperceived as being handicapped and thus discriminated against in
the job market." In a similar sense, the law should apply to *recovered*
alcoholics and drug addicts but not to alcoholics and drug addicts.
The guiding principle was that a handicap had a physical basis and
was permanent.[58]

The next question concerned what constituted discrimination on the
basis of handicap, particularly in the area of employment. Civil rights
laws for blacks and women provided little guidance because of a dilemma that the civil rights lawyers referred to as the problem of the
blind bus driver. Except for his handicap, a blind person might well
have been qualified to drive a bus, and in the language of Section 504
he might be regarded as having been "excluded from participation . . .
solely by reason of his handicap." Yet surely the law did not mandate
that blind people should drive buses. The resolution was that the law
should protect only handicapped people who qualified for the job, and
not all handicapped people. Admittedly, this is a rather fine legal distinction. Blind people were not qualified to be bus drivers. They were
excluded as a class of individuals, unlike women and blacks.

The Wodatch team also decided that the handicapped were entitled
to comparable, rather than identical, services from agencies receiving

federal funds. Failure to provide comparable services constituted discrimination. A welfare office that routinely used the telephone to communicate with its clients might have to find different ways to communicate with its deaf clients.[59]

Consideration of remedies for discrimination against the handicapped raised the delicate matter of cost. How much cost would a federal agent have to bear to employ the handicapped or to provide them with comparable services? If the economists had been in charge, they might have ordered cost–benefit analyses to determine what actions should be taken. The lawyers settled instead on the concept of "reasonable accommodation." In the case of employment, reasonable accommodation of an otherwise qualified handicapped job applicant might involve job restructuring (having the handicapped person perform duties essential to the job but not duties that could as easily be done by someone else) and architectural modifications; however, it was not to impose "undue hardship" on the employer. For all of the examples, the concept of reasonable accommodations remained murky and would occasion lively controversies after the regulations were issued.

The final question, then, was what, exactly, was an undue hardship on an employer? It soon became clear that no hard and fast rules applied. For example, "a small day care center might not be required to expend more than a nominal sum, but a large school district might be expected to provide a teacher's aide to a blind applicant for a teaching job."[60]

Applying the concept of reasonable accommodation to institutions of higher education and to public transportation posed the greatest problems. Since higher education, both private and public, was subsidized by the federal government, it had to comply with Section 504 — that is, to accommodate handicapped students and professors — in order not to lose such subsidies as student loans and research grants. Evidence mounted, however, that it would cost a great deal of money to make schools accessible to the handicapped. Peter Holmes, the director of the Office of Civil Rights under President Ford, argued that making new buildings accessible was relatively inexpensive, whereas renovation cost money. And many schools, he contended, "in physical plants built before the concept of barrier-free design was understood . . . are in precarious financial circumstances."[61]

Califano and his advisers decided that not every classroom had to be accessible, although every course did. Classes could be rescheduled from an inaccessible to an accessible classroom if a handicapped person wanted to take the course; there needed to be "an adequate selection of elective courses in accessible buildings."[62]

There remained the vexing question of standards for hiring handicapped professors and testing handicapped students. Universities routinely used subjective considerations in hiring staff and in admitting students, considerations that were widely regarded as essential to academic freedom. The problem was to preserve academic freedom while also guarding against practices that discriminated against the handicapped, such as excluding them from consideration for admission. Although Harvard, for example, could still hire the best job applicant and select the best students for its freshman class regardless of whether they were handicapped, the law required the university to accommodate the handicapped person it hired and the handicapped person it accepted. Accommodation might be a matter of hiring a reader for a blind professor or making sure that the restrooms were accessible. Providing reasonable accommodation in the area of testing handicapped students while preserving Harvard's identity as a selective and demanding institution posed a more formidable challenge. If a handicapped student's physical impairment prevented him from reading or writing as quickly as another, unimpaired student, the university might be discriminating against the handicapped student by holding him to the same standards. Students with dyslexia, for example, might need more time to take examinations. Carried too far, however, such accommodations become special privileges. The Wodatch team was unable to draw the line, requiring only that students be tested in a way that measured knowledge gained rather than their "impaired communication skills."[63]

After an initial hesitation that was caused by the expected costs of accommodating the handicapped, universities engaged in intensive reviews to determine if their classes, laboratories, and other facilities were accessible to the handicapped. Not all universities made changes in their physical plants, but most did. George Washington University, in the nation's capital, spent about $2.5 million of its own money on modifying its facilities. These modifications enabled the university to hold classes that handicapped students wanted to attend in accessible buildings. According to one university administrator, the benefits of surveying the existing programs, making the modifications, and keeping the university accessible included a "continuing level of awareness" of the handicapped; although the costs of the modifications were immediate, the benefits would stretch across many years.[64]

The controversy posed by Section 504 in higher education did not compare with the furor it raised in the transportation field. Just as the Department of Health, Education, and Welfare wrote regulations for education, so the Department of Transportation would have to write regulations that were consistent with the HEW regulations but that addressed the special problems of transportation. Like higher education, public transportation was heavily subsidized. Railroad lines required federal subsidies in order to survive and nearly all public bus and subway lines consistently lost money. As a consequence, public transportation systems, in constant need of federal assistance, were affected by Section 504 and sensitive to the costs of complying with it.

Furthermore, reasonable accommodation of the handicapped in the field of public transportation was difficult to define; no one agreed on what reasonable accommodation of the able-bodied meant. For example, New York City tourists complained that bus drivers did not announce the stops; how could similar complaints from the blind be assessed?

Ultimately, however, it was the costs associated with Section 504 compliance that generated the greatest controversy. In New York, Richard Ravitch, chairman of the Metropolitan Transit Authority, said that a state law passed to comply with Section 504, which required that subways be accessible to the handicapped and therefore equipped with elevators, imposed $100 million worth of costs on the city. Spending the money to make the New York subways, built well before the turn of the century, accessible to the handicapped, Ravitch said, would mean less money to improve the security and comfort of the subways. Millions would suffer, and only a few would gain. Ravitch stated that the Washington, D.C., subway, with its costly elevators, regularly transported only twenty-nine handicapped riders per day; the San Francisco system, which also serviced Berkeley, served only eighty-five daily wheelchair riders.[65]

The issue of making buses accessible to the handicapped created even more disputes. Not only would putting ramps for wheelchairs on buses cost a great deal of money but it also generated disagreements over the appropriate design. Both General Motors and the American Public Transit Association opposed making it mandatory for all public transit systems to use the "transbus," a special bus, designed by the federal Department of Transportation at a cost of $27 million, with a ramp for wheelchairs. Many handicapped activists strongly backed "transbus." According to B. R. Stokes, a vice-president of the American Public Transit Association, "The imposition of any such program which would imply the use of scarce federal resources, for what we believe is a non-solution in the first place, borders on the ridiculous." General Motors favored a design (a lift in the back of the bus) that would require less retooling.[66]

In the light of the problems that plagued transbus, it was indeed a nonsolution. Because of the high cost of each transbus, it was impossible for a city to purchase an entire fleet. That meant that the transbuses could operate only at certain times, on certain routes. Since the handicapped lived at locations throughout metropolitan areas, matching transbus routes with handicapped riders would be difficult. Just to give an example, the city of Baltimore, under pressure from the handicapped, secured forty buses with lifts (not transbuses with ramps) and put them in service on five different bus lines. In order to use the bus with a lift, one handicapped woman stated that she had to travel three blocks from her home, passing the closest bus stop. Whereas a college could change the location of a class to accommodate a handicapped student, changing bus routes for a greater number of people over a much wider area was much more difficult.[67]

The handicapped believed that the resistance to putting ramps on buses merely illustrated the prejudice against them. The *Disability Rag,* in a continuing series entitled "Transit Logic," pointed out that it cost twice as much to put air-conditioning in a bus as it did to install a ramp. Yet no public outcry arose over the cost of air-conditioning buses.[68]

The American Public Transit Authority and Ravitch believed the solution lay in a flexible paratransit system, such as vans, that would take the handicapped from door to door. This suggestion met with fierce resistance from Bowe and the other leaders of the handicapped rights movement. Separate facilities, they argued, implied less than equal facilities. In Boston, if a handicapped person wanted to use the dial-a-ride service, he had to notify the authorities five days in advance. This requirement would certainly take the spontaneity out of a shopping spree. In a 1982 General Accounting Office survey, 84 percent of the public transit systems with paratransit service reported that they were periodically unable to comply with requests; one-third of the systems maintained waiting lists for those who wanted to use their services. Furthermore, the hours of operation were limited in para-transit systems.[69]

The transportation issue remained unresolved by the mid-1980s. Its status reflected the state of the economy and the health of the public transportation budget. Each administration, each generation of poli-cymakers, faced a decision about how vigorously it wished to pursue reasonable accommodation or how far it wished to take compliance with the other disability rights laws.

Backlash

Even before Section 504 regulations appeared, a backlash developed against them and against the handicapped rights movement. At issue was the cost of making reasonable accommodations. A staffer in the Ford White House estimated that implementing the regulations might cost as much as $26 billion. A vice-president of the University of Mis-souri complained that not only would modifications to the university be costly, but they would also never be used. Immediately after Cali-fano signed the regulations, a story in the *New York Times* entitled "Equity for Disabled Likely to Be Costly," stated that no more than 30,000 handicapped people were expected to be in college at any one time and questioned the need to make each university accessible.[70]

The differences from earlier civil rights movements were significant. The black civil rights movement a decade earlier had reduced the cost of public accommodations in the South by reducing the need to have one facility for blacks and another for whites. Admitting James Mer-edith to the University of Mississippi cost nothing in an economic sense. All of the costs were political. Meredith required courage to attend classes, not ramps and wide toilet stalls with grab bars. In a similar sense, Rosa Parks did not need a ramp to reach the front of the bus. The very fact that people perceived discrimination to be costly eased acceptance of racial integration.

To admit James Meredith's handicapped counterpart to a university would cost money rather than save it. It would mean that the physical plant would need to be expanded or modified, and it would require the university to pay the administrative costs of complying with the federal regulations. Legal advisors to the American Council of Edu-cation warned that Section 504 would produce "sheaves of unread, unnecessary paper." Few people argued that way in Meredith's case. In the intervening decade, however, inflation had driven the cost of education to the point where major social initiatives, such as accommodating the handicapped, were subjected to substantial criticism because they were perceived to be costly.[71]

In 1977, news stories abounded on the rigidity, absurdity, and costliness of government regulation, including Section 504. The most widely reported story concerned the small town of Rudd, Iowa. This farming community of less than five hundred people had no one in a wheelchair, but it did have a public library. A regional office of HEW's Office of Civil Rights informed the town of Rudd that the library had to be made accessible. The townspeople claimed it would cost $6,500 to build a ramp for no one but the bureaucrats.[72]

With the Reagan victory, perceived as a mandate for deregulation, the leaders of the handicapped rights movement considered it a victory just to remain in the same place. Section 504, which provided for sweeping government interference in private operations, required voluminous paperwork and reporting, and cost a great deal to implement, looked like a prime target for reform.

On September 20, 1981, the Disability Rights Defense and Education Fund, concerned about a Reagan administration offensive, decided to establish a Washington office to protect the benefits secured in Section 504. The handicapped rights movement leader Evan Kemp argued that their goals and those of the Reagan administration were not dissimilar: Both accused big government of stifling initiative; both believed in welfare only for the truly needy; both denounced paternalistic government; and both were "antibureaucratic." In short, both believed in independence.

As William Roth noted, the handicapped rights movement was increasing its political sophistication by learning how to temper and tailor its rhetoric. In the past, leaders had spoken of entitlements and inherent rights. Now, with the arrival of Reagan and George Bush, who led an important Task Force for Regulatory Relief, the leaders stressed independence.[73]

Political sophistication and plain hard work paid off, and Section 504 emerged from Bush's Task Force largely unscathed. Bush and C. Boyden Gray, his counsel, had asked the Department of Justice to review a series of civil rights laws, including Section 504. In March 1982, proposed changes in Section 504 leaked to the press. By March 21, 1983, however, Bush sent Kemp a letter informing him that the administration would not press for changes in Section 504. Toward the end of Reagan's first term, Bush and others prominent in the administration were singing the praises of the handicapped. Gray said that the administration and the handicapped wanted the same thing, "to turn as many of the disabled as possible into taxpaying citizens." W. Bradford Reynolds, the Reagan administration's chief civil rights lawyer, said that the "point they're making is the difference between giving a man a fish and teaching him to catch his own. No good Republican can fault that."[74]

Beyond the efforts of Kemp and the other leaders, the administration's about-face on Section 504 resulted in part from public protest over revised regulations for the Education of All Handicapped Children Act. When the administration received 27,000 letters protesting the revisions, it gained new respect for the handicapped as a potential interest group. In addition, the administration needed Section 504 for Baby Doe.[75]

At issue was the right of parents and the other caretakers to withhold food from deformed or otherwise handicapped infants, on the grounds that these infants were better off dead or would die soon anyway. The handicapped rights community believed that such actions amounted to genocide. Many of the handicapped realized they might not have been alive if opponents of the Baby Doe regulations had had their way, so they viewed the issue as one concerning *their* right to life. To the Reagan administration, the issue formed part of a broader social agenda that included eliminating abortion. But both the Reagan administration and the handicapped rights community considered Section 504 to be applicable to the situation; killing deformed babies discriminated against the handicapped.

Here, then, the handicapped community and the liberals parted company. The *Disability Rag* wrote in an editorial, "We want the disability rights movement to be liberal, but liberals, in this issue, are siding with parents who want to withhold food from 'deformed' infants so they will die."[76]

The alliance between the administration and the handicapped community, however, like most pragmatically formed political liaisons, was unstable. Within weeks of Bush's agreement not to dismantle Section 504, Reynolds restricted its scope. He argued that a recipient of federal funds was responsible for complying with Section 504 only in those areas of his activities for which the funds were used. If a school received only student aid money from the federal government, then

224   Corrective response

only its student aid activities could be investigated by the federal government for Section 504 violations. "The paper victory is over," said handicapped rights leader Arlene Myers.[77]

Toward independence

Whatever the political problems of the moment, Section 504 remains the component of disability policy with the widest scope. It covers all of the handicapped, not just the industrially injured, the mentally retarded, the blind, those whose handicap keeps them from being employed, those who are covered by social security and cannot engage in substantial gainful activity, or those wounded in war.

The handicapped community can claim Section 504 and independent living centers as its special contributions to the nation's disability policy. Unlike the income-maintenance programs of the Progressive Era and the New Deal, Section 504 opens doors to participation rather than to retirement. Independent living centers also emphasize the participation of the handicapped in society rather than their withdrawal. Just as Section 504 is a partial answer to workers' compensation and disability insurance, independent living centers, which stress the autonomy of the handicapped and their need for independence from professional domination, are a response to vocational rehabilitation.

The rise of the handicapped as a minority group has therefore created alternatives to the nation's traditional disability policies. No longer do the handicapped have to wear artificial limbs to conform to able-bodied society or drop out of the mainstream and accept welfare benefits. There are now the possibilities of autonomy and independence.

But civil rights protection and independent living are not for everyone. They apply best to the young and to those whose mobility is impaired. Disability policy also must serve the demoralized worker at the disability hearing who wishes to retire. Reforming disability policy successfully depends on protecting his right to retire without at the same time consigning a whole new class of handicapped individuals to a life of dependency. The minority model has, for the first time in the nation's history, supplied an alternative to dependency. The problem for public policy is to incorporate that alternative into a set of programs that were built before the nation understood the capabilities of the handicapped.

Summary and conclusion

It should come as no surprise that no one has mastered all of the details of America's complex array of disability programs.

In the first place, no one person has all the expertise necessary to comprehend all the diverse legal, economic, and social phenomena encompassed by disability policy. Few have achieved mastery of such disparate subjects as nonacquiescence, the methods of compensating permanent partial disabilities, labor supply economics, the legal bases of civil rights law, and the principles of rehabilitation counseling. Even with such technical competence, a person would have to acquire a working knowledge of the massive details of all the programs before he could be proclaimed a well-rounded expert. And, as Elizabeth Boggs has noted, those details keep changing as policymakers consider and reconsider the proper direction for programs to help the disabled.

In the second place, we have, in general, lost the ability to see our social welfare system "whole." We have allowed cadres of experts to work out the details of single programs, often by using the specialized tools that come from training in the law and economics. Because few people understand the language of these experts, it is difficult to engage in general conversation about disability; conversation among the experts tends to be narrow, focusing on one program. Not only the experts but the politicians and others who interpret the analysis to the public have difficulty seeing the social welfare system whole. Congressmen, for example, operate by means of subcommittees that are heavily dependent on experts, interest groups, and others who have learned the specialized language of policy discourse. A congressman may discover that, outside of those immediately affected by a program, few people care about disability policy. Rarely, then, does the level of analysis rise above individual programs to include the larger picture. Congress and the nation debate Social Security Disability Insurance, not disability policy.

The profusion of detail and the inability to rise above it have had significant consequences for disability policy. Simply put, disability has not received the attention it deserves as a policy problem.) As mentioned earlier, no single agency, except for a very small, uninfluential one, called the National Council on the Handicapped, and no single congressional committee monitor disability policy or observe how programs interact with each other.

Everyone, it seems, is locked into a particular academic or political concern. Academics denigrate those whose knowledge is merely institutional; academia engages in explorations of theory, rather than coming to grips with the details of disability and other social welfare programs. The more politically minded analysts too faithfully mirror the concerns and hence the limitations of Congress itself.

That is why history is so important. It brings order to the labyrinth of disability programs. It enables us to see a progression from one generation to another and to compare outcome with expectations. It allows us to observe changing conditions and to perceive the dilemmas caused by the tug of modern problems on old programs. Even as these dilemmas come into focus, history reveals the resistance of programs to change. The historian understands in ways that other policy analysts might not that the present follows logically from the past: With these insights, a historian can open up a clear view of the larger picture that is denied by the structure of modern policymaking. Because of the vision that history affords, it can help to guide reform.

Perhaps the most significant insight afforded by this historical overview of disability policy is that we use old programs to cope with new problems. Consider the policy problems posed by occupational illnesses. Epidemiologists continue to discover new links between working conditions and diseases. Workers' compensation programs, the nation's major program for compensating and rehabilitating those who have the diseases, were simply not designed to handle these new conditions. Nonetheless, instead of a national law to cover industrial diseases, this country relies on more than fifty state and territorial laws, financed in ways reminiscent of practices in the nineteenth century.

This anachronistic approach to occupational disability resembles our policy toward dependency and poverty in general. In the case of welfare, we maintain state "widow's pension" laws (which we now call Aid to Families with Dependent Children), created in the same era as workers' compensation laws. Critics condemn both laws for their inability to return clients to the labor force. Yet why should these laws accomplish this modern objective, when both were created to keep their clients at home with their families? The purposes to which society desires to put social welfare policy have changed faster than the programs designed to accomplish those objectives.

Disability does not represent an exception to the general pattern of anachronistic and uncoordinated programs that are resistant to change. Efforts to change workers' compensation and welfare laws serve to illustrate this point. As the experience of the National Commission on State Workermen's Compensation demonstrates, interest groups, which have learned to handle the politics of workers' compensation, have a stake in the program's survival. Consequently, recurrent discussions about federalizing workers' compensation have yielded little in the way of substantive reform. Benefit levels, by way of contrast, have been raised in response to interest-group pressure. Reform has therefore taken place within the existing contours of the program and involved incremental, rather than fundamental, change. In a similar manner, efforts to federalize Aid to Families with Dependent Children (the nation's major welfare program), which took place at roughly the same time as the meetings of the National Commission on State Workermen's Compensation Laws, produced little in the way of substantive change.

In disability, as in social welfare in general, the only avenue of fundamental reform is to add another program to existing programs and to cope with the resulting confusion. To a certain extent, the administrators of programs learn from one another; the creators of the next layer of programs try to avoid the mistakes and remedy the problems of the previous layers. The creators of Social Security Disability Insurance were clearly aware of the limitations of workers' compensation and strove to avoid them in their new program. Even this advance knowledge of potential problems, however, could not save the Social Security Disability Insurance program from the pitfalls of state administration and prevent it from becoming more litigious as it developed. What happened in this case, as in so many others, is that the science of public administration failed to overcome the patterns of partisan politics. The creators of Disability Insurance discovered that they could not create a self-executing blueprint that would be immune from the give-and-take of congressional, judicial, and federal politics.

Because of these tendencies, our disability policy, viewed in its historical context, consists of layers of outdated programs. Ever since the

Progressive Era at the beginning of the century, significant events have occurred in each decade that have altered the course of social welfare policy in general and of disability policy in particular.

A first generation of disability programs, workers' compensation, mirrors the prevailing outlook of the Progressive Era and its condemnation of asylums and other institutions as poor substitutes for the home and the family. The program also reflects the progressive-era preference for specialists to cope with societal problems – in this case, a specialized industrial commissioner to settle industrial accident cases – rather than a judge in a court of law who handles a wide range of cases.

In the 1920s, vocational rehabilitation joined the ranks of the nation's disability programs. It was to be the corrective program that would complement the work of the compensation agencies by helping the handicapped, many of whom would be referred by the compensation agencies, to get jobs. To accomplish this objective, the program used the same methods the social welfare agencies were then applying to the poor: social diagnosis by means of psychologically oriented casework.

In the 1930s, it made less sense to diagnose the individual problems of the poor and more to get money into their hands quickly. Although the Social Security Act borrowed from existing programs, it also established new social insurance programs that viewed poverty not as a form of pathology so much as the result of the insecurities that were an inevitable part of the modern industrial economy. The old age insurance program established a means by which people could set aside money during their working lifetimes and retire on a modest pension at age sixty-five. In 1956, disability was placed in the general framework established for the old age insurance program.

The 1940s and 1950s represented the heyday of the professional approach toward social welfare programs as exemplified by the investment that Congress made in medical research and technology. During the 1950s, as part of the resurgence of faith in the ability of professionals to manage social problems, vocational rehabilitation enjoyed a revival, and policymakers optimistically expected rehabilitation counselors to transform the applicants for disability pensions into productive members of the labor force. This transformation failed to occur, just as policymakers had proved unable to change a culture of poverty into a culture of opportunity.

In the 1960s, a crisis occurred that had a profound effect on social welfare policy. Minority groups, such as blacks and women, began to assert their claim to basic rights and to challenge the authority of the professional groups, such as social workers, who acted as the gate-keepers of social programs. As the rights movements questioned the effectiveness of programs that sought to change minorities, the costs of entitlement programs, such as social security, began to rise. People feared that as the large baby-boom generation reached the age of re-tirement, it would create an unmanageable drain on public funds. In the 1970s, such fears were heightened by the fact that the costs of social security, already high, were growing at a precipitious rate, even though the baby-boom generation had not begun to retire. Both the challenge of minority groups from the left and the alarm over the cost of entitlement programs generated by the right caused policymakers to rethink their commitment to social welfare programs.

As in previous decades, the disabled were swept up in the trends of the 1960s and 1970s. Rising disability insurance costs precipitated a major effort to reduce incentives to go on the disability rolls, produc-ing first a major reform of the Social Security Disability Insurance program (in 1980) and then a major reform of the reform (in 1984). The actions of minority groups provided a model for the disabled to follow and led to the enactment of civil rights laws and independent living programs.

One result is the presence of two generations of ameliorative (or income-maintenance) programs stemming from the Progressive Era and the New Deal and two generations of service (or corrective) programs, one originating in the 1920s and the other in the 1970s. Another leg-acy of these layers of programs is the continued presence of unsolved policy problems such as litigation, which inhibit efforts at reform, and a failure to devise a way to rehabilitate those on disability pensions.

Litigation, as we have seen, has become a feature of the workers' compensation, disability insurance, vocational rehabilitation, and civil rights programs, despite an explicit desire to eliminate it in the first two programs and the near impossibility of its ever having arisen in the third. Wasteful, whatever the context, litigation poses particular problems in disability policy. Because it is a time-consuming process, it delays rehabilitation. Because of the fragmentation of disability pol-icy, however, administrators, congressmen, and members of the hand-icapped community are not aware of the trend toward more litigation.

Unless they become aware of the trend, they will hardly be able to take measures to reverse it. Yet here, as elsewhere, the desired direction for change is clear. Instead of fighting about who owes what to whom, the focus should be on making disability itself an anachronism.

The failure to blend income maintenance and rehabilitation, repeated through two generations of ameliorative programs, is another example of a problem that policymakers have never squarely faced but whose history can be clearly discerned. Congressmen, for example, have preferred to talk about the dilemmas of dependency rather than to make changes in programs that would encourage independence. At the time, no plans exist for members of the House Subcommittee on Social Security to work with members of the Subcommittee on the Handicapped on a realistic plan to rehabilitate disability beneficiaries. On the contrary, Congress hopes to ignore Social Security Disability Insurance for a bit, its political resources exhausted from the triple play of the 1980 disability amendments, the 1983 social security financing amendments, and the 1984 disability amendments. For the moment, the window of opportunity remains shut.

The historian's frustration with our disability policy, then, is that so much of it looks backward when we have the means to move forward. The central problem of disability policy is not hard to discern. The nation concentrates too much of its money on granting tickets out of the labor force and gives too little attention to the demands of the handicapped for tickets into the labor force. Social Security Disability Insurance is our best-run and, in a strictly administrative sense, our most successful disability program; vocational rehabilitation is among our worst programs. Social security transfers money to the handicapped far more efficiently than vocational rehabilitation prepares the handicapped to enter the labor force. Somewhere we have misplaced our priorities. Equal concern, creativity, and energy should go into rehabilitation as into financial compensation for disability or early retirement.

But such a fundamental reorientation of disability policy means coming to grips with our legacies from the past. We cannot simply wipe the slate clean. As a generation of modern reformers has discovered, the trick of social welfare policy lies not so much in designing better programs as in getting from here to there. A good working assumption is that existing programs will not disappear and will prove to be highly resistant even to incremental change, particularly if that change threatens to limit the size or importance of the program. Idealism sets the broad outlines of change; hard-headed realism brings about change.

With those words of caution, let me suggest desirable changes in our disability programs, beginning with workers' compensation. We need to examine closely the benefit structure of these state programs, which will remain an integral part of the nation's response to disability. Benefits must be divorced completely from the concept of fault; instead, a wage-loss approach to compensating for disability should be adopted. A disabled person should receive a substantial portion of lost wages – at least two-thirds of his weekly wage – plus all of his disability-related medical care and all of his rehabilitation expenses from the program. Instead of being compensated from a schedule of impairments, or from an estimate of his total physical disability, he should be compensated for the actual wages he has lost. Employers who wish to rehabilitate a worker in order to reinstate him in his former job should be encouraged to do so.

Is such a change possible? Florida already has the beginnings of such a system. In other states, employers might be encouraged to accept these changes on the grounds that they will save money. In return, workers need the assurance that employers will make every effort to bring them back to work after an accident and that, should the effort at working fail, they can return to the benefit rolls.

This suggested change in benefit structure places a large obligation on employers to prevent disability. Some employers have begun to respond to the challenge by instituting a system called disability management at the workplace; it takes many different forms but always stems from the realization that a short window of time exists in which to prevent disability and thereby reduce its costs. The slower and less coordinated an employer's intervention after an accident or illness, the more likely an employee will progress from illness to disability.

The Boise Cascade company has been involved with disability management since 1979, when it discovered that 250 of its employees at a Minnesota plant were disabled and drawing workers' compensation. Since the increase in workers' compensation costs showed no signs of abating, management grew concerned about disability expenses. The company called in a consulting psychologist who studied the physical requirements of each job and determined that many jobs could be modified to allow disabled employees to return to work. Eventually

100 of the 250 returned, and the company's workers' compensation liability dropped from $13 million to $3 million. The company also increased the size of its medical department, became directly involved in the rehabilitation of injured workers, and prepared a special training film to make supervisors sensitive to the needs of the handicapped workers.[1]

I realize that we cannot base national policy on anecdotal evidence. Disability management applies to the particular needs of particular companies facing particular problems. It is therefore a highly heterogeneous movement that often owes its prominence within companies to the zeal of individual corporate managers. Neither the circumstances nor the zeal of the managers can be translated from one setting to another. Nonetheless, the case of Boise Cascade illustrates how the private sector can aid in the reform of workers' compensation and disability policy generally. Simply put, the private sector needs incentives not to put people on the disability rolls.

Social Security Disability Insurance, the nation's largest disability program, has even more need of these incentives than workers' compensation. That is why I think the time is right to introduce "experience rating" into Social Security Disability Insurance. Employers with fewer employees on the disability rolls than is the norm should receive a discount on the 0.5 percent of the first $42,000 of an employee's wages that they pay into the disability insurance trust fund.[2]

I know that this suggestion will not sit well with the Social Security administrators who have rejected experience rating as a tool of social policy. In part, their attitude stems from their analysis of experience rating in the workers' compensation program. Does it encourage safer behavior among employers and reduce disability? The evidence is difficult to evaluate, in part because it is difficult to differentiate the effects of a general rise in wages and insurance costs from the effects of experience rating and in part because insurance arrangements under workers' compensation are so complicated. Experience rating affects larger firms more than small firms. The insurance rates of large firms that generate from half a million dollars worth of premium income for an insurance company are based directly on "actual" experience. Less emphasis is placed on such experience in the computation of the insurance premiums of smaller firms. The largest companies, such as the Ford Motor Company or General Motors, which self-insure in the states that permit this practice, have the purest form of experience rating. Many of the companies that are active in disability management at the workplace are self-insurers.[3]

The workers' compensation precedent suggests a potential problem with experience rating in Social Security Disability Insurance; larger firms may gain an advantage over smaller firms. If the discount is based on the number of employees who entered the social security disability rolls, a small firm would be penalized far more heavily for having one worker enter the rolls, even though its investment in disability prevention would be proportionately greater. In general, the discount would have a much more powerful effect on companies with large payrolls than on companies with smaller ones.

Applying experience rating to Social Security Disability Insurance also would undermine an important tradition in social security, which is that workers and employers bear an equal part of the social security tax burden. To grant employers a discount would mean that they would pay less for social security than employees (unless, of course, the discount applied to employees as well, to give them an incentive to reduce disability costs). Furthermore, if experience rating were applied to disability insurance, it would be logical to extend the discount to medicare as well, since the two programs are directly related. And might it not make sense to allow experience rating in old age insurance, since old age insurance includes early retirement which, in many cases, stems from disability? If carried to this extreme, experience rating would represent a significant and unwise change in the entire social security program.

Then come the perplexing econometric questions concerning the effect of a relatively small payroll tax on economic behavior. Would changes in the tax induce significant change in employer behavior, or would the differences be too slight to be noticed? After all, the present annual tax rate amounts to $210 per employee for the highest-paid employees. How much should the discount for "safe" behavior be in order to produce the optimal effect and still keep the disability trust fund solvent?

Nor do the questions end there. Administrative difficulties also would arise. What if the worker's disability had nothing to do with his employer, or what if the worker had worked for many employers before becoming disabled? One reason for the success of social security is that the program has stayed away from such questions (which are characteristic of workers' compensation); experience rating would introduce the questions to Social Security Disability Insurance.

Aware of these difficulties, I nonetheless propose that legislators experiment with experience rating in the Social Security Disability Insurance program. We need to send a signal to the nation's employers that disability represents a significant social cost. Experience rating sends that signal in a way that encourages employers to prevent disability.

Before experience rating can be passed, congressmen will have to consider the effects of such a move on disability policy, breaking their habit of considering the solvency of social security first and disability second. If policymakers begin to consider disability a significant problem in its own right, then they will come to understand the need for a fundamental rethinking of Social Security Disability Insurance. It may make sense for all sixty-five-year-olds to receive essentially the same level of social security benefits; it makes less sense for all of the disabled to receive similar benefits. It would not shatter the integrity of disability insurance or lessen its political appeal to recognize differences among people who apply and to end the all-or-nothing quality of disability insurance. There should be a middle ground, one that encourages independence, between receiving and not receiving benefits.

I propose a division between income-maintenance benefits, as in the present program, and what I call "independence initiatives." Some people should be allowed to retire and receive income-maintenance benefits, just as they do today. We should not waste money trying to rehabilitate those who have spent time in the labor force, broken down, and now want to retire. Let those people retire. But the program should have room for younger individuals, like Judy Heumann or Lex Frieden, who are disabled but who have much to contribute to the labor force. These people should be encouraged to accept independence initiatives in the form of vouchers that could be exchanged for attendant care or the modification of transportation and architectural barriers. These independence initiatives should include a lifetime entitlement to medicare, since experience indicates that access to medical care constitutes the most severe barrier to sustained employment. No one wants to lose his health insurance coverage, and many will hesitate to accept a job if it means that they might ultimately find themselves unemployed and uncovered.

Under the terms of my proposal, an applicant for disability insurance would fall under one of four categories: He might be rejected for any benefits; he might be eligible for retirement benefits, although without having to submit to continuing disability investigations or other forms of periodic surveillance; he might be given independence initiatives; or he might be given interim benefits. This last category would be valid only for a short period of time, such as a year, during which a person would attempt to find a job. If he found a job, he would be released from the disability rolls; if he failed to find a job, he could reapply to the program and achieve a permanent status.

Does such a program stand a chance of passage and is it feasible? Senator Reigle has proposed a somewhat similar bill and discovered that, although the Senate Committee on Finance will entertain the idea and hold hearings, the measure will not be passed in the near future; its ultimate chances depend on estimates of its potential cost. Having passed two major disability bills recently, Congress is in no position to contemplate Reigle's bill soon. My proposal, like Reigle's, must be considered a goal to aim for over the long term.

One consideration that stands in the way of implementing this proposal is that it will make the job of the disability determination offices even more complicated than at present. No one can predict the future course of an individual's impairment or make rules that take both individual differences and the future performance of the economy into account. Disability, as we have seen, resists precise measurement: It simply is not like poverty or old age. To expect more than fifty disability determination offices to put people into four complex categories in an equitable and consistent manner may be to expect the impossible. Nor does it appear likely that the job will be made easier by federalizing the disability determination services or by eliminating the control that the administrative law judges and the courts exercise over the process. However, the new system might take some of the pressure off the state agencies by allowing them to use the interim status essentially to defer a decision.

The difficulties of implementation suggest that the time between now and passage of the bill might profitably be used by attempting to establish a set of rules that the disability examiners would be able to follow. In the past, we have simply dumped new tasks on the state agencies, such as the black lung program, the Supplemental Security Income program, and the periodic disability reviews, without analyzing how these new tasks could be meshed with existing routines. Successful implementation of disability reform means paying attention to the needs and capabilities of state workers.

A final problem with this proposal must be faced before Congress can seriously consider its passage. Just what would the independence initiatives consist of? Beyond entitlement to medicare, most of the suggestions (such as the elimination of architectural barriers) apply to the mobility impaired far more than to other disabled individuals, such as the mentally retarded or someone suffering from a debilitating form of cancer. Could independence initiatives be designed for these other groups? I believe they could: It would first require serious study and then hard bargaining with representatives of the various handicapped groups. My blueprinting, in other words, would no more be able to transcend politics than any other legislative proposal.

If the social welfare programs of the past twenty years are any indication, even the most carefully devised plans can produce adverse affects. For that reason, I believe that changes in Supplemental Security Income, the welfare program for the handicapped, must accompany changes in Social Security Disability Insurance. States should be allowed to use more liberal definitions of disability than they do at present and still receive federal funding to pay for benefits. As matters stand, this program continues to use the stringent definition of disability developed for the Social Security Disability Insurance program, last modified in 1967. When tightening occurs in the disability insurance program, as happened in the early 1980s, those cut from the disability insurance rolls find themselves with no place to turn; ineligible for disability, they also are ineligible for supplemental security income. This part of the safety net should be strengthened. Further, I suspect that this line of reasoning will appeal to congressmen who have not subjected Supplemental Security Income, the program of the "worthy" poor, to the severe cuts that have been made in other welfare programs. They might entertain a liberalization of social security income.

The fact that I have devoted so much attention to the ameliorative programs merely reflects the priorities of our present system; it does not mean that changes are not desirable in the two generations of corrective programs. I believe, for example, that the time may have come to reconsider the emphasis that we currently place on vocational rehabilitation. I do not think that the program should be eliminated; I know it will not be. The Reagan administration tried and failed to fold the program into a social service block grant and in the process discovered the power wielded by state vocational rehabilitation directors. Besides, moderately impaired people benefit from the job counseling and other services that the program provides. Keep the present program, I would argue, but do not expand it.

Instead, one generation of programs needs to yield to another, and rehabilitation should give way to independent living. Instead of spending so much money on rehabilitation research and training projects that are peripheral to the basic rehabilitation program and that do not directly benefit the handicapped, the nation should dedicate funds for the establishment and maintenance of independent living centers. I propose the creation of "independent living block grants" to localities. Money from these grants should be used to start independent living centers and to coordinate independent living services. Although local rehabilitation counselors, with their knowledge of job placement and their many other skills, would be very useful in such an effort, the emphasis should be on independent living, not vocational rehabilitation.

I think that independent living block grants could facilitate disability management in both the private and public sectors. Employers could turn to the center for help in accommodating an injured employee; they might appropriately use workers' compensation funds to pay for the services rendered. As their handicapped employees prepared to return to work and to resume their lives with disabilities, they might profit from contact with an independent living center, which would provide practical advice from one handicapped person to another. The block grants could help fund an employee's continuing association with the center, even after he returned to work. The centers also could help applicants to the disability insurance program who have been put on an interim status or who have been granted independence initiatives. The independence initiative vouchers would provide another source of funds for the centers. In short, independent living centers could serve as focal points for a disability policy that favors participation over withdrawal, work rather than retirement.

I must stress again, however, that independent living centers are not for everyone. They will continue to serve more of the younger, mobility-impaired people than developmentally disabled individuals. They will only be as good as the level of resources and of interest in a particular community can make them. Nor are the practical policy problems associated with social service block grants, of the type that would fund the centers, insignificant. Federal policymakers hesitate to create grants that can be used for a wide variety of purposes, for fear that the money will be wasted or will not reach the groups that Congress intends to aid. Consequently, regulation writers typically build in rules to limit the ways in which the money can be spent. As the red tape unravels, it becomes progressively more costly to implement the services; only the groups with the patience and resources to endure expensive regulatory battles end up with the money from the grants. To gain the flexibility necessary to reach across programs, we must be prepared to sacrifice a bit of what policymakers call accountability.

As the nation explores more fully the notion of independence for the handicapped, I think it will recognize the value of Section 504 and other civil rights measures and endorse their vigorous enforcement. As the handicapped become integrated into the daily life of America, the nation should and will, I believe, express its commitment to their full participation in society by passing a law that expands civil rights protection to cover private sector, as well as public sector, activities. After all, independence will only become a reality if jobs are accessible and if physical and attitudinal barriers are lowered. Realistically, however, I think that the nation's policymakers will need to be impressed with the capabilities of the handicapped before such a law is passed. Civil rights laws tend to restate reality rather than serve as the leading edge of change. But that does not diminish their effectiveness or their symbolic importance.

As we work harder at accommodation, we should not lose sight of the goal of prevention. None of the present programs, with the partial exception of workers' compensation, emphasizes prevention. One way to encourage thinking about prevention would be to put experience rating into Social Security Disability Insurance. Another way would be to make this topic the research mission of the National Institute of Handicapped Research and to stress the mission's importance by putting this institute into the National Institutes of Health, where it would gain prestige and visibility.

In recommending changes in individual disability programs, I do not want to lose sight of the big picture; each disability program has to be reconsidered in relation to the others and to its effect on disability policy.

That is why I strongly urge, no matter what other changes are made, that a committee in Congress and an agency in the executive branch of the federal government be created that will consider disability policy as a whole, not little pieces of it. I have in mind a congressional joint oversight committee on disability that will monitor trends, such as the rise in litigation; prepare an annual disability budget that would enable the country to observe its disability expenditures from year to year; and provide a forum for fundamental change in disability policy. In the executive branch, I recommend giving the National Council on the Handicapped more staff and funding so that it could enlarge its mission. It would have the task of making sure that the nation's disability policy recognizes the capabilities of the handicapped.

Recognition of these capabilities and a willingness to part with anachronistic practices are the keys to disability reform. Enlarging or reshuffling the bureaucracy will not produce change; at most it will produce the awareness that might lead to change. Nor, as I have tried to stress, is the reform of disability policy a simple matter of bringing our programs up to date. Consider, for a moment, the various people described in this book: the woman from Pennsylvania who was mentally and physically ill as well as old and demoralized, yet who was denied disability benefits; the man who injured his back laying carpet and who appeared at a workers' compensation hearing; the man affected by mental illness who came to the administrative hearing in Chicago; the man who worked with asbestos in Baltimore and suffered from shortness of breath; Linda Ross, articulate yet manic-depressive; Judy Heumann, Lex Frieden, and Ed Roberts, who use a wheelchair to walk; Frank Bowe, who is deaf. Are all of these people members of the same minority group? Should the same policies be applied to all?

The answer to these questions is no. But the truth is that we have used diversity among the handicapped as a means to subsume disability under other headings and to create a policy that impugns the integrity of those who deserve to retire while making it difficult for the handicapped to work. Strip away all the complexity and fragmentation with which we have surrounded disability and the choice is simple. Do we wish to continue to perpetuate policies that keep all of the people mentioned in this book from working?

For now it is no exaggeration to say that America remains without a disability policy. I believe it needs one.

Notes

Introduction

1 For a comprehensive overview of disability expenditures, see Monroe Berkowitz, *Disability Expenditures 1970–1982* (New Brunswick, N.J.: Rut-
gers Bureau of Economic Research, 1985). These expenditures, it should be
emphasized, represent estimates, and many simplifying assumptions have
been used. Other important surveys of disability policy that have preceded
and influenced this one include Deborah Stone, *The Disabled State* (Philadelphia, Pa.: Temple University Press, 1984); Robert Haveman et al., *Public Policy toward Disabled Workers: Cross National Analyses of Economic
Impacts* (Ithaca, N.Y.: Cornell University Press, 1984); Monroe Berkowitz
et al., *Public Policy toward Disability* (New York: Praeger, 1976); Frank
Bowe, *Handicapping America: Barriers to Disabled People* (New York:
Harper and Row, 1978); John Gliedman and William Roth, *The Unexpected Minority: Handicapped Children in America* (New York: Harcourt,
Brace, Jovanovich, 1980). In addition, this book has relied heavily on sources
in social welfare history and social security policy. Among the most helpful
of these books for my purposes were James T. Patterson, *America's Struggle
against Poverty, 1900–1980* (Cambridge, Mass.: Harvard University Press,
1981); Roy Lubove, *Struggle for Social Security* (Cambridge, Mass.: Harvard University Press, 1968); Paul Starr, *The Social Transformation of
American Medicine* (New York: Basic Books, 1982); William Graebner, *A
History of Retirement* (New Haven, Conn.: Yale University Press, 1980);
and the indispensible Martha Derthick, *Policymaking for Social Security*
(Washington, D.C.: Brookings Institution, 1979).
2 John D. Worrall and David Appel, "Some Benefit Issues in Workers' Compensation," in *Workers' Compensation Benefits: Adequacy, Equity, and
Efficiency*, ed. Worall and Appel (Ithaca, N.Y.: ILR Press, 1985), p. 18.
3 *Social Security Bulletin: Annual Statistical Supplement, 1984–1985* (Washington, D.C.: Social Security Administration, 1985), pp. 1, 82.
4 Lawrence D. Haber, "Trends and Demographic Studies on Programs for
Disabled Persons," in *Social Influences in Rehabilitation Planning: Blueprint for the 21st Century*, ed. Leonard G. Perlman and Gary F. Austin
(Arlington, Va.: National Rehabilitation Association, 1985), pp. 34–35.
Haber provides an introduction to the various definitions. This volume follows the definitions developed by Nagi. See Saad Nagi, "Measuring Disability," in *Disability Programs and Government Policies*, ed. Edward Berkowitz (New York: Praeger, 1979), pp. 1–15. Impairments and functional
limitations refer to physical phenomena; disability and handicap are social
phenomena.

5 "Memorandum on Maria Deaver," June 12, 1958, Box 1, Accession 67-270, Records of the Social Security Administration, Washington National Records Center, Suitland, Md.

6 *Social Security Bulletin: Annual Statistical Supplement 1981* (Washington, D.C.: Social Security Administration, 1981), pp. 11, 100–101.

7 Harlan Hahn, *The Issue of Equality: European Perceptions of Employment for Disabled Persons* (New York: World Rehabilitation Fund, 1984), pp. 10–11.

Part I: Income maintenance programs

1 Elizabeth M. Boggs, "A Taxonomy of Federal Programs Affecting Developmental Disabilities," in *Mental Retardation and Developmental Disabilities,* ed. John Wortis (New York: Brunner/Mazel, 1978), vol. 10, p. 214.

Chapter 1

1 Among the many books that discuss the legal origins of workers' compensation is Herman M. Somers and Anne Somers, *Workmen's Compensation: Prevention, Insurance and Rehabilitation of Occupational Disability* (New York: John Wiley and Sons, 1954), pp. 17–26. Although more than thirty years old, this excellent book remains the standard account of workers' compensation. The book combines a historical survey of workers' compensation with a discussion of policy problems that, it turns out, have not changed much since the book was written. Like Somers and Somers, I try to combine history and policy analysis in this chapter. It is not a chronology of workers' compensation. Rather, it is a historical essay on how practices in the program originated and how they led to problems as time passed. These "first-generation problems" recur in the second-generation disability programs, such as Social Security Disability Insurance, of which I have provided a full chronological account in chapters 2 and 4.

2 *Report of the Employee's Liability Commission of the State of Illinois* (Chicago: Stromberg, Allen, 1910), p. 42.

3 Roy Lubove, "Workmen's Compensation and the Prerogatives of Voluntarism," *Labor History* 8 (Fall 1967), p. 261.

4 See Edward Berkowitz and Monroe Berkowitz, "Challenges to Workers' Compensation: A Historical Analysis," in *Workers' Compensation Benefits: Adequacy, Equity, and Efficiency,* ed. David Appel and John D. Worrall (Ithaca, N.Y.: ILR Press, 1985), pp. 158–79; Lubove, "Workmen's Compensation"; Lawrence M. Friedman and Jack Ladinsky, "Social Change and the Law of Industrial Accidents," *Columbia Law Review* 67 (1967), p. 59.

5 Friedman and Ladinsky, "Social Change," pp. 59–67.

6 Walter Dodd, *Administration of Workmen's Compensation* (New York: Commonwealth Fund, 1936), p. 21.

7 Lubove, "Workmen's Compensation," p. 258.

8 Joseph F. Tripp, "An Instance of Labor and Business Cooperation: Workmen's Compensation in Washington State (1911)," *Labor History* 17 (Fall 1976), p. 537; Friedman and Ladinsky, "Social Change," p. 59.

9 Dodd, *Administration of Workmen's Compensation,* p. 24; *Report of the*

Employee's Liability Commission of the State of Illinois (Chicago, 1910), p. 76.

10 Robert Asher, "The Convenient Reform" (unpublished manuscript), p. 109.

11 The Laws of the State of Washington, "Chapter 51.04 RCW General Provisions, RCW 51.040.010, Declaration of Policy Power – Jurisdiction of Courts Abolished," in *Industrial Insurance Laws of the State of Washington* (Olympia, Wash.: Department of Labor and Industry, 1983), p. 1.

12 Tripp, "Labor and Business Cooperation," pp. 540, 543; *Report of the Employee's Liability Commission of the State of Illinois*, p. 14; Asher, "Business and Workers' Welfare in the Progressive Era: Workmen's Compensation Reform in Massachusetts, 1880–1911," *Business History Review* 43 (Winter 1969), p. 470. Asher's article provides an exhaustive look at the political forces that produced the worker's compensation law in Massachusetts.

13 Asher, "Radicalism and Reform: State Insurance of Workmen's Compensation in Minnesota, 1910–1933," *Labor History* 14 (Winter 1973), pp. 34–5.

14 U.S. Congress, Senate, *Workmen's Compensation – Report upon Operations of State Laws*, 63d Cong., 2d sess., 414, 416, 419.

15 Gerald Nash, "The Influence of Labor on State Policy," *California Historical Society Quarterly* 62 (September 1963), p. 251; Dodd, *Administration of Workmen's Compensation*, p. 215.

16 Quoted in "Submission of Industrial Accident Commission of California to Conrad Moss, Chairman, Workmen's Compensation Study Commission," 4 June 1964, Record Group 220, Records of the National Commission on State Workmen's Compensation Laws, National Archives, Washington, D.C. This record group is used to store the records of most presidential commissions, not just those of the commission on state workers' compensation laws.

17 Ibid.

18 Walton Hamilton to Arthur Altmeyer, 16 January 1937, Record Group 47, Records of the Social Security Administration, File 156.3, National Archives, Washington, D.C.; Mr. Joseph to William Haber, 26 June 1940, Record Group 47, File 056.11. The social security records are divided between the National Archives, Washington, D.C., and the Washington National Records Center, Suitland, Md. (WNRC). Those in WNRC, which are designated by record group and accession number, are closed to researchers without written permission from the Social Security Administration, Baltimore, Md.

19 Dodd, *Administration of Workmen's Compensation*, pp. 279–86.

20 Ibid., pp. 273–77.

21 "Injury on Public Sidewalk Not Compensible," *Workmen's Compensation Bulletin* 2 (July 1983), p. 3.

22 Dodd, *Administration of Workmen's Compensation*, p. 733; Bryce B. Moore, "Determining Compensation Due under the Kansas Workmen's Compensation Act," *Journal of the Kansas Bar Association* (Fall 1983), p. 223.

23 Evelyn Ellen Singleton, *Workmen's Compensation in Maryland* (Baltimore, Md.: Johns Hopkins University Press, 1935), pp. 67, 69.

24 James Gaffney, Massachusetts State Industrial Commissioner, quoted in Patrick Thomas, "Attorneys – The Least of the System's Problems," *Business Insurance,* clippings file, Record Group 220.

25 Remarks of Abe Weberman at Conference on Social Security Law, 22 May 1984, Detroit, Mich.

26 Personal correspondence from Abby Struck, legal technician, State of Minnesota, 19 June 1984.

27 Wisconsin Department of Industry, Labor and Human Relations, *Facts for Injured Workers about the Wisconsin Workers' Compensation Law* (Madison, Wisc.: July 1983).

28 Interview with Larry Tarr and observation of hearing, 2 July 1984, Alexandria, Va.

29 Ronald Conley and John H. Noble, Jr., *Workers' Compensation Reform: Challenge for the 80's,* Interdepartment Workers' Compensation Task Force (Washington, D.C.: Government Printing Office, 1979), pp. 99–103.

30 Arthur Larson, "Workmen's Compensation: Tensions of the Next Decade" (unpublished manuscript), p. 23; State of Washington, Department of Labor and Industries, *Workmen's Compensation Industrial Insurance Employees Guide* (Olympia, 1982), p. 9; Moore, "Determining Compensation," p. 218.

31 On the development of schedules in Illinois, Wisconsin, and elsewhere, see Dodd, *Administration of Workmen's Compensation,* pp. 43–44; Evelyn Singleton, *Workmen's Compensation in Maryland,* pp. 50–51; Wisconsin Department of Industry, Labor and Human Relations, *100th Anniversary of the Department of Industry, Labor and Human Relations* (Madison: State of Wisconsin, 1983) pp. 12–14; Monroe Berkowitz, "Trends and Problems in Workmen's Compensation," *Social Service Review* 32 (1958), p. 177; Arthur H. Reede, *Adequacy of Workmen's Compensation* (Cambridge, Mass.: Harvard University Press, 1947), pp. 117–18, 124.

32 Industrial Accident Commission of California to Conrad Moss, 4 June 1964, Record Group 220.

33 Dr. Henry Kessler made this observation; cited in Dodd, *Administration of Workmen's Compensation,* p. 631.

34 Tony Korioth, ed. and comp., *Digest of Texas Workers' Compensation Law* (Austin: Workers' Compensation, 1982), pp. 17–18; Department of Labor and Industrial Relations, Disability Compensation Division, *Hawaii Workers' Compensation Law* (Honolulu, 1982), p. 17.

35 Kansas Workers' Compensation Agency, "Table of Maximum Benefits, Kansas Workers' Compensation Law," obtained from State of Kansas; Moore, "Determining Compensation," pp. 16–22.

36 Abby Struck to author, 19 June 1984.

37 State of Hawaii, Department of Labor and Industrial Relations, *Work Injury Statistics* (Honolulu, 1982), p. 2.

38 Reede, *Adequacy,* pp. 49–50.

39 Singleton, *Workmen's Compensation in Maryland,* pp. 25–29.

40 Larson, "Workmen's Compensation: Tensions of the Next Decade," p. 7; "Exposure Draft," Report of the National Association of Insurance Commissioners Occupational Disease Advisory Committee, November 19, 1984, pp. 2-1, 3-1, 5-2, 5-7.

41 Conley and Noble, *Workers' Compensation Reform,* pp. 33–4, 110–11.

42 Ibid., p. 158.

43 "Exposure Draft," Report of the NAIC Occupation Disease Advisory Committee, pp. 2-1 (quotes Congressman Miller), 2-6.

44 Anthony Pipitone, "Ex-Shipyard Worker Settles Asbestos Suit," *Evening Sun,* 1 November 1984, p. B-1.

45 Representative George Miller, "National Tragedy of Asbestos Disease," material reprinted from *Congressional Record,* 26 May 1983; available from Representative Miller's office.

46 Department of Labor, *1954 Annual Report,* quoted in Monroe Berkowitz, "Trends and Problems in Workmen's Compensation," p. 168; address by Arthur Larson delivered 28 October 1954, TS, Box 11-A, Nelson Cruikshank Papers, Wisconsin State Historical Society, Madison, Wisc.

47 See the material in Departmental Subject Files, 1957, Box 193, Records of the Department of Labor, Record Group 174, National Archives, Washington, D.C.

48 Paul E. Gurske to Walter Wallace, 10 October 1957, Box 193, Record Group 174.

49 See the material in Record Group 47, Accession 67-270, Carton 3, WNRC, for the quotation and other relevant material.

50 The following paragraphs rely heavily on the clippings file in Records of the National Commission on State Workmen's Compensation Laws, Record Group 220, hereafter cited as clippings file, Record Group 220.

51 The quotations come from unmarked clippings that appeared in *Business Insurance* between 1970 and 1972, clippings file, Record Group 220.

52 The following section relies on the verbatim transcripts of commission meetings that are available in Records of the National Commission on State Workmen's Compensation Laws, Record Group 220. Since not all of these transcripts are paginated, I refer to them by date and, where possible, by page number.

53 Quotations are taken from transcript of commission meeting, 21, 22, and 23 February 1972, Record Group 220.

54 Transcript of commission meeting, 21 March 1972, Record Group 220, p. 98.

55 Transcript of commission meeting, 14 December 1971, Record Group 220, pp. 356–96; John L. Lewis gave the lecture on permanent partial disability.

56 Remarks of Mr. Flournoy, transcript of commission meeting, 21 March 1972, Record Group 220, p. 141.

57 Transcript of commission meeting 15 December 1971, Record Group 220, p. 93; transcript of commission meeting 22 March 1972, Record Group 220, p. 403.

58 Transcript of commission meeting, 22 March 1972, Record Group 220, pp. 22, 51, 66–67.

59 National Commission on State Workmen's Compensation Laws, *The Report of the National Commission on State Workmen's Compensation Laws* (Washington D.C.: Government Printing Office, 1972), pp. 14, 25, 70, 79, 102.

60 Ibid., pp. 62–4.

61 Ibid., p. 26.

62 See the testimony of John Burton, in U.S. Senate, Committee on Labor and Public Welfare, Subcommittee on Labor, *National Worker's Com-*

pensation Act 1976, 94th Cong. 2d sess., 2, 3, 4 March 1976; Department of Labor, Division of State Worker's Compensation Programs, *State Worker's Compensation Laws in effect on April 1, 1984 compared with the 19 essential recommendations of the National Commission on State Workmen's Compensation Laws* (mimeographed).

Chapter 2

1 Interview with Judge Francis O'Bryne, 21 March 1984, Chicago, Ill.
2 This chapter relies heavily on the archival sources of the social security program stored in the National Archives and the Washington National Records Center, Suitland, Md., as well as on interviews with some of the participants in the legislative enactment over disability insurance, including Nelson Cruikshank and Wilbur Cohen. My reading of the secondary sources depends upon Edward Berkowitz and Kim McQuaid, *Creating the Welfare State* (New York: Praeger, 1980), pp. 96–116; Deborah Stone, *The Disabled State* (Philadelphia, Pa.: Temple University Press, 1984); Robert Haveman, Richard V. Burkhauser, and Victor Halberstadt, *Public Policy toward Disabled Workers: Cross-National Analyses of Economic Impacts* (Ithaca, N.Y.: Cornell University Press, 1984); W. Andrew Achenbaum, *Social Security: Visions and Revisions* (New York: Cambridge University Press, 1986); Martha Derthick, *Policymaking for Social Security* (Washington: Brookings Institution, 1979). A definitive source of information on social security is Robert J. Myers, *Social Security*, 3d ed. (Homewood, Ill.: Richard D. Irwin, 1985), which could be supplemented with Robert M. Ball, *Social Security: Today and Tomorrow* (New York: Columbia University Press, 1978).
3 "The Wagner Bill and a critical review of its provisions," 21 May 1940, Record Group 47, Records of the Social Security Administration, File 056.11, National Archives, Washington, D.C.; Falk to Wilbur J. Cohen, 3 December 1938, Record Group 47, File 056.11.
4 "Extended Disability Benefits: Administrative and Medical Considerations," 15 February 1949, Arthur Altmeyer Papers, Box 7, Wisconsin State Historical Society, Madison, Wisc.; Lucille Smith, consultant on medical social work, to Jane Hoey, 5 February 1942, Record Group 47, 1942, File 056.11, Accession 56-533, Washington National Records Center, Suitland, Md.; W. R. Williamson to Oscar Pogge, 16 December 1941, Record Group 47, January-December 1941, File 056.11, Box 20, Accession 56-533, Washington National Records Center (hereafter WNRC).
5 Oscar Pogge to Arthur Altmeyer, 21 February 1946, Record Group 47, 1944–7, File 056.111, Box 20, Accession 56-533, WNRC.
6 Arthur Altmeyer, "Formulating a Disability Insurance Program," January 1942, Record Group 47, 1942, File 056.11, Box 20, Accession 56-533, WNRC.
7 Definition quoted in Arthur Altmeyer, "Social Insurance for Permanently Disabled Workers," *Social Security Bulletin* 4 (March 1941), p. 4.
8 1947–8 Advisory Council, "Extended Disability Insurance," Record Group 47, Box 6, Accession 56-533, WNRC.
9 Pogge to Altmeyer, 21 February 1946, Record Group 47, 1944–7, File 056.11, Accession 56-533, WNRC.

10 Ibid.

11 Arthur Altmeyer, "Preservation of Insurance Rights under the Federal Old-Age and Survivors System of Permanently Disabled Persons," 15 July 1952, Record Group 47, File 056.11, Box 38, Accession 64A-751, WNRC; Social Security background material, p. 86, 1949, no box, n.d., Record Group 47, WNRC. Hereafter cited as Background Material 1949.

12 Background Material, 1949, p. 86.

13 Altmeyer, "Social Insurance for Permanently Disabled Workers," p. 34; "National Health Conference Program 18–20 July 1938," Arthur Altmeyer Papers, Box 3, Wisconsin State Historical Society; I. S. Falk to Wilbur J. Cohen, 3 December 1938, Record Group 47, File 056.11, National Archives; Arthur Altmeyer to Gerald Morgan, 26 November 1938, Record Group 47, 1935–47, File 025, National Archives, Box 10.

14 Pogge to Altmeyer, 21 February 1946, Record Group 47, 1944–7, File 056.11 Accession 56-533, WNRC; Background Material, 1949, p. 89.

15 Falk to Cohen, 3 December 1938, Record Group 47, File 056.11, National Archives.

16 Background Material, 1949, p. 89.

17 Preliminary outline of Plan AC-14, 21 January 1939, Record Group 47, Box 10, National Archives; for a more detailed examination of the relationship between workers' compensation and disability insurance, see Edward Berkowitz and Monroe Berkowitz, "The Survival of Worker's Compensation," *Social Service Review* 58 (June 1984), pp. 259–80.

18 Oscar Pogge to Corson, 21 April 1941, and Corson to Falk, 15 April 1941, January–December 1941, Record Group 47, File 056.11, Box 20, Accession 56-533, WNRC.

19 Preliminary Outline of Plan AC-14, 21 January 1939, Record Group 47, Box 10, National Archives.

20 Background Material, 1949, p. 121; Pogge to Altmeyer, 21 February 1946, Record Group 47, 1944–7, File 056.11, Accession 56-533, WNRC.

21 Arthur Altmeyer, "Formulating a Disability Insurance Program," January 1942, Record Group 47, 1942, File 056.11, Box 20, Accession 56-533, WNRC.

22 Falk to Social Security Board, 22 August 1941, Record Group 47, File 056.11, Box 20, Accession 56-533, WNRC.

23 Plan 41-A, 2 September 1941, Record Group 47, File 056.11, Box 20, Accession 56-533, WNRC.

24 Falk to Cohen, 3 December 1938, Record Group 47, File 056.11, National Archives; American Medical Association, "Report of Reference Committee on Consideration of the National Health Program," 24 September 1938, Box 3, Arthur Altmeyer Papers, Wisconsin State Historical Society.

25 Background Material, 1949, p. 117.

26 Arthur Altmeyer, 'Formulating a Disability Insurance Program," January 1942, Record Group 47, 1942, File 056.11, Box 20, Accession 56-533, WNRC; Background Material, pp. 104, 122.

27 W. R. Williamson to Wilbur J. Cohen, 9 November 1938, Record Group 47, File 056.11, National Archives; Mrs. Van Eenan to Mr. Williamson,

19 March 1940, Record Group 47, File 056.11, National Archives; R. K. McNickle, "Editorial Research Report," Arthur Altmeyer Papers, Box 7, Wisconsin State Historical Society, 1949.

28 Elizabeth Otley, "Cash Benefits," *Social Security Administration Publication,* June 1940, pp. 22–33; Falk to Cohen, 3 December 1938, Record Group 47, File 056.11, National Archives; Stone, *The Disabled State,* pp. 73–6.

29 Falk to Cohen, 3 December 1938, Record Group 47, File 056.11, National Archives.

30 Ibid.; Otley, "Cash Benefits," p. 18.

31 W. R. Williamson to Arthur Altmeyer, 8 November 1938, Record Group 47, File 056.11, National Archives.

32 Williamson to Cohen, 29 October 1941, Record Group 47, January–December 1941, File 056.11, Box 20, Accession 56-533, WNRC.

33 Interview with Robert Ball, 22 May 1984, Detroit, Mich.

34 Robert J. Meyers to D. C. Bronson, 10 December 1941, Record Group 47, File 056.11, Box 20, Accession 56-533, WNRC.

35 Falk to Cohen, 3 December 1938, Record Group 47, File 056.11, National Archives.

36 M. Jarvis Farley to Williamson, 21 July 1942, Record Group 47, 1942, File 056.11, Box 20, Accession 56-533, WNRC.

37 W. R. Williamson to Arthur Altmeyer, 27 April 1942, Record Group 47, 1941–2, File 056.11, Box 20, Accession 56-533, WNRC.

38 Williamson to Altmeyer, 29 November 1945, Record Group 47, 1945, File 056.11, Box 20, Accession 56-533, WNRC; Wilbur J. Cohen, *Retirement Policies under Social Security* (Berkeley: University of California Press, 1957), pp. 46–7.

39 Edwin Witte to Arthur Altmeyer, 14 May 1937, and Witte to Altmeyer, 3 January 1939, Record Group 47, File 095, National Archives; Witte to Theresa McMahon, 7 December 1938, Edwin Witte Papers, Box 34, Wisconsin State Historical Society.

40 Edward Berkowitz, "The First Social Security Crisis," *Prologue* 15 (Fall 1983), pp. 132–49; see also Edward Berkowitz and Kim McQuaid, "Businessman and Bureaucrat," *Journal of Economic History* 38 (March 1978), pp. 120–42.

41 Statements of Douglas Brown in transcript of Advisory Council meeting, 10 December 1938, p. 13, Box 12, and statements of Arthur Altmeyer in transcript of Advisory Council meeting, 22 October 1938, Record Group 47, Box 12, National Archives. The verbatim transcripts of the meetings of this advisory council are housed in the National Archives.

42 Statement of Albert Mowbray in transcript of Advisory Council meeting, 22 October 1938, Record Group 47, Box 12, pp. 49–50.

43 Wilbur J. Cohen to Arthur Altmeyer, 13 October 1938, Record Group 47, File 025, Box 10.

44 Statement of W. R. Williamson in transcript of Advisory Council meeting, 21 October 1938, Record Group 47, Box 13, p. 59.

45 Statement of Lee Pressman in transcript of Advisory Council meeting, 10 December 1938, Record Group 47, Box 12, p. 37.

46 Edwin Witte to Gerald Morgan, 7 November 1938, Witte Papers, Box 34, Wisconsin State Historical Society.

47 Statement of Paul Douglas in transcript of Advisory Council meeting, 10 December 1938, Record Group 47, Box 12, p. 43.

48 Edwin Witte to Arthur Altmeyer, Record Group 47, File 025, Box 10, National Archives; discussion in Minutes of Advisory Council meeting, 10 December 1938, Record Group 47, p. 53.

49 Wilbur J. Cohen to Corson, 5 April 1941, Record Group 47, File 056.11, Box 20, Accession 56-533, WNRC; Social Security Board, *Report of the Social Security Board to the President and the Congress* (Washington, D.C.: Government Printing Office, 1941), p. 12; U.S. Congress, House, *H.R. 7534*, 77th Cong., 2d sess., 9 September 1942.

50 Cohen to Corson, 5 April 1941, Record Group 47, File 056.11, Box 20, Accession 56-533, WNRC.

51 Falk to Social Security Board, 23 February 1942, Record Group 47, File 056.11, Box 20, Accession 56-533, WNRC; Falk to Social Security Board, 22 August 1941, Record Group 47, 1942, File 056.11, Accession 56-533, WNRC; Falk to Cohen, 12 April 1941, Record Group 47, 1941–3, File 056.11, Box 20, Accession 56-533, WNRC; Falk to Corson, 19 November 1941, Record Group 47, January–December 1941, File 056.11, Box 20 Accession 56-533, WNRC.

52 Witte to Altmeyer, 4 September 1939, Record Group 47, National Archives; W. R. Williamson, "The Change of Mood in Reference to Social Insurance," 27 February 1942, Record Group 47, 1942, File 056.11, Box 20, Accession 56-533, WNRC.

53 Falk and Corson to Oscar Powell, "Preparation of the Disability Rating Schedule for Civilian War Benefits Program," 5 June 1943, Record Group 47, File 847.2, Box 119, Accession 56-533, WNRC.

54 Oscar Pogge to Wilbur J. Cohen, 20 October 1942, Record Group 47, File 055.4, Box 20, Accession 56-533, WNRC; Pogge to Altmeyer, 3 April 1942, Record Group 47, 1942, File 056.11, Box 20, Accession 56-533, WNRC.

55 W. R. Williamson, "New Formulae for the Extension of OASI," 19 January 1943, Record Group 47, 1943, File 056.11, Box 25, Accession 56-533, WNRC; "H. R. Gordon Sounds the Battle Cry against Federal Disability Insurance," Record Group 47, 1941–2, File 056.11, Box 20, Accession 56-533, WNRC.

56 Altmeyer, "Desirability of Expanding the Social Insurance Program Now," *Social Security Bulletin* 5, no. 11 (November 1942).

57 "Temporary Disability," 23 June 1937, Record Group 47, File 56.112, National Archives. For more on the development of temporary disability insurance, see Edward D. Berkowitz, "The American Disability System in Historical Perspective," in *Disability Programs and Government Policies*, ed. Edward D. Berkowitz (New York: Praeger, 1979), pp. 16–74.

58 Williamson to Altmeyer, 9 July 1942, Record Group 47, 1941–2, File 056.11, Box 20, Accession 56-533, WNRC.

59 Letter by John B. Andrews, "Health Insurance," *New York Times*, 5 June 1942, in Edwin Witte Papers, Box 201, Wisconsin State Historical Society.

60 J. Douglas Brown to William J. Ellis, 13 January 1941, Record Group 47, January–December 1941, File 056.11, Box 20, Accession 56-533, WNRC.

61 Altmeyer, "Improving and Extending Unemployment and Temporary Disability Insurance," 7 May 1948, Record Group 47, Box 97, Accession 64A-751, WNRC.

62 "Governor's Message on Cash Sickness Compensation," 1950, Witte Papers, Box 201, Wisconsin State Historical Society.

63 "Research and Statistics Note 29," 20 July 1955, Edwin Witte Papers, Box 201, Wisconsin State Historical Society; U.S. Government Policy Relating to Temporary Disability Insurance Legislation, Record Group 47, 4 June 1951, File 056.112, Box 38, Accession 64A-751, WNRC.

64 U.S. Congress, Senate, *S. 1161*, 78th Cong., 1st sess., Record Group 47, File 011.1, Box 4, Accession 56-533, WNRC; U.S. Congress, Senate, *S. 1050*, in Robert F. Wagner Papers, Folder 2, Box 329, Georgetown University.

65 Wilbur J. Cohen to Edwin Witte, 25 September 1947, Witte Papers, Box 35, Wisconsin State Historical Society.

66 Edwin Witte to Wilbur J. Cohen, 8 October 1947, Witte Papers, Box 35, Wisconsin State Historical Society; Witte to Cohen, 28 November 1947, Witte Papers, Box 35, Wisconsin State Historical Society.

67 Interview with Nelson Cruikshank, 24 August 1983, Washington, D.C.

68 Cohen to Witte, 7 November 1947, Witte Papers, Box 34, Wisconsin State Historical Society.

69 Cohen to Witte, 17 February 1948, Box 35, Witte Papers, Wisconsin State Historical Society.

70 Agenda for first meeting of Senate Advisory Council, 4 and 5 December 1947, Record Group 47, File 025, Box 6, Accession 56-533, WNRC.

71 Cohen to Witte, 17 February 1948, Box 35, Witte Papers, Wisconsin State Historical Society.

72 Robert Beasley to William L. Mitchell, 8 January 1948, Record Group 47, 1948, File 025, Box 5, Accession 56A-533, WNRC.

73 Cohen to Altmeyer, 29 March 1948, Record Group 47, 1948, File 025, Box 6, Accession 56-533, WNRC.

74 Robert J. Myers to Wilbur J. Cohen, 2 April 1948, Record Group 47, 1948, File 025, Box 6, Accession 56-533, WNRC.

75 Cohen to Altmeyer, 13 April 1948, Record Group 47, 1948, File 025, Box 6, Accession 56-533, WNRC.

76 M. Albert Linton, "Should Total Disability be Included in a Federal Old-Age Security Program?" in Stettinius Papers, Box 783, University of Virginia Library, Charlottesville.

77 Pogge to Altmeyer, 15 September 1948, Record Group 47, 1948, File 056.11, Box 20, Accession 56A-533, WNRC.

78 U.S. Congress, Senate, *Permanent and Total Disability Insurance,* 80th Cong., 2d sess., S. Doc. 1621, 1948, p. 6.

79 Jane Hoey to Frank Bain, 20 February 1948, Record Group 47, 1948, File 056.11, Box 20, Accession 56-533, WNRC.

80 Cohen to Witte, 27 February 1949, Witte Papers, Box 5, Wisconsin State Historical Society; statements of Arthur Altmeyer, Record Group 47, Box 97, Accession 64A-751, WNRC.

81 "Report of the Washington Office to the House of Delegates at the Interim Session – 1949," Wilbur Cohen Papers, Box 13, p. 7, Wisconsin State Historical Society.

82 Transcript of American Forum of the Air, 23 September 1950, Record Group 47, Box 97, Accession 64A-751, WNRC.

83 Arthur Altmeyer to Oscar Pogge, 14 August 1951, Record Group 47, File 056.1101, Box 38, Accession 64A-851, WNRC.

84 For more on the freeze and related matters, see Edward Berkowitz and Kim McQuaid, "Welfare Reform in the Fifties," *Social Service Review* 54 (March 1980), pp. 45–58.

85 Interview with Arthur Hess, Columbia Oral History Collection, pp. 87–8.

86 Ibid., p. 34.

87 "Preservation of Insurance Rights of Permanently and Totally Disabled Persons under the Federal Old-Age and Survivors Insurance System," 17 November 1952, Cohen Papers, Box 13, Wisconsin State Historical Society.

88 Altmeyer to Cohen, 18 November 1953, and Cohen to Altmeyer, 5 November 1953, Cohen Papers, Box 47, Wisconsin State Historical Society.

89 Perkins to Mitchell, 12 August 1954, Record Group 47, File 056.11, Box 38, Accession 64A-751, WNRC.

90 Wilbur J. Cohen and Fedele F. Fauri, "The Social Security Amendments of 1956," *American Public Welfare Association – Public Welfare*, October 1956, in Social Security Legislative Archives, Baltimore, Md.; material in Nelson Cruikshank Papers, Jere Cooper File, Box 11A, Wisconsin State Historical Society.

91 Quoted in David Koitz, *Work Disincentives and Disability Insurance*, Congressional Research Service, Report 80-160, EPW, 24 October 1980, p. 340.

92 Nelson Cruikshank to Arthur Altmeyer, 22 March 1956, Cruikshank Papers, Box 11-A, Wisconsin State Historical Society.

93 Cohen to Witte, 22 February 1956, Cohen Papers, Box 7, Wisconsin State Historical Society.

94 Arthur Altmeyer to Senator Byrd, Cruikshank Papers, Box 11A, Wisconsin State Historical Society.

95 Interview with Nelson Cruikshank, Columbia Oral History Collection, p. 17.

96 Cruikshank interview with author, 24 August 1983, Washington, D.C.

97 George Meany to Walter George, 22 May 1956, Cruikshank Papers, Box 9B, Wisconsin State Historical Society.

98 Remarks of Senator Byrd, in U.S. Congress, Senate, *Congressional Record*, 17 July 1956, pp. 13046–9.

99 Cruikshank interview, 24 August 1983; Nelson Cruikshank, "Disability Insurance in 1956," Cruikshank Papers, Box 11A, Wisconsin State Historical Society.

100 Cruikshank, "Disability Insurance in 1956."

101 Nelson Cruikshank to Arthur Altmeyer, 18 July 1956, Cruikshank Papers, Box 11A, Wisconsin State Historical Society.

102 Cruikshank interview, 24 August 1983.

103 Arthur Altmeyer to Nelson Cruikshank, 21 July 1956, Cruikshank Papers, Box 11A, Wisconsin State Historical Society; Witte to Cohen, 27 July 1956, Cohen Papers, Box 7, Wisconsin State Historical Society.

104 Victor Christgau to Employees, in *Director's Bulletin*, no. 239 (July 18, 1956), in Social Security Archives, Social Security Library, Baltimore, Maryland.

105 U.S. Congress, House, *HR 2936, Social Security Amendments of 1956*, 84th Cong., 2d sess., 1956, p. 26.

Chapter 3

1 The interpretation is mine but the descriptive facts are from U.S. Congress, Senate, Committee on Governmental Affairs, Subcommittee on Oversight of Government Management, *Oversight of the Social Security Administration Disability Reviews,* 97th Cong., 2d sess., August 1982. This chapter, like the first chapter, uses history as a means of examining some administrative problems that have arisen in a representative disability program. It is not a chronology of developments. Readers who want a firmer chronology of events in the Social Security Disability Insurance program should consult Chapter 4. Readers who wish to know more about how the effort to rehabilitate disability beneficiaries proceeded should see Chapter 5.

2 "Processing Time for Disability Claims," 27 November 1957, Record Group 47, Records of the Social Security Administration, File 752.1, Box 92, Accession 64-751, Washington National Records Center (WNRC), Suitland, Md. Unless otherwise noted, all references to Record Group 47 in this chapter refer to materials stored in WNRC.

3 The GAO responded to a congressional query on federalizing the state disability determination services and concluded that the political obstacles were too great; interview with Cam Zola and Barry Tice, April 1985, Baltimore, Md.

4 General Accounting Office, "A Plan for Improving the Federal Disability Determination Process by Bringing It under Complete Federal Management Should Be Developed," HRD 78-146, 31 August 1978, pp. 7–8.

5 "The Social Security Administration Should Provide More Management and Leadership in Determining Who Is Eligible for Disability Benefits," GAO Report, 1976, reprinted in U.S. Congress, House, *Disability Insurance Amendments of 1976: Report to Accompany H.R. 15630,* 94th Cong., 2d sess., 30 September 1976, WMCP, 94-151, pp. 24–5.

6 Ibid., p. 6.

7 U.S. Congress, House, Committee on Ways and Means, Subcommittee on Social Security, *Status of the Disability Insurance Program,* 97th Cong., 1st sess., 16 March 1981, WMCP 97-3, p. 21; U.S. Congress, Senate, Committee on Finance, *Staff Data and Materials Related to the Social Security Disability Insurance Program,* Committee Print 97-16, August 1982, p. 112; Deborah Stone, *The Disabled State* (Philadelphia, Pa.: Temple University Press, 1984), pp. 122–3; U.S. Congress, Senate, Committee on Finance, *Issues Related to Social Security Act Disability Programs,* 96th Cong., 1st sess., Committee Print 96-23, October 1979, p. 12, (hereafter Committee on Finance, 1979); U.S. Congress, House, Ways and Means Committee, *Committee Staff Report on the Disability Insurance Program,* July 1974 (Washington, D.C.: Government Printing Office, 1974), pp. 8–9 (hereafter Ways and Means Committee, 1974).

8 David Koitz, *Staff Report: Current Legislative Issues in the Social Security Disability Insurance Program,* prepared for the Office of the Assistant Secretary for Management and Budget (Washington, D.C.: U.S. Department of Health, Education, and Welfare, 1977), p. 75.

9 U.S. Congress, Senate, Committee on Finance, 1979, p. 109; David Koitz, *Work Incentives and Disability Insurance,* Congressional Research Service Report 80-160, EPW, 24 October 1980, pp. 5–12.

10 John S. Lopatto II, "The Federal Black Lung Program: A 1983 Primer," *West Virginia Law Review* 85 (1983), pp. 678–87; U.S. Congress, House, Ways and Means Committee, 1974, p. 1.

11 For an overview of SSI, including the statistics cited, see U.S. Congress, Senate, Committee on Finance, 1979, pp. 4–7, 103–6; Koitz, *Work Incentives and Disability Insurance*, p. 11; Annual Statistical Supplement, *Social Security Bulletin*, 1981, p. 222; U.S. Congress, House, Ways and Means Committee, Subcommittee on Social Security, *Status of the Disability Insurance Program*, 16 March 1981, pp. 34–5.

12 U.S. Congress, Senate, Committee on Finance, 1979, p. 27; interview with Rhoda Greenberg Davis, 20 January 1984, Baltimore, Md.; interview with Hale Champion, 31 January 1984, Cambridge, Mass.; interview with Stanford Ross, 13 March 1984, Washington, D.C. For a view of the politics of the 1980 measure, see U.S. Congress, House, Ways and Means Committee, Subcommittee on Social Security, *Summary of Testimony on Disability Insurance*, 1 August 1979, WMCP, 96-31, p. 13.

13 Memorandum of James LaBianca, 26 July 1961, Record Group 47, Siegel Correspondence, Box 1, Accession 67A-278.

14 Memorandum of Thomas C. Fisher, 6 September 1960, Record Group 47, Louisville Correspondence, Box 22, Accession 67-278.

15 U.S. Congress, Senate, Committee on Governmental Affairs, Subcommittee on Oversight of Government Management, *Social Security Disability Reviews: The Role of the Administrative Law Judge*, 98th Cong., 1st sess., 8 June 1973, p. 49.

16 U.S. Congress, House, Committee on Ways and Means, Subcommittee on Administration of the Social Security Laws, *Administration of Social Security Disability Insurance Program: Preliminary Report*, 11 March 1960, p. 31; George Wyman to Robert Forsythe, 25 May 1959, Record Group 47, File 752.1, Box 92, Accession 64-751; Marvin Schwartz, *The Trial of a Social Security Disability Case* (New Paltz, N.Y.: Social Security Foundation, 1983), p. 1.02; U.S. Congress, Senate, Committee on Finance, *Staff Data and Materials Related to the Social Security Disability Insurance Program*, 97th Cong., 2d sess., CP 97-16, August 1982, pp. 69–70.

17 U.S. Congress, Senate, Special Committee on Aging, *Social Security Disability: Past, Present, and Future*, 97th Cong., 2d sess., 1982, pp. 1, 10; U.S. Congress, Senate, Committee on Finance, *Staff Data and Materials Related to the Social Security Act Disability Programs*, September 1983, CP 98-93, pp. 35, 74.

18 L. Steele Trotter to Robert B. Hennings, Director, Program Division, Office of Hearings and Appeals, 30 March 1960, Charleston Correspondence File, Box 22, Accession 67-270, Record Group 47.

19 Robert G. Dixon, *Social Security Disability and Mass Justice: A Problem in Welfare Adjudication* (New York: Praeger, 1973), p. 35; *Baltimore Sun T.V. Week*, 5 August 1984, p. 21.

20 Schwartz, *The Trial of a Social Security Disability Case*, p. 102.

21 Interview with Thomas Ploss, 21 March 1984, Chicago, Ill.

22 Interview with Judge James Cullen, 8 February 1984, Baltimore, Md.

23 U.S. Congress, Senate, Committee on Finance, *Staff Data and Materials Related to the Social Security Act Disability Programs*, September 1983, CP 98-93, p. 36.

24 Charles H. Bono in U.S. Congress, Senate, Committee on Governmental Affairs, Subcommittee on Oversight of Government Management, *Social Security Disability Reviews: The Role of the Administrative Law Judge,* 98th Cong., 1st sess., 8 June 1983, p. 43; Judge Francis J. O'Byrne, address to the American Society of Law and Medicine, 25 October 1983, Chicago, Ill., p. 2.

25 Howell Hefflin, "Should Federal Administrative Law Judges Be Independent of Their Agencies," *Judiciature* 67 (March 1984), pp. 412–13.

26 Robert Hannings, acting director, Program Division, to Hearing Examiners, 23 October 1959, Record Group 47, Hannings File, Box 22, Accession 67-270.

27 Letter of Hearings and Appeals Office to State Rehabilitation Departments, 5 October 1959, Record Group 47, Louisville Correspondence, Box 22, Accession 67-270.

28 Claire W. Harding to Martin Tieburg, 7 September 1959, Record Group 47, File RHR, Tieburg, Box 22, Accession 67-270.

29 On the definition, see, for example, U.S. Congress, Senate, Committee on Finance, *Staff Data and Materials Related to the Social Security Disability Insurance Program,* CP 97-16, August 1982, p. 5; Dixon, *Disability and Mass Justice,* p. 53; U.S. Congress, House, Committee on Ways and Means, *Social Security Amendments of 1967,* 90th Cong., 1st sess., August 7, 1967, H. Rept. 544, pp. 29–30.

30 Lance Leibman, "The Definition of Disability in Social Security and Supplemental Security Income: Drawing the Bounds of Social Welfare Estates," *Harvard Law Review* 89 (March 1976), p. 851; Dixon, *Disability and Mass Justice,* p. 95.

31 U.S. Congress, House, Ways and Means Committee, 1974, p. 48.

32 Ibid., p. 32.

33 Victor Christgau to Robert Ball, 7 December 1962, Record Group 47, Civil Activities File, Box 3, Accession 67-270; Dixon, *Disability and Mass Justice,* pp. 48–9; U.S. Congress, Senate, Committee on Finance, 1979, p. 55; information from Fred Arner.

34 Fred Arner, *Proposed Book on the Social Security Disability Program* (unpublished manuscript), p. 22.

35 U.S. Congress, Senate, Committee on Finance, 1979, p. 58.

36 Andrew Kachmar v. Celebrezze, Record Group 47, Civil Actions File, Box 3, Accession 67-270.

37 Ora P. Hall v. Celebrezze (USCA, circuit 6, Kentucky), reported in Thomas C. Parrott, director of Division of Claims Policy, to Robert Ball, 28 August 1963, Record Group 47, Civil Actions File, Box 3, Accession 67-270.

38 Cecil E. Farley v. Celebrezze (USCA, circuit 3, Pennsylvania), reported in Parrott to Ball, 28 August 1963, Record Group 47, Civil Actions File, Box 3, Accession 67-270; the disability insurance law passed in 1984 changed the program's rules toward multiple impairments.

39 Otis Jarvis v. Ribicoff (USCA, circuit 6, Kentucky), reported in Parrot to Ball, 8 June 1963, Record Group 47, Civil Actions File, Box 3, Accession 67-270; Horace Little v. Celebrezze (USCA, circuit 7), reported in ibid.

40 Leibman, "The Definition of Disability in Social Security and Supplemental Security Income," p. 851; Dixon, *Disability and Mass Justice,* pp. 92–3, 97.

41 Stone, *The Disabled State,* pp. 74, 137, 160–1; Dixon, *Disability and Mass Justice,* pp. 92–3; U.S. Congress, House, Ways and Means Committee, 1974, p. 32; Koitz, *Staff Report: Current Legislative Issues in the Social Security Disability Insurance Program.*

42 U.S. Congress, House, Ways and Means Committee, Subcommittee on the Administration of the Social Security Laws, *Administration of Social Security Disability Insurance Program: Preliminary Report,* 11 March 1960, p. 30 (hereafter *Harrison Report*); U.S. Congress, House, Ways and Means Committee, Subcommittee on the Administration of the Social Security Laws, *Administration of Social Security Disability Insurance Program: Hearings,* 86th Cong., 1st sess., 4, 5, 6, 9, 10, 12, 13 November and 7 December 1959, p. 29 (hereafter *Harrison Hearings*).

43 *Harrison Hearings,* p. 39; *Harrison Report,* pp. 17, 33.

44 Arthur E. Hess, "Old Age Survivors and Disability Insurance: Early Problems and Operations of Disability Provisions," *Social Security Bulletin* 20 (December 1957), p. 4; statement by William Roemmich, chief medical officer, Division of Disability Operations, 5 November 1959, Record Group 47, Box 22, Accession 67-270.

45 U.S. Congress, Senate, Special Committee on Aging, *Social Security Disability: Past, Present, and Future,* 97th Cong., 2d sess., 1982, p. 9; U.S. Congress, House, Ways and Means Committee, 1974, p. 46; U.S. Congress, Senate, Committee on Finance, 1979, p. 20; U.S. Department of Health, Education, and Welfare, *Disability Evaluation under Social Security Handbook for Physicians,* no. 79-10089, August 1979, p. iv.

Chapter 4

1 "Social Security Administration Press Release," 10 December 1960, Record Group 47, Records of the Social Security Administration, File OASI, Memos, Box 22, Accession 67-270, Washington National Record Center, Suitland, Md. All of the material from Record Group 47 cited in this chapter is stored in the Washington National Records Center rather than the National Archives. As the notes make clear, this chapter depends heavily on congressional sources as well as on interviews with Carter administration officials and congressional committee staff conducted for this study. I am particularly grateful to the staff of the Senate Special Committee on Aging and to the staff of Senator Jim Sasser for providing me with memoranda and other materials I would not otherwise have been able to consult. It is also important to point out, with regard to the notes of this chapter, that all conclusions and inferences are mine and are not to be attributed to any member of Congress or congressional committee. This caveat applies in particular to my interpretation of the activities of Senator Robert Dole; Carolyn Weaver, a scholar on the subject of social security and a former staff member of the Senate Committee on Finance, is preparing her own account of the 1984 amendments, which, when they are published, should be read along with this one.

2 Linda Ross, "Disabled and Victimized," *New York Times,* 21 April 1983, p. A27.

3 Remarks of Senator Hartke, U.S. Congress, Senate, *Congressional Record,* 23 August 1960, p. S17234; Joseph Califano quoted in James W. Singer,

"It Isn't Easy to Cure the Ailments of the Disability Insurance Program," *National Journal,* 16 May 1978, p. 718; Joseph A. Califano, Jr., *Governing America* (New York: Simon and Schuster, 1981), p. 384.

4 Interview with Frank Bowe, 1 May 1984, East Lansing, Mich. For program statistics see U.S. Congress, Senate, Committee on Finance, *Staff Data and Materials Related to the Social Security Disability Program,* CP 97-16, August 1982, 97th Cong., 2d sess., pp. 19–20.

5 U.S. Congress, Senate, Committee on Governmental Affairs, Subcommittee on Oversight of Government Management, *Oversight of Social Security Disability Benefits Terminations,* 25 May 1982, 97th Cong., 2d sess., p. 3.

6 Harold B. Siegel to Joseph M. Mandell, 19 July 1960, Record Group 47, File Charleston, Box 22, Accession 67-270.

7 Representative John E. Henderson to Charles Schottland, 24 June 1958, Record Group 47, File 752.1, Box 92, Accession 64-751; Robert Forsythe to William Mitchell, 1 May 1959, Record Group 47, File 752.1, Box 92, Accession 64-751; remarks of Representative Perkins, U.S. Congress, House, *Congressional Record,* 31 July 1958, pp. 15737, H15764.

8 George K. Wyman to William Mitchell, 5 November 1959, Record Group 47, 1959, File 326.102, Box 70, Accession 64A-751.

9 Interview with Fred Arner, 7 February 1984, Baltimore, Md.; statement of William L. Mitchell, 7 December 1959, Record Group 47, File Identical Memorandum, Box 22, Accession 67-270; William L. Mitchell, "Legislation in the 86th Congress," *Social Security Bulletin* 23, (November 1960), p. 15.

10 Arthur Hess, Columbia Oral History Collection, p. 40; statement of Arthur Fleming before U.S. Congress, House, Committee on Ways and Means, 23 March 1960; Flemming testimony before U.S. Congress, Senate, Committee on Finance, 29 June 1960, both in Social Security Legislative Archives, Social Security Library, Baltimore, Md.

11 Donald O. Parsons, "Disability Insurance and Male Labor Force Participation: A Response to Haveman and Wolfe," *Journal of Political Economy* 92 (June 1984), pp. 542–9; U.S. Congress, Senate, Committee on Finance, *Staff Data and Materials Related to the Social Security Act Disability Programs,* 98th Cong., 1st sess., 1983, CP 98-93, p. 9.

12 U.S. Congress, House, Committee on Ways and Means, *Committee Staff Report on the Disability Insurance Program,* July 1974 (Washington, D.C.: Government Printing Office, 1974), p. 15 (hereafter cited as Committee on Ways and Means, 1974); U.S. Congress, Senate, Committee on Finance, *Issues Related to the Social Security Act Disability Programs,* CP 96-23, 96th Cong., 1st sess., October 1979, p. 68 (hereafter cited as Committee on Finance, 1979).

13 U.S. Congress, Senate, Committee on Finance, 1979, pp. 60–1.

14 Ibid., p. 69.

15 U.S. Congress, Senate, Committee on Finance, *Staff Data and Materials Related to the Social Security Disability Insurance Program,* August 1982, pp. 126–8.

16 David Koitz, *Work Disincentives and Disability Insurance,* Congressional Research Service, Report 80-160, EPW, 24 October 1980, pp. 14–15; interview with Janice Gregory, 27 June 1984, Washington, D.C.

17 Koitz, *Work Disincentives and Disability Insurance,* pp. 26–7, 29–30.
18 Gregory interview; interview with Stan Ross, 13 March 1984, Washington, D.C.
19 I draw my account of what followed from personal interviews with Janice Gregory, Stan Ross, Hale Champion (31 January 1984, Cambridge, Mass.), Dan Marcus (6 October 1984, Washington, D.C.), and a number of informal conversations with Wilbur Cohen.
20 Ross interview; interview with Pat Harris, 14 April 1984, Washington, D.C.
21 Gregory interview.
22 Statement by the AFL–CIO Executive Council, 6 August 1979, obtained from the AFL–CIO; U.S. Congress, House, Committee on Ways and Means, *Disability Insurance Amendments of 1979,* 96th Cong., 1st sess., 1979, pp. 4–9.
23 Committee on Ways and Means, *Disability Insurance Amendments of 1979,* pp. 8–9.
24 Statements of Representative Pickle, U.S. Congress, House, *Congressional Record,* 6 September 1979, pp. 7397ff.
25 Statements of Representative Pepper in ibid., pp. H7408–9.
26 Koitz, *Work Disincentives and Disability Insurance,* p. 33.
27 Remarks of Senator Kennedy, U.S. Congress, Senate, *Congressional Record,* 5 December 1979, p. S17800.
28 Remarks of Senator Robert Dole in ibid., p. S17778.
29 Public Law 96-265.
30 U.S. Congress, House, Committee on Ways and Means, Subcommittee on Social Security, *Status of the Disability Insurance Program,* 97th Cong., 1st sess., WMCP 97-3, 16 March 1981, pp. 2–3; U.S. Congress, Senate, Committee on Finance, 1979, pp. 112–13.
31 Koitz, *Staff Report,* pp. 6, 82; Committee on Ways and Means, Subcommittee on Social Security, *Summary of Testimony on Disability Insurance Legislation,* 96th Cong., 1st sess., WMCP 96-31, 1 August 1979, p. 14.
32 U.S. Congress, Senate, Committee on Finance, 1979, p. 31; Koitz, "Social Security: Reexamining Eligibility for Disability Benefits," Issue Brief 82078 (Washington, D.C.: Congressional Research Service, 1983), p. 5 [hereafer Issue Brief 82078].
33 "More Diligent Followup Needed to Weed out Ineligible SSA Disability Beneficiaries" (Washington, D.C.: General Accounting Office, 3 March 1981), pp. 3–6; interview with Phil Gambino, 14 May 1982, Baltimore, Md.
34 Interview with Bert Van Engel, 17 April 1984, Baltimore, Md.; interview with Barry Tice, Joseph Law, and Jeff Chaney of the General Accounting Office, 7 May 1984, Baltimore, Md.
35 Tice, Law, Chaney interview; Van Engel interview; interview with Paul Simmons, 13 April 1984, Washington, D.C.
36 "More Diligent Followup Needed," pp. 8–10.
37 Simmons interview.
38 Peter J. McGough, director, Office of Program Planning, General Accounting Office, testimony before U.S. Congress, House, Committee on Ways and Means, June 30, 1983, p. 2 (obtained from GAO).
39 Interview with Rhoda Greenberg Davis, 31 January 1984, Baltimore, Md.;

interview with Pat Owens, 2 April 1984, Baltimore, Md., Simmons interview. It is also important to note that the entire discussion about disability took place in an atmosphere of perceived crisis in the social security program that led to the 1983 amendments. See W. Andrew Achenbaum, *Social Security: Visions and Revisions* (New York: Cambridge University Press, 1986); and Paul Light, *Artful Work* (New York: Random House, 1985).

40 U.S. Office of Management and Budget, *Budget Revisions,* April 1981, pp. 172–5.

41 U.S. Congress, House, Committee on Ways and Means, Subcommittee on Social Security, *Status of the Disability Insurance Program,* March 1981, WMCP 97-3, p. 4.

42 Fred Schutzman to all regional commissioners, 13 March 1981; memorandum from Sandy Crank, associate commissioner for operational policy and procedures, to acting deputy commissioner (operations), 6 March 1981; and Andrew J. Young, associate commissioner, Office of Hearings and Appeals, to chief and deputy chief ALJs, 7 May 1981; all in U.S. Congress, Senate, Committee on Governmental Affairs, Subcommittee on Oversight of Government Management, *Oversight of Social Security Disability Benefits Termination,* pp. 151, 152, 274 [hereafter Subcommittee on Oversight]. See also House Select Committee on Aging, *Impact of the Accelerated Review Process on Cessations and Denials in the Social Security Disability Insurance Program,* 21 May 1982, 97th Cong., 2d sess., pp. 9–10 [hereafter Impact].

43 Impact, pp. 10–11; Margaret Shapiro and Spencer Rich, "Hill Alters Rules for Disability," *Washington Post,* 20 September 1984, p. 1; Robert Pear, "Dispute Continues on Aid to Disabled," *New York Times,* 12 August 1984, p. 1.

44 Testimony of Peter J. McGough, director of Program Planning, before U.S. Congress, House, Committee on Ways and Means, Subcommittee on Social Security, 30 June 1983 (mimeographed), p. 1; testimony of McGough prepared for U.S. Congress, Senate, Committee on Aging, 7 April 1983 (mimeographed), p. 5; testimony of Gregory Ahart, U.S. Congress, Senate, Subcommittee on Oversight, pp. 242, 251.

45 Jack Anderson, "Bureaucratic Nightmare for the Disabled," *Washington Post,* 2 September 1981 (reprinted in U.S. Congress, Senate, Subcommittee on Oversight, p. 475).

46 Cited by Senator Pryor in Special Committee on Aging and Subcommittee on Civil Service, Post Office, and General Services, *Social Security Disability: The Effects of the Accelerated Review,* 97th Cong, 2d sess., 19 November 1982, Fort Smith, Arkansas [hereafer Fort Smith hearings].

47 "Fairness of Reagan's Cutoff of Disability Aid Questioned," *New York Times,* 9 May 1982 (reprinted in U.S. Congress, Senate, Subcommittee on Oversight, p. 468).

48 Jack Moseley, "Social Security Cutbacks Border on Terrorization," *Southwest Times Record,* 14 November 1982 (reprinted in Fort Smith Hearings, p. 7).

49 "In the matter of Frank Williams' Back," *Detroit News,* 25 July 1982 (reprinted in U.S. Congress, Senate, Subcommittee on Oversight, p. 499).

50 Ingrid Kindred, "Disabled Husband's Benefits Terminated, Wife Goes into

Battle," *Birmingham News,* 26 January 1982 (reprinted in U.S. Congress, Senate, Subcommittee on Oversight, p. 476).

51 "Medal of Honor Winner Fears Benefit Loss," *Baltimore Sun,* 28 May 1983, p. A-3.

52 Spencer Rich, "War Hero Told He Wouldn't Lose Disability," *Washington Post,* 13 July 1982, p. A-2.

53 Transcript of "Through the Safety Net," *Frontline,* obtained from WGBH, Boston.

54 Testimony of Jonathan Stein, U.S. Congress, Senate, Subcommitte on Oversight, pp. 75–81; testimony of Kathleen Grover, U.S. Congress, Senate, Subcommittee on Oversight, p. 68.

55 Fort Smith Hearings, pp. 27, 30.

56 Interview with Linda Gustitus and Susan Collins, 10 May 1984, Washington, D.C.

57 Testimony of Ethel Kage in U.S. Congress, Senate, Subcommittee on Oversight, p. 61.

58 Gustitus and Collins interview; John Rother and Frank McArdle to John Heinz, Special Committee on Aging, 26 May 1982.

59 Lance Simmens to Senator Jim Sasser, 15 March 1982, Senator Sasser Files; statement of Jim Sasser before U.S. Congress, Senate, Committee on Finance, 18 August 1982, Senator Sasser Files; Lance Simmens to Senator Sasser, 21 October 1982, Senator Sasser Files.

60 Interview with Senator John Heinz, 25 February 1985.

61 Rother and McArdle to Heinz, Special Committee on Aging, 26 May 1982, and 12 April 1982.

62 U.S. Congress, Senate, Committee on Finance, *Social Security Disability Insurance Program,* 97th Cong., 2d sess., 18 August 1982, pp. 13–15; U.S. Congress, Senate, Special Committee on Aging, *Social Security Disability: Past, Present and Future: An Information Paper,* 97th Cong., 2d sess., March 1982.

63 Heinz interview.

64 Peter J. McGough, associate director, Human Resources Division, GAO, testimony prepared for U.S. Congress, Senate, Committee on Aging, 7 April 1983 (mimeographed), p. 7.

65 Statement of Peter M. McGough before U.S. Congress, Senate, Committee on Aging, p. 20 (quotation is on p. 12).

66 C. Fraser Smith, "Mentally Ill Hard Hit by Purge of Disability Rolls," *Baltimore Sun,* 9 May 1983, p. 1.

67 Carl Levin in U.S. Congress, Senate, Subcommittee on Oversight, p. 3.

68 Fort Smith Hearing, p. 16.

69 Owens interview; Simmons interview.

70 "Disability Benefit Reviews: Fairness Counts," letter from John Svahn to the editor, *New York Times* (reprinted in U.S. Congress, Senate, Subcommittee on Oversight, p. 472).

71 O'Byrne quoted in Pat Doyle, "Crackdown on Disability Aid 'a Disgrace' " *Sunday Herald* (Arlington, Ill.), p. 1; Fort Smith Hearing, p. 18.

72 Social Security Administration, *Annual Report to the Congress for the Fiscal Year 1981* (Washington, D.C.: Government Printing Office, May 1982), pp. 10–11.

73 "The Bellmon Report," *Social Security Bulletin* 45, no. 5 (May 1982), p. 3.

74 Confidential interviews; transcript of testimony of Secretary Richard Schweiker before U.S. Congress, Senate, Budget Committee, Senator Sasser Files.

75 Interview with Francis O'Byrne, 8 February 1984, Chicago, Ill.; Spencer Rich, "Administrative Law Judges File Suit over Pressure to Pare Disability Rolls," *Washington Post*, 28 January 1983, p. A-17.

76 Fort Smith Hearings, p. 44; Spencer Rich, "Heckler Says She Is Foe of Abortion," *Washington Post*, 26 February 1983, p. A-4.

77 U.S. Congress, Senate, Subcommittee on Oversight, p. 128.

78 Koitz, Issue Brief 82078, pp. 7–8; Lou Enoff to Social Security Administration Executive Staff, Senate Special Committee on Aging Files, 27 August 1984.

79 Peter M. McGough, associate director, Office of Program Planning, before U.S. Congress, House, Committee on Ways and Means, Subcommittee on Social Security, 30 June 1984, pp. 9–10; transcript obtained from General Accounting Office; Jesus Rangel, "Court Assails U.S. on Mentally Ill," *New York Times*, 29 August 1984, p. 1; also see "Dear Colleague" letter from Senator Heinz, Special Committee on Aging Files, 24 January 1984.

80 Robert Pear, "Disability Spurs Legal 'Crisis,' " *New York Times*, 9 September 1984, p. 1; "Litigation Management Project Statement," in Lou Enoff to Social Security Administration Executive Staff, U.S. Congress, Senate, Special Committee on Aging, 27 August 1984.

81 Robert Pear, "Fairness of Reagan's Cutoff of Disability Aid Questioned," *New York Times*, 9 May 1982 (reprinted in U.S. Congress, Senate, Subcommittee on Oversight, p. 470); Peter M. McGough, associate director, Human Resources Division, GAO, testimony prepared for U.S. Congress, Senate, Special Committee on Aging, 7 April 1983 (mimeographed), p. 11.

82 Anonymous memo to Senator Jim Sasser, 12 February 1982, Senator Sasser Files.

83 Interview with Ivan Cottman, 22 May 1984, Detroit, Mich.

84 Peter Kihss, "Cut from U.S. Benefits, Disabled Seek Welfare," *New York Times*, 19 May 1982 (reprinted in U.S. Congress, Senate, Subcommittee on Oversight, p. 470); Eric R. Kingson, "The Participation of Older Persons in General Assistance Programs," report to the Andrus Foundation, 1 March 1984; statement of Edward Koch and Carol Bellamy before U.S. Congress, Senate, Subcommittee on Oversight, p. 292; statement of Ken Patton before Fort Smith Hearings, p. 41.

85 For a good background and data on the revolt of the states that describes these actions, see Koitz, Issue Brief 82078.

86 National Senior Citizens Law Center, *Washington Weekly* 9, no. 31 (August 5, 1983), p. 113.

87 Governor Richard Celeste, Executive Order 83-52, 11 October 1983.

88 Agnes Mansour and Patrick Babcock to Governor James Blanchard, 18 October 1983, privately obtained; "Governor Signs Executive Order on Social Security Disability," News Release, 7 September 1983; "Robb Shelves Social Security Cutoff," *Washington Post*, 30 September 1983, p. 34.

89 Interview with Janice Gregory, 27 June 1984.
90 Larry Atkins and Paul Stietz to Senator Heinz, Special Committee on Aging Files, 23 January 1984.
91 U.S. Congress, House, *Disability Amendments of 1982*, House Report 97-588 to accompany HR 6181, 97th Cong., 2d sess., 26 May 1982.
92 Gregory interview; Gustitus and Collins interview – which is the source of the quotation; testimony of Sieglinde Shapiro before U.S. Congress, Senate, Committee on Finance, 18 August 1982 (obtained from disability coalition).
93 "Congress Pressed to Revamp Disability Review Procedures," *Congressional Quarterly*, 4 June 1983, p. 1117.
94 Robert Pear, "U.S. Plans to Ease Disability Criteria in Social Security," *New York Times*, 7 June 1983, p. 1; Koitz, Issue Brief 82078, p. 14; statement of Margaret Heckler in U.S. Department of Health and Human Services, Press Release, 7 June 1983; C. Fraser Smith, "What Drives Public Policy," *Baltimore Sun*, 12 June 1983, p. K1; Felicity Barringer, "Disability Rules Revamped," *Washington Post*, 8 June 1983, p. 1.
95 Koitz, Issue Brief 82078, p. 11.
96 Association of Retarded Citizens, *Action Alert*, 29 November 1983.
97 Spencer Rich, "Purge of Disability Rolls is Challenged," *Washington Post*, 28 October 1983, p. A21; Thomas Hassler, "Dole Says Bill May Deplete Disability Fund," *Baltimore Evening Sun*, 11 May 1984, p. 1.
98 "Long: On Guard against Disability Abuses," *Congressional Quarterly*, 31 March 1984, p. 725; interview with Joseph Humphrys, 29 May 1984.
99 "Joint Statement by Richard S. Schweiker and John A. Svahn," *Health and Human Services News*, 28 April 1982; telegraph from James Brown to Social Security offices, 30 August 1982 (obtained from the Department of Health and Human Services).
100 Morrow Carter, "Trimming the Disability Rolls – Changing the Rules during the Game, *National Journal*, 4 September 1982, p. 1512; "Congress Pressed to Revamp Disability Procedures," *Congressional Quarterly*, 4 June 1983, p. 118; Thomas Hassler, "U.S. Cracking Down on Disability Reviews," *Baltimore Evening Sun*, 26 January 1984, p. 1; "Administration against Changing Disability Review System Again," *Washington Post*, 26 January 1984, p. A-4; Spencer Rich, "Heckler Sees Social Security Disability Cut," *Washington Post*, 8 February 1984, p. A4.
101 Gustitus and Collins interview, 10 May 1984; Carter, "Trimming the Disability Rolls," p. 1512.
102 Smith, "Mentally Ill Hit Hard by Purge of Disability Roles"; Koitz, Issue Brief 82078, p. 10; Teddi Fine, Division of Government Relations, to Committee on Rehabilitation, American Psychiatric Association, 15 August 1983; Gustitus and Collins interview; Spencer Rich, "House Votes Curbs on Disability-Roll Removals," *Washington Post*, 28 March 1984, p. A-6.
103 Pear, "Dispute Continues on Aid to Disabled."
104 Humphrys interview.
105 Humphrys interview; conversation with Robert Ball, 22 May 1984; U.S. Congress, Conference Committee, *Social Security Disability Benefits Re-*

form Act of 1984, House Report 98-1039 to accompany HR 3755, 19
September 1984, pp. 23–6.
106 Humphrys interview; H. Rept. 98-1039, pp. 23–4.
107 H. Rept. 98-1039, pp. 25–8.
108 H. Rept. 98-1039, p. 36.

Part II. The corrective response

1 Robert Haveman et al., *Public Policy toward Disabled Workers: Cross National Analyses of Economic Impacts* (Ithaca, N.Y.: Cornell University Press, 1983), p. 3.

Chapter 5

1 John Gardner quoted by Representative Curtis in U.S. Congress, House, *Congressional Record,* 1967, p. H10684.
2 For background on the origins of vocational rehabilitation, see Mary E. MacDonald, *Federal Grants for Vocational Rehabilitation* (Chicago: University of Chicago Press, 1944), p. 12; U.S. Federal Board for Vocational Education, *Vocational Rehabilitation in the United States,* Bulletin 120, 1927, p. 34; Record Group 235, Records of the Federal Security Administration, 26 July 1948, File 450, National Archives, Washington, D.C.
3 G. Lyle Belsey to Administrator, 13 September 1959, Record Group 235, 1950, File 450.
4 W. Oliver Kincannon to David Bernstein, 24 July 1950, Record Group 235, 1950, File 450.
5 Phillip Schaefer to Michael Shortley, 3 March 1950, quoted in Edward Berkowitz and Monroe Berkowitz, "The Survival of Workers' Compensation," *Social Service Review* 58 (June 1984), p. 271; Mary Switzer to the Secretary, 17 November 1954, Record Group 235, 1954, File 450.
6 Oscar M. Sullivan and Kenneth O. Snortum, *Disabled Persons: Their Education and Responsibility* (New York: Century, 1926), p. 187.
7 Sullivan and Snortum, *Disabled Persons,* p. 208.
8 Edward D. Berkowitz, "The Federal Government and the Emergence of Rehabilitation Medicine," *The Historian* 53 (August 1983), pp. 530–45.
9 Interview with Peter Griswold, director of the Michigan Rehabilitation Program, 14 October 1983, Lansing, Mich.; interview with Altamount Dickerson, 19 August 1983, Richmond, Va.
10 Arthur Altmeyer to Edwin Witte, 30 January 1935, Record Group 47, "Records of the Social Security Administration," File 095 Witte, National Archives, Washington, D.C.
11 Interview with Arthur Hess, Columbia Oral History Collection, pp. 1, 45; George Wyman to Victor Christgau, 28 September 1959, File 055.4, 1957–59, Box 7, Accession 68-888, Record Group 47, Records of the Social Security Administration, Washington National Records Center, Suitland, Md. (all material from Record Group 47 cited in this chapter is from Washington National Records Center).
12 Arthur Hess to Robert Ball, 25 November 1959, Record Group 47, 1957–59, File 055.4, Box 7, Accession 68-888.

13 U.S. Congress, House, Committee on Ways and Means, Subcommittee on the Administration of Social Security Laws, *Administration of Social Security Disability Insurance Program*, 86th Cong., 1st sess., 1960, p. 26.

14 Commissioner's Bulletin, 30 October 1963, Record Group 47, Accession 67-270, Carton 3.

15 Mary F. Smith, *Rehabilitation Services under the Social Security Act: Recent Changes and Legislative Proposals* (Washington, D.C.: Congressional Research Service, EPW Division, 7 January 1982), p. 4.

16 Ibid., p. 3.

17 U.S. Department of Health, Education and Welfare, *Staff Report: Current Legislative Issues in the Social Security Disability Program*, prepared for the Office of the Assistant Secretary for Management and the Budget by David Koitz (Washington, D.C., 1977), p. 5.

18 Ibid., p. 5; David Stockman, "The Social Pork Barrel," *Public Interest* 39 (Spring, 1975), pp. 3–30.

19 Smith, *Rehabilitation Services under the Social Security Act*, pp. 5–7.

20 Oveta Culp Hobby, address before officers' wives, 8 October 1953, Record Group 235, 1953, File 450.

21 Oscar Ewing to Governor Dan E. Garvey, 21 February 1949, Record Group 235, 1949, File 450.

22 Mary Switzer to Secretary, 16 November 1953, Record Group 235, 1953, File 450.

23 U.S. Congress, House, *Rehabilitation Act of 1973*, 93d Cong., 1st sess., 4 June 1973, H. Rept. 93-244, p. 6; Mary F. Smith, *Programs Authorized by the Rehabilitation Act*, Congressional Research Service report no. 83-518 EPW, 2 February 1983, p. 6.

24 These points come directly from Monroe Berkowitz and Edward Berkowitz, "Benefit–Cost Analysis," *Rehabilitation Research Review* (Washington, D.C.: The National Rehabilitation Information Center, 1983).

25 Quoted in George Nelson Wright, *Total Rehabilitation* (Boston: Little, Brown, 1980), pp. 6–7.

26 Wright, *Total Rehabilitation*, p. 171; Charles Burt Cole, "Social Technology, Social Policy and the Severely Disabled: Issues Posed by The Blind, The Deaf and Those Unable to Walk" (Ph.D. diss., University of California, Berkeley, 1980), pp. 140, 154–5.

27 Wright, *Total Rehabilitation*, pp. 142, 174; Cole, "Social Technology," pp. 159–60.

28 U.S. Congress, House, *Rehabilitation Act Amendments*, 6 February 1984, H. Rept. 98-565, p. 29.

29 Interview with William Burnside, 21 October 1983, northern Virginia; Griswold interview.

30 U.S. Congress, Senate, Committee on Labor Relations, Subcommittee on the Handicapped, *Implementation of the Rehabilitation, Comprehensive Services, and Developmental Disabilities Amendments*, 96th Cong., 1st sess., 5 and 7 November 1979; Record Group 235, 26 July 1948, File 450; U.S. Congress, House, H. Rept. 95-1780, p. 46; Rehabilitation Services Administration (RSA), *Annual Report 1982* (Washington, D.C.: Government Printing Office, 1983), p. 23.

31 Wright, *Total Rehabilitation*, p. 128.

32 "Programs for the Rehabilitation of the Physically Handicapped," 5 Feb-

ruary 1942, Record Group 235, 1942, File 450; "Minutes of Vocational Rehabilitation Conference," 22 December 1941, Record Group 235, 1941, File 450; Federal Board for Vocational Education, *Fifth Annual Report* (Washington, D.C.: Government Printing Office, 1921), p. 29.

33 Gabriel Farrell to Basil O'Connor, 23 December 1942, Record Group 235, File 450, 1943–4, and Watson Miller to Stella M. Marks, 26 March 1943, both in Record Group 235, File 450, 1943–4.

34 Wright, *Total Rehabilitation*, p. 131.

35 Ibid., pp. 11, 15.

36 Sullivan and Snortum, *Disabled Persons*, pp. 268, 272–3.

37 "Programs For the Rehabilitation Of the Physically Handicapped," 5 February 1942, Record Group 235, 1942, File 450; Tracey Copp, quoted in Edward Berkowitz, *Rehabilitation: The Federal Government's Response To Disability, 1935–1954* (New York: Arno, 1980), pp. 90–1.

38 "Summary of Legislation Proposed by Office of Vocational Rehabilitation," December 1948, Record Group 235, File 450; Mrs. Sarah Mobley to Honorable Virgil Chapman, 31 July 1949, Record Group 235, 1949, File 450.

39 "Vocational Rehabilitation During Fiscal 1955 – Accomplishments," 4 August 1955, Record Group 235, 1955, File 450; Martha Lentz Walker, *Beyond Bureaucracy: Mary Elizabeth Switzer and Rehabilitation* (Lanham, Md.: University Press of America, 1985).

40 RSA, *Annual Report 1982*, pp. 39, 55; Smith, "Appropriations for Vocational Rehabilitation Programs Authorized under the Rehabilitation Act of 1973 – P.L. 93-112 as amended, and under the Social Security Act FY 1979–FY 1984," Congressional Research Service, 27 January 1984.

41 Wright, *Total Rehabilitation*, pp. 21, 34, 36, 168.

42 Ibid., pp. 21–2, 24.

43 Ibid., pp. 32–3.

44 Ibid., p. 53.

45 Interview with Peter Griswold, 14 October 1983; Cole, "Social Technology," p. 132; Virginia Department of Rehabilitative Services, RS-4 Work Sheet.

46 Interview with Richard Batterton, 18 June 1984, Baltimore, Md.

47 Cole, "Social Technology," p. 131; Saya Schwartz to Anne Geddes, Bureau of Public Assistance, 1 July 1943, and Anne Geddes, chief, Statistics and Analysis Division, Bureau of Public Assistance, to Jane Hoey, 15 July 1943, Record Group 47, July–September 1943, File 011.1, Accession 56-533.

48 For an overview of the different pieces of legislation, see Wright, *Total Rehabilitation*, pp. 143–5, and also the various congressional reports (e.g., H. Rept. 93-244) that accompanied the legislation.

49 The figures come from Smith, *Programs Authorized by the Rehabilitation Act*, pp. 1, 3, 5; RSA, *Annual Report 1982*, pp. 8, 13.

50 See, for example, Daniel Patrick Moynihan, *The Politics of a Guaranteed Annual Income* (New York: Random House, 1970).

51 RSA, *Annual Report 1982*, pp. 5, 20.

52 Cole, "Social Technology," pp. 214–17.

53 Martha Derthick, *Uncontrollable Spending for Social Services Grants* (Washington, D.C.: Brookings Institution, 1975).

54 Congressional leader quoted in *New York Times,* 16 March 1973, p. 19.
55 U.S. Congress, House, "Rehabilitation Act of 1973," H. Rept. 93-244, 93d Cong., 1st sess., 4 June 1973, pp. 5, 9.
56 U.S. Congress, Senate, Committee on Labor and Human Resources, Subcommittee on the Handicapped, *Rehabilitation Act 1973,* 93d Cong., 1st sess., 10 January, 6 February 1973 [hereafter Rehabilitation Hearings, 1973], pp. 17, 173, 181.
57 U.S. Congress, Senate, *Rehabilitation Act of 1973,* 93d Cong., 1st sess., 26 February 1973, S. Rept. 93-148, pp. 13, 30.
58 Richard Nixon veto message of 27 October 1972, quoted in U.S. Congress, Senate, Rehabilitation Hearings, 1973, p. 198.
59 Michigan Rehabilitation Services, a division of the Bureau of Rehabilitation and Disability Determination, State Board of Education, *1982 Annual Report.*
60 For a discussion of this concept, see *The Clinical Model in Rehabilitation and Alternatives,* ed. Diane E. Woods, Arnold Wolf, and David Brubaker (New York: World Rehabilitation Fund Inc., 1983).
61 U.S. Congress, Senate, S. Rept. 93-148, p. 25.
62 Smith, *Programs Authorized by the Rehabilitation Act,* p. 13; U.S. Congress, House, *Rehabilitation Act Amendments,* 6 February 1984, H. Rept. 98-565, p. 27.
63 Commonwealth of Virginia, Department of Rehabilitation Services, "Individual Written Rehabilitation Plan," obtained from Virginia Department of Rehabilitation Services.
64 Batterton interview; Griswold interview.
65 These cases come from the narratives of the client assistance program in the state of Michigan. I obtained these narratives courtesy of the Michigan program.
66 Much of this section derives from Edward Berkowitz, "Professionals as Providers: Some Thoughts on Disability and Ideology," *Rehabilitation Psychology* 29 (1984), pp. 211–16.

Chapter 6

1 Oscar M. Sullivan and Kenneth O. Snortum, *Disabled Persons: Their Education and Responsibility* (New York: Century, 1926), pp. 105, 124.
2 U.S. Department of Education, National Council on the Handicapped, *National Policy for Persons with Disabilities, Adopted 29 August 1983* (privately distributed).
3 Gerben DeJong, "Independent Living: From Social Movement to Analytic Paradigm," *Archives of Physical Medicine and Rehabilitation* 60 (October 1979), p. 438; John Gliedman and William Roth, *The Unexpected Minority: Handicapped Children in America* (New York: Harcourt Brace, Jovanovich, 1980), pp. 3, 12; U.S. Commission on Civil Rights, *Accommodating the Spectrum of Individual Abilities,* Clearinghouse Publication, 81 (Washington, D.C.: Commission on Civil Rights, 1983), p. 25.
4 Gliedman and Roth, *The Unexpected Minority,* p. 35.
5 Ibid., p. 43.
6 Ibid., p. 261.
7 Constantina Saflios-Rothschild, "Disabled Persons Self Definition and Their

Implications for Rehabilitation," *Cross National Rehabilitation Policies: A Sociological Perspective,* ed. Gary Albrecht (Beverly Hills, Calif.: Sage, 1981), p. 39.

8 Harlan Hahn, "Changing Perception of Disability and the Future of Rehabilitation," *Social Influences in Rehabilitation Planning: Blueprint for the 21st Century,* ed. Leonard G. Perlman and Gary F. Austin (Alexandria, Va.: National Rehabilitation Association, 1985), p. 54; Renee R. Anspach, "From Stigma to Identity Politics: Political Activism among the Physically Disabled and Former Mental Patients," *Social Science and Medicine* 13 (1979), pp. 765–73.

9 Frank Bowe, *Rehabilitating America: Toward Independence for Disabled and Elderly People* (New York: Harper and Row, 1980), p. 96; Edward D. Berkowitz and Monroe Berkowitz, "Widening the Field, Economics and History in the Study of Disability," *American Behavioral Scientist* 28 (January/February 1985), pp. 405–18.

10 Saad Z. Nagi, "The Concept and Measurement of Disability," *Disability Policies and Government Programs,* ed. Edward D. Berkowitz (New York: Praeger, 1979), p. 115; Monroe Berkowitz, William Johnson, and Edward Murphy, *Public Policy toward Disability* (New York: Praeger, 1976).

11 Robert H. Haveman, Victor Halberstadt, and Richard V. Burkhauser, *Public Policy toward Disabled Workers: Cross-National Analysis of Economic Impacts* (Ithaca, N.Y.: Cornell University Press, 1984), p. 845.

12 Cornelius J. Peck, "Employment Problems of the Handicapped: Would Title VII Remedies Be Appropriate and Effective?" *Journal of Law Reform* 16 (Winter 1983), pp. 348–52.

13 John Howe to Art Quern, 26 August 1975, Spencer Johnson Papers, Box 3, Ford Library, Ann Arbor, Mich.

14 Terry Martin, "Interview with the President," KMPC Radio, 18 June 1976, Sara Massengale Papers, Box 9, Ford Library.

15 Robert Allen Bernstein, "Do-Good Pitythons," *New York Times,* 6 September 1983; "Evan Kemp, Aiding the Disabled: No Pity Please," *New York Times,* 3 September 1981.

16 "Freedom in a Wheelchair," *Time,* 21 June 1976, p. 44; Laurence Cherry and Rona Cherry, "New Hope for the Disabled," *New York Times Magazine,* 5 February 1984, p. 52; Anne Peters, "When the Cheering Stops," *Disability Rag,* March/April 1985.

17 "Michigan Woman Awarded Damages by Discriminating Hotel," *Disability Rag,* May 1985, p. 8; personal communication with James Jeffers; Sonny Kleinfeld, *The Hidden Minority* (Boston: Little, Brown, 1979), p. 114.

18 "Ragtime: Killing Babies Left and Right," reprinted from *Disability Rag,* May 1983, and distributed in mimeograph.

19 William Roth, "The Politics of Disability: Future Trends As Shaped by Current Realities," *Social Influences in Rehabilitation Planning: Blueprint for the 21st Century,* ed. Pearlman and Austin (Alexandria, Va.: National Rehabilitation Association, 1985), pp. 8–11; Harlan Hahn, "Changing Perception of Disability and the Future of Rehabilitation" (paper presented at the 9th Mary E. Switzer Memorial Seminar, New York, 30 November 1984), p. 21.

20 This section and the sketch of Lex Frieden is based on an interview with

Lex Frieden, 10 November 1984, Houston, Texas; interview with Judge James Cullen, 8 February 1984, Baltimore, Md.

21 Esther Blaustein, "She Fought to Teach," *Redbook,* September 1971; "A Unique and Inspiring Atmosphere," *Seawanhanka,* 20 April 1966; *New York Sunday Daily News,* 19 January 1969, p. b22; *New York Times,* 2 April 1970; *New York Daily News,* 5 and 6 April 1970; "Polio Victim, 22, is Denied License to Teach in City's Schools," *New York Times,* 1 April 1970; *New York Post,* 2 April 1970. I am grateful to Mrs. Ilsa Heumann for providing me with these clippings from her personal collection.

22 Richard K. Scotch, *From Goodwill to Civil Rights* (Philadelphia, Pa.: Temple University Press, 1984), pp. 84–5; interview with Judy Heumann, 10 April 1984, Berkeley, Calif.

23 *Sunday New York Daily News,* 5 January 1975, clipping supplied by Ilsa Heumann.

24 This section is based on an interview with Ed Roberts, 10 April 1984, Berkeley, Calif.

25 Interview with Fred Collignan, 1 May 1984, East Lansing, Mich.; Roberts interview; Charles Burt Cole, "Social Technology, Social Policy, and the Severely Disabled: The Issues Posed by the Blind, the Deaf, and Those Unable to Walk" (Ph.D. dissertation, University of California, Berkeley, 1979), pp. 368–425.

26 Center for Independent Living, Inc., *Disabled People Are on the Move* (Berkeley, Calif.: Center for Independent Living, Inc.), p. 15; Gerben DeJong, *The Movement for Independent Living: Origins, Ideology, and Implications for Disability Research* (East Lansing, Mich.: Michigan State University, Center for International Rehabilitation, 1979), p. 15.

27 Georgie Ann Geyer, "Wheelchair Power! The Disabled Go Public" [her column of 5 July 1975, supplied by Mrs. Ilsa Heumann].

28 Judy Heumann, testimony before U.S. Congress, House, Committee on Education and Labor, *Oversight Hearings on the Rehabilitation Act of 1973,* 95th Cong., 2d sess., 1978, p. 77 [hereafter Oversight Hearings].

29 Jean A. Cole, et al., *New Options,* (Houston, Tex.: Institute for Rehabilitation and Research, 1979), p. 2; "Independent Living Concerns for the 80's," a videotape produced by Dick Brundle in collaboration with Denise Tate (East Lansing, Mich.: Michigan State University, Center for Rehabilitation, n.d.).

30 Edward D. Berkowitz, "The Federal Government and the Emergence of Rehabilitation Medicine," *The Historian* 43 (August 1981), pp. 530–45. See also Glenn Gritzer and Arnold Arluke, *The Making of Rehabilitation: A Political Economy of Medical Specialization* (Berkeley: University of California Press, 1985).

31 Edward Berkowitz, *Rehabilitation: The Federal Government's Response to Disability* (New York: Arno, 1980).

32 Oversight Hearings, pp. 60, 32.

33 George Wright, *Total Rehabilitation* (Boston, Mass.: Little, Brown, 1980), p. 154; Mary Smith, "Appropriations for Vocational Rehabilitation Authorized under the Rehabilitation Act of 1973" (Washington, D.C.: Library of Congress, 1984); U.S. Congress, House, *Comprehensive Rehabilitation Services Amendments of 1978: Report to Accompany H.R. 12467,*

95th Cong., 2d sess., 1978, H. Rept. 1780, p. 425; statement of Robert Humphreys, U.S. Congress, Senate, Committee on Labor and Human Resources, *Implementation of the Rehabilitation, Comprehensive Services, and Developmental Disabilities Amendments, 1979*, 96th Cong., 1st sess., 1979, p. 346.

34 Charles Cole, "Social Technology, Social Policy, and the Severely Disabled," p. 425.

35 The Institute for Educational Leadership, *Challenges of Emerging Leadership: Community Based Independent Living Programs and the Disability Rights Movement* (Washington, D.C.: Institute for Educational Leadership, Inc., 1983), p. 201; DeJong, *The Movement for Independent Living*, pp. 31, 41, 589.

36 Institute for Educational Leadership, *Challenges of Emerging Leadership*, pp. 32, 123; Donald E. Galvin, "Policy Issues in Independent Living Rehabilitation" (photocopy, World Congress on Rehabilitation, Winnepeg, Canada, 1980).

37 "Developmental Disability Bill of Rights," quoted in Commission on Civil Rights, *Accomodating the Spectrum of Individual Abilities*, p. 61.

38 Erwin L. Levine and Elizabeth M. Wexler, *P. L. 94142, An Act of Congress* (New York: Macmillan, 1981); Bowe, *Rehabilitating America*, p. 215; Commission on Civil Rights, *Accommodating the Spectrum of Individual Abilities*, p. 59.

39 Gliedman and Roth, *The Unexpected Minority*, p. 182.

40 Warren Rustand to Dr. James Cavanaugh, 12 October 1974, Central Files, Box 22, File WE 8, Ford Library; transcript of meeting between President Ford and representatives of area handicapped, 15 October 1974, Sarah Massengale Papers, Box 9, Ford Library.

41 The White House Conference on Handicapped Individuals, *Final Report*, Vol. 2, Part A (Washington, D.C.: Government Printing Office, 1977); "The White House Conference on Handicapped Individuals, Fact Sheet," (n.d.), Sarah Massengale Papers, Box 10, Ford Library.

42 Jim Cannon to President Ford, 29 May 1975, Sarah Massengale Papers, White House Conference File, Box 11, Ford Library; HEW Secretary to President, 22 April 1975, Spencer Johnson Papers, Box 5, Ford Library.

43 "Report on Major Activities at the White House Conference on Handicapped Individuals," 4 November 1976, Sarah Massengale Papers, Box 10; "Issues and Recommendation Development for Participants," n.d., Sarah Massengale Papers, Box 10, Ford Library. Other conferences of this era, it should be noted, also failed to achieve their purposes, such as the White House Conference on the Family; see Gilbert Steiner, *The Futility of Family Policy* (Washington, D.C.: Brookings Institution, 1980).

44 Scotch, *From Goodwill to Civil Rights*, pp. 33, 105.

45 Paul Strachan, quoted in Edward D. Berkowitz, "Strachan and the Limits of the Federal Government," *International Review of History and Political Science* 42 (February 1980), pp. 65–81.

46 Interview with Frank Bowe, East Lansing, Mich., 12 May 1984.

47 29 U.S.C. 794 (Supp V 1981).

48 Commission on Civil Rights, *Accommodating the Spectrum*, p. 49; Scotch, *From Goodwill to Civil Rights*, p. 26.

49 Ibid., pp. 49–54.

50 Ibid., pp. 62, 72.

51 Ibid., p. 75.

52 Michael Lottman to David Lissy, 18 February 1976, Sarah Massengale Papers, Box 9, Ford Library; David Lissy to Sarah Massengale, 29 January 1976, ibid.; David Lissy to William Morrill and Peter C. Holmes, 24 November 1975, ibid., Box 10; President Ford, *Executive Order 1194*.

53 Bowe, *Rehabilitating America*, p. 61; David Lissy to Spencer Johnson, 5 March 1976, Spencer Johnson Files, Box 10, Ford Library; Peter Holmes to HEW Secretary, 30 June 1975, Sarah Massengale Papers, Box 10, Ford Library; *Higher Education Daily*, 6 May 1976, Sarah Massengale Papers, Box 9, Ford Library; *Washington Post*, 18 May 1976; Scotch, *From Goodwill to Civil Rights;* Nancy Hicks, "Handicapped Use Protests to Push HEW to Implement '73 Bias Law," *New York Times*, 11 April 1977, p. 12; Frank Bowe, *Handicapping America: Barriers to Disabled People* (New York: Harper and Row, 1978), pp. 205–7.

54 Joseph A. Califano, Jr., *Governing America, An Insider's Report from the White House and the Cabinet* (New York: Simon and Schuster, 1981), p. 258; Scotch, *From Goodwill to Civil Rights*, p. 110; interview with Joseph Califano, 21 November 1983, Washington, D.C.; interview with Dan Marcus, 6 October 1983, Washington, D.C.

55 Califano interview; Marcus interview.

56 Califano interview; Marcus interview; Bowe interview.

57 Scotch, *From Goodwill to Civil Rights;* Bowe, *Handicapping America*, pp. 209–12; Marcus interview.

58 U.S. Department of Health, Education, and Welfare, Office of the Secretary, *Programs and Activities Receiving or Benefiting from Federal Financial Assistance, Nondiscrimination on the Basis of Handicap, Proposed Regulations (45 CFR Part 84)* (hereafter cited as Draft Regulations), 2 February 1976, Spencer Johnson Papers, Box 10, Ford Library; Peter E. Holmes to HEW Secretary, 30 June 1975, Sarah Massengale Papers, Ford Library.

59 Draft Regulations, p. 12.

60 Ibid., pp. 16–17.

61 Peter Holmes to HEW Secretary, 30 June 1975, Sarah Massengale Papers, Ford Library.

62 Draft Regulations, p. 22.

63 Holmes to HEW Secretary, 30 June 1975, Sarah Massengale Papers, Ford Library; Draft Regulations, pp. 20, 26.

64 Scotch, *From Goodwill to Civil Rights*, p. 124–5; interview with Marianne R. Phelps, 12 April 1984, Washington, D.C.

65 Ari L. Goldman, "MTA Asks Exception from Wheelchair Law," *New York Times*, 9 June 1983, p. B-5.

66 Bowe, *Rehabilitating America*, pp. 70–5.

67 Michael A. Fletcher, "Handicapped Rider Tests MTA Test," *Baltimore Evening Sun*, 28 September 1983, p. F-1.

68 "Transit Logic," *Disability Rag*, 5 May 1985, p. 10.

69 Commission on Civil Rights, *Accommodating the Spectrum*, p. 39.

70 David Lissy to Douglas S. Harlan, 5 November 1975, Sarah Massengale Papers, Box 10, Ford Library; Bowe, *Rehabilitating America*, p. 12; Nancy Hicks, "Equity for Disabled Likely to be Costly," *New York Times*, 1 May 1977, p. A-29.

71 Scotch, *From Goodwill to Civil Rights,* p. 99.
72 Califano, *Governing America,* p. 262.
73 Roth, "The Politics of Disability," p. 6; Michael Landwehr, "The Evolution of the Disability Rights Education and Defense Fund, Inc.," *Law Reform in Disability Rights,* vol. 2 (Berkeley, Calif.: Disability Rights, Education, and Defense Fund, Inc., 1982); Evan Kemp, "Stop Caring for the Disabled," *Washington Post,* 7 June 1981, p. D-3.
74 Felicity Barringer, "How Handicapped Won Access Rule Fight," *Washington Post,* 12 April 1983, p. A-3; Vice President Bush to Evan Kemp, 21 March 1983, Evan Kemp Archives; Robert Bernstein, "Disabled Seek Independence, Not Pity" (unpublished manuscript), Evan Kemp Archives.
75 Interview with Justin Dart, Jr., 22 October 1984, Washington, D.C.; interview with Evan Kemp, 25 March 1984, Washington, D.C.; Association for Retarded Citizens, *ARC's Government Report* (Washington, D.C.: Association for Retarded Citizens-National Governmental Affairs Office, 1983), p. 3.
76 "Killing Babies: Left and Right," *Disability Rag,* May 1983.
77 Barringer, "Staffer Faults Reynolds in Protecting Handicapped," *Washington Post,* 26 April 1983, p. A-3; "Justice Narrows Reading of Disabled Access Law," *Washington Post,* 19 April 1983, p. A-10.

Conclusion

1 Donald E. Galvin, "Employer-Based Disability Management and Rehabilitation Programs," *Review of Rehabilitation* (in press), pp. 45, 20.
2 These are estimated 1986 contribution rates. See *Social Security Bulletin: Annual Statistical Supplement, 1984–1985* (Washington, D.C.: Social Security Administration, 1985), p. 23.
3 See *ABC's of Experience Rating* (New York: National Council on Compensation Insurance, 1981).

Index